THE METRICAL VERSION
OF
MANDEVILLE'S TRAVELS

EARLY ENGLISH TEXT SOCIETY
No. 269
1973

Here begynnuth the boke of Maundevile

Almyghtin god in trenite
Oo god and persones thre
ffadir and sone and holi goostr
Es lessid god of myghtis moste
Nowe spede vs atte oure begynnynge
And saue all this fair gaderynge
And graunt vs grace so bigynne
To lyue out of dette and dedeli synne
And teche vs the right way
Vn to p blisse p lasteth ay Amen.

Nowe lordis and ladies leues der
Yif ye woll of wondris her
A litill stounde yif ye woll dwell
Of grete mruails I wai you tell
Som tyme in Engelonde was a knyght
A fers man boothe stronge and wyght
he was a man of noble fame
Sir john maundevile was his name
And in seynt Albours he was born
And his auncestres hym bi forn
And putte in Engelonde were ye weld
Of his kynne he liuen ful fele
A worp soudiour forsothe was he
And wel trauilis bi yonde the see
In many a dyuers kinges londe
As aftir ye shal vnderstonde
ffor he was out of this lond her
So litche fone and thrtti yer
And euer he trauailid with out wene
The wondres of ps worlde to sene
And all p he seye he condutoke
And eft he wrote it in a boke
And als men hym tolde he to
he wrote it in e boke also
But in p boke is moch thinge
That nedeth naught in ps talkinge
And ps forsoth hit nedeth naught
As I haue herde men sein offt
Be it in geste othir in songe

And it be made on songe
hit maketh men werie and lothe to here
Thoug hit be neu so good matere
And fre for this first tretis
Out of that boke drawe it ys
That of alle merueilis tells
That he sawe and some yinge elles
A thousand and thre hundris also
And two and twenti put yt to
Was cristus gate yement
When he out of ps londe went
And euen on wygesmasse day
That worthi knyght toke his way
Atte Dover p is a toune in kent
The gentil knyght to shipe he went
Thei drowe up saile and forth thei yede
Nowe crist of heuen be our spede
To whom he made his praier
As dauid saith in his sauter
Quas tuas die demonstra muthi et se
mitas tuas edoce me. Salui me fac
tisum main tuam
Bi twene ps and p numtre of stone
Offten times men gone and come
That toune wel tel w oute mps
Of al p thei knowen and howe it is
But forsothe thei knowen nat all
And before I you tell here shall
Ere that Cite was furst bi gonne
And howe p toun is forth ronne
And for canse p staine Cite
Is thief of all cristiante
And also hede of holichurch
There woll I begynne frist to worth
As seith anjse clerk in his vers
The which I shalto you rehers

He seith that Cite was thieff founde
Empire of all ps worlde rounde
lesteneth and ye shall wetin

THE METRICAL VERSION
OF
MANDEVILLE'S
TRAVELS

FROM THE UNIQUE MANUSCRIPT IN THE
COVENTRY CORPORATION RECORD OFFICE

EDITED BY

M. C. SEYMOUR

Published for
THE EARLY ENGLISH TEXT SOCIETY
by the
OXFORD UNIVERSITY PRESS
LONDON   NEW YORK   TORONTO
1973

Printed in Great Britain
at the University Press, Oxford
by Vivian Ridler
Printer to the University

TO
BARBARA

PREFACE

THIS second volume in the projected series of four editions of *Mandeville's Travels* owes its existence largely to the kindness of others. Mr. Neil Ker drew my attention to the Coventry manuscript and read a first draft. Dr. A. I. Doyle and Mr. R. A. Waldron commented on points of detail. And Miss Dorothy Leech, formerly the Coventry archivist, gave me every facility for study, including a set of xerox sheets. Their courtesy and generosity are gratefully acknowledged.

The Lord Mayor and Corporation of the City of Coventry and the Trustees of the British Museum have kindly allowed me to print from manuscripts in their care.

Much of this book was prepared during four 'summer' months spent in New Zealand in 1963 where the hospitality of the Librarian and his staff at Victoria University provided a pleasant refuge from the gales and grosser elements that howled outside his windows.

Though originally prepared for this book, the description of the manuscript and the classification of manuscripts in Appendix B have been printed, respectively, in the *Transactions of the Edinburgh Bibliographical Society* in 1966 and in the Clarendon Press edition of *Mandeville's Travels* in 1967. I am grateful to the editor of that journal and the Delegates of that Press for permission to reproduce them here in revised form.

More than most, I am indebted to the Council for their continuing support.

M. C. S.

8 December 1967

CONTENTS

INTRODUCTION

THE ORIGIN OF THE METRICAL VERSION

IT seems reasonable to assume, as a working hypothesis, that the Metrical Version of *Mandeville's Travels* was based upon a version of the book circulating in England rather than on the Continent. None of the versions made outside England is known to have crossed the sea before the sixteenth century except the archetype of the Insular Version (an Anglo-French copy of the original French text, from which all extant versions of *Mandeville's Travels* made in England ultimately derive)[1] and a degenerate and unfinished French manuscript.[2]

The deliberate editing which lies behind the Metrical Version, as well as the recasting of the author's original prose source into verse, makes an investigation of its origins difficult. The author has omitted much matter which may have contained those scribal errors and contaminations by which the interrelationship of the various versions may be determined. Yet sufficient evidence of this kind is discernible in the Metrical Version to make inquiry worth while.

The extant manuscripts of the Insular Version are clearly divisible into three major sub-groups.[3] The Metrical Version contains a number of readings which collectively indicate its derivation from a precise point in the manuscript tradition of Sub-Group B of the Insular Version:

1. *Malleleuile* 470, a corrupt form of *Maleville*, a town near Belgrade. The form is correctly given in Sub-Group B of the

---

[1] See Appendix B below. Hakluyt printed an abridged text of the Latin Vulgate Version in 1589, probably from an earlier edition printed on the Continent. Extracts from this Vulgate Version in Royal Library, Copenhagen MS. S 172, ff. 135–8 (owned and partly written by William Horton, a monk of Lewes *c.* 1475) were added after 1500, also probably from an edition printed on the Continent.

[2] Durham University Library MS. Cosin B. i. 10, a text of Sub-Group C of the Insular Version and written in France *c.* 1425, has the English name *Ludlow R* (perhaps a former owner) on f. 3 in a contemporary hand.

[3] See Appendix B below.

Insular Version, but in Sub-Group A and its affiliates it is written *male ville* 'evil town'.[1]

2. *þe yatis of helle* 1427 translates a corrupt variant *chemins denfer* of the better *chimineez denfer* found in all manuscripts of Sub-Group B and its affiliates and, independently, elsewhere.[2]

3. *Cleperone* 468, a corrupt form of *Chipron*, i.e. Sopron in Hungary, which is paralleled in Sub-Group B (i) and the affiliated Harley Version.

4. *Grece* 657, a corruption of the better *Crete* which is found in Sub-Group B (i) and, independently, elsewhere.[3]

5. *iuys of þe same tree* 2082, a reading traceable to a corrupt variant *foilles* 'leaves' of the better *fiens* 'dung' found in Sub-Group B.

6. *foure and xx*[ti.] 1888, a scribal corruption of the better *xviii.* found in Sub-Group B.

7. *Sinosople* 2462, a corrupt form of the better *Gynosophe* which occurs in Sub-Group B and some of its affiliates.

8. *Ronnemare* 2499 and *Rennomare* 2548, corrupt forms of the better *Buemar* which are found in Sub-Group B and some of its affiliates.

9. *Cleophe* 1462, a corrupt form of the better *Eliopole* which is paralleled in Sub-Group B (i) and the affiliated Harley Version.

These readings suggest that the Metrical Version is closely affiliated to Sub-Group B (i) of the Insular Version and to the Harley Version, and this suggestion is reinforced by detailed comparison of the scribal forms of place-names in the relevant manuscripts.[4]

There is precise evidence that the Metrical Version does not derive from any of the four English prose versions of *Mandeville's Travels* as they are now extant. Each of these four texts gives a corrupt reference to *Maleville* (reading 1 above) by following an Insular manuscript which contained the *male ville* distortion; and each, from an earlier confusion of *cheual* and *cheualer*, obscures a reference to the horse of a Knight of Rhodes which the Metrical

---

[1] M. C. Seymour, 'The scribal tradition of *Mandeville's Travels*: the Insular Version', *Scriptorium* xviii (1964), 37.

[2] Ibid., p. 38 n. 14. This and other cited readings are discussed more fully in the Commentary.

[3] This easily made error occurs independently in one manuscript of Sub-Group A (MS. Royal 20 B. x f. 7ᵛ); in the Bodley Version (MS. e Musaeo 116 f. 10ᵛᵃ); and in the Defective Version (MS. Queen's 383 f. 26ᵛ).

[4] See pp. xiv–xv below.

Version 691–5 preserves correctly.[1] And the Metrical Version contains matter, such as the description of the Pepper Forest 1883–1912, which is omitted in two of the English versions.[2]

On the other hand, there are readings in the Metrical Version which suggest that the author may have followed a Latin translation of the Insular Version as extant in Sub-Group B (i):

10. *Sterens* 492, i.e. the medieval Sofia, appears to be a Latinized form of the better *Sternes* of Sub-Group B of the Insular Version, cf. *ciuitatem Sterrensem* of the Harley Version 150/4; although the word occurs in rhyme and may, like other place-names in the text, have been distorted by the author.[3]

11. *leuke* 891, 892, 896 ('continental league' < Latin *leuca*) is used by the author to express distances; although he may have intentionally adopted the word to avoid mistranslating OF. *lieux* as 'miles'.[4]

12. *Peroun* 897, a grossly distorted reference to the river Belus in Palestine, one explanation of which may be a misreading of *riuulus paruus* (as in the Harley Version 157/38); although, in view of the extensive corruption of names in the Metrical Version, *Peroun* may possibly be a distortion of an earlier and better *Beloun*.

13. *Nembras Galeas* 1330 is apparently corrupted from *Nembrot gigas* (as in the Harley Version 160/23) or similar Latin forms.

14. *Salemount* 1753, an otherwise unnamed hill of salt, has apparently evolved from *salis mons* (cf. the Harley Version 174/36), rather than from *montaigne de siel* in an Insular manuscript.

15. *gripes* 2632, a rendering of Latin *gryphes* 'griffons', appears in its context to have confused the author.

These readings do not, of course, provide evidence of a sufficient weight to argue conclusively that the Metrical Version is based on a Latin version of *Mandeville's Travels*. And there is nowhere discernible in the forms of place-names in the Metrical Version any trace of Latin case endings (except in the interpolated description

[1] In the latest editions cited in Appendix B below, Bodley 5/13 and 19/4; Cotton 5/21 and 17/4; Egerton 12/24, omitting the first reference at 4/8; and in the Defective (MS. Queen's 383 ff. 17ᵛ, 27).

[2] Bodley Version (note to 86/21) and Defective Version (MS. Queen's 383 f. 80).

[3] See p. xiv below. This and other readings cited as evidence of a possible Latin derivation are more fully discussed in the Commentary.

[4] See note to 1246 below.

of Rome 62–462) which ultimately derive from a Latin source.
None the less, these cited readings suggest the possibility and
prompt some detailed comparison of the scribal forms of place-
names in the Metrical Version and the relevant Latin translations
of the Insular Version.[1]

None of the three Latin affiliates of Sub-Group B of the Insular
Version exactly corresponds in the scribally corrupt forms of its
place-names with the Metrical Version, as a selective comparison
shows:[2]

Metrical	Harley	Leiden	Ashmole
Cleperone	Clipron	Chipponiam	Cipron
Neyesburghe	Neselburgh	Nersobrugia	Neysburgh
Malleleuile	Malleuillam	maleuillam	Maleuile
Dayneby	Damaby	dambi	*omitted*
Mace	Traciam	rachie	*omitted*
Bungrece	Bulgariam	terram Bulgrorum	Boygres
Marraone	Marro	Mar	Marray
Pyncerasse	Pynseras	Pinteras	Pyncerach
Sterens	Sterrensem	Sturnes	Stereneth
ffynepaie	fympapam	fines Epapie	Synopapo
Dandrenople	Dandrenopolim	dantrennople	Candropolis
Arthanie	Hircania	Hircamia	terra hicanorum
Dago	Dabago	Charodabago	Clarotu dabago
Despaine	hispanie	yspanie	hyspanicum
Ephan	Temar	Theamar	Thenar
fflorencie	ffinecia	finees	fenicis
Grece	Cretam	Orecia	Cretesem
Morecan	Moretanam	Moretanam	Mericanorum
Cleophe	Cleopolis	Elyopolis	Eliephili
Sinosople	Synosepulis	gynosopolia	ginosple
Traprophan	Taprobana	taprobania	Capprobana
Rennomare	Remmare	Bentuar	Benemar
Ribooth	Ryboht	Riboth	Reboth

It will be useful to have for comparison parallel forms occurring
in the sub-groups of the Insular Version and the affiliated Defec-
tive Version. Sub-Group A is quoted, with page and line reference,
from the printed text; Sub-Group B (i) from MS. Sloane 1464;

---

[1] i.e. those derived from a manuscript of Sub-Group B, and excluding the
Royal Version which derives from a manuscript of Sub-Group A. See Appendix
B, p. 194 below.

[2] The forms in the first two sections occur in the Metrical Version 468–93,
1632–1778; in the Harley Version, pp. 149–50, 172–5 below; in the Leiden
Version MS Vulcan 96 ff. 73^v–77; in the Ashmole Version MS. Ashmole 769 ff.
2^v, 41^v–45. The forms in the last section occur at various points in the text.

Sub-Group B (ii) from MS. Vossius Lat. 75; the Defective Version
from MS. Queen's 383, supplemented by MS. Royal 17 B. xliii:

Sub-Group A	Sub-Group B (i)	Sub-Group B (ii)	Defective
Cipron 4/27	Clipron f. 4	Chipron f. 1^v	Chippron f. 17^v
Neiseburgh	desie Seburgh	Nesseburgh	Newbur3
la male ville	Maleuille	Malleuylle	(ile towun)
Dambe	Damby	Danuby	Damuby
Trachie	Trachie	Trachie	Trachie
Bourgres	*omitted*	Bolgres	Bugrys
Marroc	Marro	Marres	Marrok
Pincemarcz	Pinseras	Pinceras	Pynceras
Ny	Sternes	Sternes	Sternes
Fenepape	Phinepape	Afinepape	Affympayne
Dandrenople	Dandernople	Drandenople	Bradenople
Hircanie 72/37	Hirtanie f. 80	hirtanie f. 23^v	*omitted*
char Dabago 75/45	char Dabago	char dabago	(Cardabago)
de Spaigne 72/33	Despaine	de Spayn	*omitted*
Theman 76/29	Themar	Themar	(Thomar)
Phenicie 72/32	fineez	ffinees	ffimes f. 72
Crete 12/37	Grece f. 12	Orete f. 4	Grece f. 26^v
Morikane 23/29	Mortanez f. 23	Morecane f. 7	*omitted*
Eliopole 25/33	Cleophe f. 24^v	Clipole f. 7	*omitted*
Gysonophe 145/42	Sinosople f. 152	Synosople f. 47^v	(Synople)
Taprobane 148/34	Taphane f. 154^v	Traprobane f. 49^v	Tabrobane f. 126^v
Buemar 147/33	Renemar f. 153^v	Renemar f. 49	Renemare f. 125
Byboth 152/37	Riboth f. 158	Ryboth f. 50^v	Ryboth f. 130

In these selective lists the forms of the Metrical Version are
closely related to those of the Harley Versions and to Sub-Group
B (i) of the Insular Version. But the Metrical Version contains a
number of forms (e.g. *Bungrece, ffynepaie, Despaine, Sinosople,
Rennomare*) which better preserve the original French forms than
the Latinized forms of the Harley Version, and cannot therefore
derive from the Harley Version. Equally, the Metrical Version does
not derive from either of the extant manuscripts of Sub-Group B
(i) of the Insular Version, which give some grossly corrupt forms
avoided by the Metrical Version.[1]

This inquiry into the origins of the Metrical version is thus

[1] e.g. *desie Seburgh* and *Taphane* of MS. Sloane 1464 quoted above. The
corresponding forms of MS. Additional C 280 are *Clipton, de Sieseburgh,
Maleuille, Danuby, Traci, Marro, Pinseras, Sternes, Phinopapa, Dandernople
hircayme, char dabago, despaine, Themar, fineez, grece, moretanez, Cleophe,
Sinosople, Taxbane, Renemar, Roboch*. Both manuscripts of Sub-Group B (i)
omit by eyeskip the reference to Bungrece 486, reading *entre homme en la terre
de Marro* instead of the better *entre homme en la terre de Bougres. Et la passe
homme vn pont de piere qest sur la riuere de Marroc*. And cf. note to 696 below.

inconclusive. It is certain that the author worked from a lost text closely affiliated to Sub-Group B (i) of the Insular Version, and possible that this lost text was a Latin translation, but no final conclusion may be reached on the evidence at present available.

DATE AND PROVENANCE

Mandeville's Travels was written on the Continent *c.* 1357 and, on the evidence of the extant manuscript tradition, seems to have appeared in England, perhaps in Lincolnshire, *c.* 1375. The earliest dated manuscript of the book known to have been written in England, a copy of the degenerate Latin Leiden Version, was made at Abingdon in 1390,[1] and the degree of its scribal corruption suggests that it is at some removes from the lost ancestor of all versions made in England.

Among these the Metrical Version is, without doubt, the most corrupt in the preservation of its place-names, but it is impossible to say whether its many unique corruptions not protected by rhyme were introduced by scribes before or after versification. The extant manuscript, written in the reign of Henry VI, is a most carefully penned work and remarkably free from copying errors, but this excellence throws no light on the state of the author's holograph. All one can say with assurance is that the Metrical Version was composed between *c.* 1375 and *c.* 1460, though an informed guess that dated its composition between 1400 and 1425 might not be wildly misleading.[2]

Whatever its date, there seems some ground for believing that the Metrical Version was composed in the North-east Midlands, perhaps in Lincolnshire or near its borders. The language of the text, as it survives in the unique manuscript, has been carefully and thoroughly 'modernized' in the emerging standard literary language of the fifteenth century,[3] as exemplified by Hoccleve

---

[1] Leiden University MS. Vulcan 96 f. 147: scriptum in Anno iubileo per manus Ricardi Bledelewe monachi Abendonensis Anno domini m.ccc. nono-gesimo.

[2] Based on the development of the scribal tradition and evidence that *Mandeville's Travels* was especially popular in the Midlands and the North at that time. See M. C. Seymour, 'The English Manuscripts . . .', *Trans. Edin. Bibl. Soc.* iv (1966), 173–4. The Metrical Version's derivation from a non-English version is a further argument for an early, rather than later date when English translations were readily available. Cf. *Mum and the Sothsegger*, ll. 1414–56.

[3] Some of the forms suggest that an intermediary manuscript between the

whose poems precede the Metrical Version in the manuscript;
perhaps the most spectacular example of this altering is *fright* 134
which replaces the earlier and better *frith* as a rhyme for *with*.
This distortion of rhyme is unusual; generally the scribe is at pains
to give an exact eye-rhyme, even where his forms are irregular, as
in *medicyim* 2078, *folle* 2167. However, some evidence of the
original language of the Metrical Version survives these scribal
practices. It is discernible, first of all, in verb forms in rhyme, e.g.

(*a*) *pr. 3 s.* in *-s*: *tellys* 45, *sais* 145, *telles* 326, *heles* 1946.
(*b*) *pr. 3 pl.* in *-s*: *shines* 332, *sees* 496, *saies* 1221.
(*c*) *pr. ppl.* in *-ande, -ende*: *passande* 967, *fleende* 1472.
(*d*) *p. ppl.* form *tane* 651; *pr. 3 s.* form *es* 1290.

Since medieval poetic practice tolerated the use of abnormal dia-
lectal forms in rhyme, the evidence of verbal forms is not neces-
sarily conclusive.[1] But in this case their evidence is supported by
that of some non-verbal forms in rhyme in which the original
language of the Metrical Version is discernible. Thus, the scribal
rhymes *church/worch* 72–3, *waxen/asshen* 1485–6, *kinge/yonge* 1803–
4, *drinketh/thenketh* 2395–6, *ys/flessh* 2165–6, *fyre/clere* 2729–30
appear to have replaced the earlier and better *kyrke/werk*, *waxen/*
asken, *kinge/yinge*, *drenke/thenke*, *es/flessh*, *fere/clere*. And the forms
mare/thare 1098–9 (cf. 832–3), *rawe/shawe* 1255–6 (cf. 163–4),
lyf/yif 1986–7 are found in North-east Midland and Northern
dialects in the early fifteenth century.

The evidence of the rhymes cited above suggests that the
original language of the Metrical Version belongs to the North-
east Midlands, but in view of the fragmentary nature of that
evidence (and indeed in the present state of knowledge about late
Middle English dialects)[2] that suggestion is subject to caution.
There is no obviously dialectal colouring discernible in the vocabu-
lary of the Metrical Version, apart from the forms cited above, but

---

author's holograph and this extant copy (perhaps the scribe's exemplar) was
written in the Central Midlands, possibly in or near Northampton.
  [1] e.g. the 3 s. and pl. form *geth* 'go' in rhyme at 915, 936, 1231, cf. the 3 s. and
pl. forms ending in *-s* cited above (possibly eye-rhymes formed on *goth*); the
pr. pl. forms in rhyme *goon* 1027, *gone* 1792, *kenne* 1187 (perhaps earlier *gan*
and *kennes*), *bene* 276, 801, 1815, 1834, *lyne* 1109.
  [2] See R. Kaiser, *Zur Geographie des mittelenglischen Wortschatzes* (1937).
Studies of the language, rhymes, and romance elements of the Metrical Version
will appear elsewhere.

in view of the extensive 'modernizing' of the language by the scribe this absence is unremarkable. Some otherwise unrecorded forms (e.g. *ravenne* 'gall-nuts' 2262, *shoilinge* 'sloping' 2901), which are discussed in the Commentary, may be dialectal. The poetic archaism *he(e)* 'they', which occurs in rhyme alongside the more general forms *thei*, *thay* at 130, 827, 1372, 1788, 1793, 1811, 1891, 2267, 2520, 2636, 2906, and which probably indicates an earlier, rather than a later, date of composition, has no regional significance here.[1]

THE AUTHOR

Without further evidence it is impossible to discover the author of the Metrical Version. An attractive suggestion that he was Capgrave does not, unfortunately, bear investigation. Capgrave (d. 1461) was a most careful and consistent orthographer, as his extant holographs show,[2] and his forms do not show any admixture of North Midland spellings. But, despite this anonymity, it is possible to learn something of the author of the Metrical Version.

He was, clearly, an experienced and fluent writer. His familiarity with the conventional form of romance is apparent from the stylized invocation (1–10) and his interpolated reference to Brut, the eponymous founder of Britain (109), both common features of this genre. And everywhere he makes use of those conventional metrical formulae which meet the requirements of rhyme and metre when invention flags. Thus, in the first three hundred lines (excluding the conventional opening 1–14) occur these instances: *wete ye wele* 21, *without wene* 29, *withouten mys* 64, *As I you rede and telle can* 90, *I vndirstonde* 119, *as þe boke sais* 145, *as I you say* 167, *or I goo hens* 194, *nowe wol I neven* 213, *ye shal here* 228, *knoweth many a man* 268, *as Y you telle* 273, *as I wene* 296. Such tags notwithstanding, the Metrical Version contains no bad rhymes which cannot be attributed to corruption.

Moreover, the author adopts an unhesitating approach to his task of drawing a *litille tretis* out of his source:

---

[1] *hee*, which occurs at 1793 and 1811, is the distinctive feminine form, possibly introduced by the scribe; non-rhyming *he* 'they' 2643 was originally singular after an uncorrupted *ham/man* rhyme.

[2] See *Ye Solace of Pilgrimes*, ed. C. A. Mills (1911), pp. xv–xvii; *The Chronicle of England*, ed. F. C. Hingeston, Rolls Series (1858), pp. xxv–xxix; *The Lives of St. Augustine and St. Gilbert of Sempringham*, E.E.T.S., o.s. 140 (1910); P. J. Lucas, 'John Capgrave O.S.A. . . .', *Trans. Camb. Bibl. Soc.* v (1969), 1–35.

But in þat boke is moch thinge
That nedeth naught in þis talkinge.
And þerefor seth hit nedeth nauʒt,
As I haue herde men sein offt,
Be it in geste othir in songe,
And it be made ouerlonge,
Hit maketh men werie and lothe to here
Thouʒ hit be neuer so good matere.
And þerefor this litille tretis
Out of that boke drawe it ys.   (35-44)

These lines suggest the confidence of experience, which may in part be inherited from the North Midland tradition of such works as Robert Mannyng's *Handlyng Synne*. Compared with the tentative approach of other English abridgements of *Mandeville's Travels*,[1] the Metrical Version appears a bold and successful enterprise executed to a careful design. In omitting virtually all details of itinerary except those concerned with the Holy Land and preserving all the marvellous fables of his source, the author displays a sure understanding of popular taste.

These qualities most probably derive from the practised hand of a professional writer. But if this is so, he is more likely to have been a cleric than a layman, possibly even a learned friar with an interest in antiquity.[2] He clearly had access to a library which contained a copy of the *Mirabilia Urbis Romae* and Bartholomaeus' *De Proprietatibus Rerum*[3] as well as other unidentified learned works and chronicles, and within a little compass he reveals a range of reference comparable to that of Lydgate or Capgrave, for example. Moreover, he appears to have had a fluent command of Latin. Even if he used English texts of the *Mirabilia Urbis Romae* and *Mandeville's Travels*, he quotes familiarly from the Bible and other Latin sources and adds stylistic flourishes, like *archa federis* 1030, which indicate the scholar.

---

[1] See my notes in *NQ* ccvi (1961), 169-71; *Anglia* 84 (1966), 27-58; *English Studies in Africa* iv (1961), 148-58; and *AUMLA* xxi (1964), 39-52.

[2] It seems unlikely, in view of the anachronisms and errors in the account of Rome (62-462), that he had visited Rome.

[3] Over twenty manuscripts of English provenance of this work survive in English libraries, and in fifteenth-century England its readers seem to have been mainly academics and ecclesiastics. Trevisa's English translation, made in 1398 and of more limited circulation, had a somewhat less academic readership. Bartholomaeus Anglicus is also cited in the Bodley Version 87/6 fn. and the Egerton Version 79/21.

Alongside these indications of experience and learning are discernible more remarkable characteristics. In writing his *litille tretis* the author has not merely abridged and rearranged his material. He has also deliberately and frequently distorted it for the sake of sensationalism in a manner which is alien to his source; for 'Mandeville' compiled his account of the world, apart from the fabrication of personal details, entirely from works which he undoubtedly believed to be accurate. The most obvious example of this striving after sensationalism is the account of the Greek faith (569–90). Where 'Mandeville' accurately reproduced the account of Jacques de Vitry, the author has substituted the later description of the belief of the Mohammedans. Many similar examples are recorded in the Commentary. One and all, they are inspired by the author's developed sense of narrative, which is also responsible for his many interpolations and expansions, for example the story of Noah's Ark (1695–1736). And where his sources fail him, he does not hesitate to invent details, such as the names of islands like *Calopide* 2084.

By such spirited editing the author avoids any suggestion of tedium that *maketh men werie and lothe to here*. Though the verse is unrelievedly pedestrian, it is in every way superior to comparable fifteenth-century productions like the rhymed portion of William Wey's Itinerary, and it runs lightly through the wonders of the world; in the versifier's hands what 'Mandeville' himself conceived as a popular though serious encyclopaedia becomes a marvellous romance. As such, it is able to stand comparison with all but the finest in its field.

THE COVENTRY CITY RECORD OFFICE MANUSCRIPT

ff. vi+168+vi, the flyleaves being almost entirely excised. Parchment. 320×190 mm., trimmed for binding. Double-columned frame, each column 245×90 mm. and containing 39–41 lines. Until 1968 in brown leather 17th-c. binding with attached library chain.

COLLATION. 1^8 (wants 5–8), 2^8 (wants 1–3), 3–12^8, 13^8 (wants 1, 3–6, 8), 14^8 (wants 6, 7^b, 15–18^8, 19^8 (wants 2), 20–3^8. Catchwords. No text is lost through excisions in quires 1 and 2. The Mandeville item begins on 4th leaf of quire 11, ends on 4th leaf of quire 14. Quire 1 signed in black and quires 2–10 in red, respectively with the abbreviations for *et* (quire 1) and the abbreviations for *et, con*,

and a triple tittle (quires 2–4) and the letters *e, s, T, A, m, E.*
Quires 11–14, 17–23 unsigned, the signatures perhaps trimmed
away. Quires 15–16 signed *aa, bb.* These signatures suggest that
perhaps 184 leaves (in 23 quires of 8, signed a–z) may have been
detached before f. 1 and separately bound, and the make-up of
quires 1 and 2 (in effect, nine separate leaves in Hand I) supports
this conjecture. See Dr. A. I. Doyle's description of the MS. in
PLMA lxxxiii (1968), 22–6, and Mr. N. R. Ker's description in
a forthcoming volume of *Medieval Manuscripts in British Libraries.*

CONTENTS (the numbers in parentheses refer to entries in *An
Index of Middle English Verse* and its *Supplement*, 1943 and 1965):

f. 1rb Hoccleve, *Regiment* (2229)

f. 40rb Hoccleve, *Complaint* (124)

f. 43va Hoccleve, *Dialogue with a Friend* (299)

f. 49rb Hoccleve, *Tale of Jereslaus* (1561)

f. 57rb Hoccleve, *Learn to die* (3121)

f. 64vb Hoccleve, *Tale of Jonathas* (3582)

f. 70ra Lydgate, *Danse macabre*, A text (2591)

f. 75ra Chaucer, minor poems (239, 2262, 3787, 3348, 3190, 809).
Printed by G. B. Pace in *PMLA* lxxxiii (1968), 26–9

f. 77va *Mandeville's Travels*, Metrical Version (248.5). Imperfect
ff. 96–7v blank

f. 98ra *Siege of Jerusalem* (1881). Ends imperfectly, *That xl. yere
he aboode* (l. 5144 of the poem edited by J. A. Herbert for the
Roxburghe Club, 1905)

ff. 130–6v (i.e. quire 19) blank

f. 137ra Lydgate, *Siege of Thebes* (3928)

f. 167va Twenty-four quatrains (502.5) in late 15th-c. hand. Begins,
Behold we wrecches in this world present

SCRIBES. Middle of 15th-c. South-east Midlands.

Hand I (ff. 1–95, i.e. quires 1–14) *cursiva formata*: headed *a*;
ascenders of *b, h, l* looped and of *d* generally looped, occasionally
oblique; open *e*; short *r*, final *s* eight-shaped.

Hand II (ff. 98–129v, 137–67, i.e. quires 15–23 with blanks) *fere-
textura*: ascenders of *b, h, l* vertical and of *d, v, w* oblique; open *e*;
short *r*; final *s* eight-shaped.

DECORATION. Gilded initials and champ sprays, executed by one
artist throughout, *c.* 1430–60. On f. 1 a large bordered tinted

drawing, 175 × 175 mm., of figure in long white gown and round cap against a ground of green hills, competently executed (now badly faded); Dr. Doyle suggests 'Aristotle' or Egidius Romanus, two of the sources of Hoccleve's *Regiment*.

DATE. Reign of Henry VI (1422–61), perhaps *c*. 1450. Both the Hoccleve 'sequence' of poems (excluding the *Regiment*) and Lydgate's *Siege of Thebes* were completed *c*. 1421, and their texts in this MS. reflect some degree of scribal corruption. The text of the *Regiment*, completed in 1412, in this MS. is most closely affiliated to a subgroup (B.M. MSS. Addit. 18632 and Royal 17 D. vi and Bodleian MS. Digby 185) which developed after 1430.

HISTORY. The MS. may be the product of a London shop and was perhaps originally about twice its present size. Given by T. Alford, possibly the father of Thomas Alford, rector (1643–56) of Allesley, near Coventry, to the Coventry Public Library (founded in 1602 and then housed in Coventry School); see C.U.L. MSS. Addit. 4467, f. 5 (book of donors) and Addit. 4468, f. 16 (catalogue made in 1697) and Corpus Christi College, Oxford MS. 390, f. 211. Removed for safe keeping by a headmaster between 1816 and 1834 (*Report of the Charity Commissioners for 1834*, p. 131) and subsequently passed into private hands. Rediscovered in 1950 and purchased by the Coventry Corporation for £300 in 1962.

EDITORIAL PROCEDURE

The Metrical Version is edited from the unique text in the Coventry Record Office MS., ff. 77ᵛᵃ–95ᵛᵇ. Occasionally the scribal forms of *e* and *o* are impossible to distinguish; where rhyme offers no evidence, scribal intention has been interpreted in conformity with his general spelling practices. Editorial corrections are shown by italicizing altered letters and placing added letters and substituted words within square brackets. Rejected manuscript readings are printed below the text. Punctuation and word-division follow modern practice, and the scribe's initial *ff*- has been printed as *f* or *F* according to modern usage.

The scribe's corrections to the manuscript have been accepted without notice. The flourish after *-r* and the bar through *-ll* have been expanded to final *-e*; apart from the form *suffre* 1968, the final *-e* in such environments appears to have no phonetic value.

The flourish over vowels has been interpreted as a suspension sign and expanded as *m* or *n*; it seems probable that the scribe intended forms such as *toun* 431 and *adoun* 573, rather than *ton* and *adon*. But the identical mark over final *-m* and *-n* (in form indistinguishable from *-u*) has been disregarded; sometimes this mark runs above the whole word (e.g. *men* 33 and 38, *euen* 51), and if it has any value it is that of final *-e* (cf. the rhymes *borne* and *lorñ* 527–8, *Iordane* and *thañ* 1207–8). The bar through the ascender of *h*, in medial as well as in final position, is treated as otiose (e.g. *knyght* 15, *wyght* 16); in line 601, mistakenly written twice, occurs the barred form *forth* and the unbarred form *forthe*, but this appears to have no significance alongside barred forms which have written final *-e* (e.g. *nyghte* 775). For the sake of consistency barred *h* is disregarded in *Iohn* 18 etc., the name sometimes occurring without a barred *h* (e.g. *Iohnes* 687), although the form might legitimately be expanded to *Iohan* or *Iohun*. The curved mark above final and medial *p*, sometimes above a dot (e.g. *vp* 55), is also treated as otiose, but it may perhaps have the value of *-e* or even *-pe*; the form mainly affected is *vp*. The curled abbreviation indicating *-er* or *-ir* has been interpreted without exception as *-er*, but in some forms the scribe may have intended *-ir* (e.g. *othir*, *watir*, not *other*, *water*). In none of these cases do the Latin rubrics and quotations offer any guide to the scribe's intentions. All other contraction signs in the MS. are unambiguous.

Editorial correction is generally confined to the emendation of the forms of place-names and numerals which may have been distorted by a scribe of the Metrical Version. No attempt is made to restore the dialectal forms of the original text.

The marginalia of scribe or rubricator, generally very brief Latin *notae* and place-names copied from the text, have not been recorded except in those few cases, printed below the text as footnotes, where the marginal forms (perhaps those of the scribe's exemplar) differ significantly from the textual forms.

The scribe's large coloured initials are printed as bold capitals. Smaller coloured initials and paragraph marks are not distinguished in this edition.

THE BOKE OF MAWNDEVILE

Here biginnith the boke of Mawndevile

Almyghti God in trenite,
Oo God and persoones thre,
Fadir and sone and holi gooste,
Blessid God of myghtis moste,
Nowe spede vs atte oure begynnynge   5
And saue alle this faire gaderinge,
And graunte vs grace so binynne
To live out of dette and deedeli synne,
And teche vs the right way
Vnto þat blisse þat lasteth ay. Amen.   10
Nowe lordis and ladies leve and dere,
Yif ye wolle of wondris here,
A litille stounde yif ye wolle dwelle,
Of grete meruailis I mai you telle.
Som time in Engelonde was a knyght,   15
A fers man boothe stronge and wyght.
He was a man of noble fame,
Sir Iohn Mavndevile was his name,
And in Seinte Albones he was born,
And his auncestres hym biforn.   20
And yitte in Engelonde, wete ye wele,
Of his kynne þere liven ful fele.
A worþi sowdioure forsothe was he
And wel trauailid biyonde the see
In many a dyuers kinges londe,   25
As affter ye shal vndirstonde.
For he was out of this londe here
Holiche foure and thirti yere,
And euer he trauailid without wene
The wondres of þis worlde to sene.   30
And al þat he sawe he vndirtoke
And euer he wrote it in a boke,
And al þat men hym tolde þereto
He wrote it in a boke also.
But in þat boke is moch thinge   35

7 binynne] MS. bigynne

That nedeth naught in þis talkinge.
And þerefor seth hit nedeth nauȝt,
As I haue herde men sein offt,
Be it in geste othir in songe,

And it be made ouerlonge,   40
Hit maketh men werie and lothe to here
Thouȝ hit be neuer so good matere.
And þerefor this litille tretis
Out of that boke drawe it ys,
That of alle merueilis tellys   45
That he sawe and some þinge elles.
A thousand and thre hundrid also
And two and twenti put þereto
Was Cristis date verement
When he out of þis londe went,   50
And euen on Migelmasse day
That worthi knyght toke his way.
Atte Dover, þat is a toune in Kent,
The gentil knyght to shippe he went.
Thei drowe vp saile and forth thei ȝede.   55
Nowe Criste of heuen be oure spede,
To whom he made his praiere,
As David saith in his sautere:
Vias tuas domine demonstra michi
Et semitas tuas edoce me. Saluum me fac   60
Secundum misericordiam tuam.
Bitwene þis and þe cuntre of Rome
Offten times men gone and come
That conne wel tel withouten mys
Of al þat thei knowen and howe it is.   65
But forsothe thei knowen nat alle,
And þerefor I you telle here shalle
Ere that cite was first bigonne
And howe þe cours is forth ironne.
And for cause þat same cite   70
Is chief of alle cristiante
And also hede of holi church,
There wol I beginne frist to worch,
As seith a wise clerk in his vers,
The which I shal to you rehers: 75

[*Roma capud mundi tenet imperium mundi*].
He seith that cite was chieff founde
Empire of alle þis worlde rounde.
Lesteneth and ye shalle weten

Howe in croniclis it is written   80
Fro the time þat God the worlde bigan
Til þat Rome was makid than
Was iiii. m^l· and cccc. yere
And iiii. and fiffti ferre ne nere.
And fro the fundacioun of þat toun   85
Vnto Cristis incarnacioun
Were vii. hundrid yere and fiffti also,
Beth written in þe croniclis and no mo;
So þat bifore er Rome bigan,
As I you rede and telle can   90
With moch sorowe and litel ioy,
Was the grete sege of Troy.
The grettest sege forsoþe was hit
That was euer accountid ʒit,
For it endurid seuen yere   95
Or þat cite taken were.
A noble kinge Ser Eneas
Captaine and lorde þereof he was.
He had two sones of grete renoun
That were princis of that toun,   100
And Remus and Romulus
Tho two bretheren were callid iwys.
But whan þat noble cite sholde
Taken ben and vp iyolde,
Thoo twoo bretheren, as I you say,   105
Bi nyghte in shippe scaped away,
And othir seuen kingis moo
Escaped awaie with hem alsoo.
And Brute þat al þis lande wan
That same time fro Troie cam.   110
But herkeneth nowe and ye shal here
These kingis names what thei were.
There was the kinge of Sabanense,
And þe kinge of Abbanense,

76 *Latin verse partially deleted in MS.*

And the kinge of Scalane,   115
And the kinge of Spolitane,
The kinge of Camarence Calanem,
And þe kinge of Campanie with hem.
And þat time regned, I vndirstonde,
In Ierusalem and Iewerie londe   120
Kinge Achaz and kinge Ozie,
And Ioathan and Ezechie,
And also the prophete Isaie
Of Criste þat made his prophecie.
Visio Isaie prophete quam vidit super Iudam   125
Et Iherusalem in diebus Ozie, Ioathan, Achaz,
Et Ezechie, regum Iude.
But the kinges þat wee erst of spoken,
That from þe seege of Troie were broken,
Daie and nyghte so sailid he   130
Til thei come ouer the Grete See
Into þe londe of Italie
Ther Rome is nowe certainlie.
And there thei londid in þat fri*th*
And alle the meyne þat come hem with,   135
And lokid about hem and vndirstode
Howe þat cuntre was faire and goode
And profitable, as I you telle,
And there thei shope hem for to dwelle
And inhabited hem þere by and by,   140
As seith seinte Thomas in his story,
Omne solum est forti patria.
Than eueri kinge his place þere fon*ge*
And maden tovnes grete and longe,
And in eueri a tovne, as þe boke sais,   145
Eche kinge made hym a faire paleis.
Than Romulus enclosid ham inne echone
With a walle made of lyme and stone,
And so many werkemen þere he hade
That in a moneth þe walle was made,   150
That was accountid without doute
Twoo and fourtie myle aboute.
And when he had closed hem alle

f. 78rb

134 frith] MS. fright   143 fonge] MS. fonde

With that stronge stonen walle,
And for þat Romulus was his name,   155
He clepid it Rome so in his game.
And thus Rome was made and first bigonne
The chief cite vndir þe sonne.
Three hundrid and ey3te and fourti toures
f. 78ᵛᵃ   Weren on the walle of stronge socoures,   160
And yates also ben in þat walle
Eighte and [tene] principalle,
And all hir names I shal you shewe
And euery rekene hem in a rewe.
The first porte is Campanie,   165
And Porte Pauli next þere bye
And Sepulcre Remy, as I you say,
And Porte Apie þere lieth the way
To *Domine quo vadis*, that holie place,
And also forthe to Catecumbas.   170
And Porte Latyn than is next,
There þat seint Iohn þe euangelist
Alle quik in oile boiled he was,
And 3it oure lorde through his grace
Delyuered hym out of þat penaunce,   175
For in hym was alle his affiaunce.
Porte Mecroine and Porte Azinarie
And Porte Lucane þe more þere by,
Porte Taury and Porte Tiberine,
Porte Numentane and Porte Pyncine,   180
Porte Collecte and Porte Septim,
And Porte Aurea next to hym,
Porte Portuens and Porte Petri,
Porte Castelle Sancte Angeli,
And Porte Viridaun; here bethe alle   185
The grete yates in the walle.
And while that cite alle hole stoode
There were þere in castellis stronge and good
Three and fourtie without moo,
And stronge barbicans also   190
Seven thousand foure score and ten
With grete strength for fyghtynge men,

162 tene] MS. twenti   184 Castelle] MS. Castell*e* and

And othir archeris of grete defence
That I shal rekene or I goo hens.
The golden arche of seinte Alexi,   195
And the arche of Theodosii,
And the arche of Constantine þerto,
And the arche of seven lanternes also,
And the arche of Vaspasian and Tity
There were the seuen chaundelers of Moysy,   200

f. 78vb And þe arche of Iulii Cesaris—
At seinte Martynnes þat arche ys—
And þe arche also of Antonyne
Atte seinte Laurence in Lucine.
And seuen brigges certainly   205
Ben ouer the water of Tibery,
The castel brigge of seinte Aungelle,
The Iewes brigge men knoweth it welle,
The brigge also of Fabian,
And þe brigge also of Gracian,   210
And þe brigge of Theodosii,
And Valerianus brigge than next þer by,
The senatoures brigge nowe wol I neven;
And these beth the brigges alle seuen.
And hilles also in that cite   215
[Seuen] I wote welle that þer be.
The mounte Ianicle and mounte Eventine
At the church of seinte Sabine,
The mounte Tanelle at seint Alext,
And mounte Stephan in Soleo next,   220
The mounte Capitoile and seint Marie mount
The more [and], as I haue herde account,
The mounte in þe grete paleis þere tille.
þere was taken the grete clerke Virgille
And inuisible there made hym   225
And escaped vnto Neapolym.
Twenti paleicis also þere were,
And alle hir names ye shal here.
The grete paleis amyddes the toun,
And Romulus paleis (nowe som is doun)   230
And Neroes paleis Lateranense,

216 Seuen] MS. Eiȝte   222 and] MS. is

The paleis of Surrie nought ferre thense,
The holie church roode is þere nouthe,
And Rom[ul]us paleis more bi southe.
And two faire houses þere made he,　235
The hous of concorde and þe hous of pete,
And Romulus his god þere inne sette,
An ymage affter his owne mette,
And said this paleis shalle nouȝt be lorn
Til a maide a childe haue born.　240
And also asone certainly

That God was born of oure lady,
That place þat was so stronge and sounde
Alle toflattered and felle to grounde.
There is the paleis of Troiane,　245
And the paleis of Adriane,
And Claudius paleis bi Panteon,
And the paleis of Anthion.
There was a paleis faire ynowe
There þat Nero hymselff slowe;　250
From þe hospitalle of seinte sperite
Vnto seint Petris lastith hitte.
And þe paleis of Iulius Cesare—
His owne bodie is buried thare.
And the paleis of Eufemine,　255
And the paleis of Titi and Vaspasine
In the mounte of Euentine,
And þe paleis of Constantine.
There is an hors and man of bras,
An emperoure there some time he was;　260
For he was wise and so worthi
Thei made hym so in memory.
And the paleis of Domician
That is *ad micam auream*.
And þe paleis also of Olimpias　265
There seint Laurence rostid was.
And the paleis of Octovian,
That place wel knoweth many a man.
The paleis also of Veneris
That *Scala Celi* nowe callid ys.　270

234 Romulus] MS. Remus　　　270 Scala Greca *in margin*

The paleis of Camille is eke there by
That nowe is called seinte Anthony.
And þere also, as Y you telle,
Is a place men callith it helle.
And holie churcheyerdis seuentene   275
In þat cite without that þere bene,
Calipodie and Pancras hole
And seint Agace at þe Girole,
And seint Vrsus nought ferre thens,
And seint Felice in the Pynce.   280
Withoute Apize gate thare
f. 79rb   Ys þe churcheyerde of Appolinare.
Concorde also was some time
Withouten the Porte Latine.
Bitwene twoo leepres at seint Heline   285
An holie churcheʒerde was som time.
Seynt Sabines and seinte Vrsus withalle
And seint Laurencis withouten the walle,
Seint Agnes and seint Petris Wille,
Seint Eracene and seint Prescille,   290
Seint Saturnine and seint Felici,
Seinte Kalixt and seinte Ponci,
Seinte Heremite þe Domicelle,
And seint Kiriace, as I you telle.
Templis also þere were nyne[tene].   295
I shal reherce hem, as I wene.
At þe temple of Adrian thoo
Some time þere were templis twoo,
Oone of Florre, anoþer of Pheby.
Bi þe temple of Virgily   300
There was thoo, as I telle yowe,
But Newe Rome men callith hit nowe,
Temple Enee and temple Appoline,
Temple Neron and temple Anthonine,
Temple Marci, and temple Martis   305
In þat temple sette it is.
The Romaines þere her councel ches
The frist daie of Iulii without les,

271 Camille] MS. Carille   286 An] MS. And *with corrector's mark in*
margin   295 nynetene] MS. nyne

And than thei dwelled þere in fere
Vnto þe kalendis of Ianivere.   310
And by Pantheon was temple Numie
And pillers of marble yitte þer be.
The temple Veste was in þat place
There nowe is seint Kirias.
The goldene castelle, I suppose,   315
Was in the manere of Dame Rose.
Anothir castelle there was ywysse,
That castelle [Pantheon] callid ys.
That place to Romaines was ful lefe
For of alle þe worlde thei helde it chiefe,   320
With curious walles boþe hie and stronge.

f. 79va   The rooffe was copere and gelte amonge
Ful rialiche al for the nones,
Araied with golde and precious stones,
With iaspes, beches, and berilles,   325
And many othir stones as þe boke telles,
Amatistes, crisolites, and calcidoynes,
Crapotines, coteices, and sardoynes,
Diamoundes, dianes ful thik þere wore,
Emeraudes, saphiris, and vermidore,   330
Peritotes also and reflambines,
And carbuncles that bright shines,
Rubies, topaces, and onicles riche,
Sardes and garnettis for thei ben liche,
Smaragdes, ligoyns, and perles fele,   335
Moo than I can rekene wele.
Hit was so riche, men þat it knewe
And accountid it at such valewe,
Worþe þe [þrid] parte and no lasse
Wise men saiden þat it wasse.   340
Hir god that was thair maumette,
Richeli amyd he was sette.
He raught vp to the temple rounde
From the rooff vnto the grounde,
And abouten hym in the walle   345

311 Numie] MS. Ninine   318 Pantheon] MS. pito *followed by blank in*
MS. where four letters have been erased   339 þrid] MS. *om.*
341 maumette] MS. maumetee *corrected*

There stoode ymages boþe grete and smalle
Of eueri londe that thei did conquere.
Eueri lande had an ymage there
And eueri ymage, as I you telle,
About his necke he had a belle.   350
And when any cuntre come
And weren rebelle ayens Rome,
Anone the ymage of þat cuntre
Framwarde þe maumette than turned he
And ringeth his belle so loude and clere   355
That alle the Romaines myght hit here.
Than sent thei knightis when þei þis knewe
To conquere al that cuntre newe.
And nowe is that temple þat is so rounde
Callid seinte Maries the Rotounde.   360
The rooffe of copre and of bras
f. 79vb As hoole as in þe temple it was
The deuel al hole from thens hit fette
And atte seint Petris he hit sette.
And othir templis þere were many moo   365
That I shal nempne or I goo.
Temple Iouis and Numie prest
And eke the temple of þe west.
The Romaines in that temple so faire
Setten Iulius Cesare in the chaire,   370
That Iulius Cesare þat al þis [land] wan
Of a kinge þat highte Cassibilan.
And when he this lande conquerid hade
The toure of London anone he made,
And þe truage þat longeth to Rome   375
Beth the Petir Pens þat of þat conquest come.
And þere was the temple of Iovis,
Temple Ercules and temple Ofilis.
The senatours of Rome thare
Thei quelleden Iulius Cesare.   380
And in that same place þerefore
Ys nowe seinte Maries church þe more.
Also there was temple Iany,

He was keper of that capitoly.
Of Colise nowe telle I shalle,   385
Hit was moost meruailous temple of alle.
The goddis that therein were done
Weren of the sonne and of the mone.
Hit was wondirful moch and wide,
With hie wallis in eueri side,   390
Proude pynnacles and coruen toures,
And peinted alle with riche coloures.
The rooff was made verament
Euenliche vnto the firmament,
With sonne and moone and sterris briȝte   395
That shined bothe daie and nyȝte.
Thundir and lightenenge, hayle and rayn,
Wheneuer thei wolde in certayn,
Thai shewed it in dede apertly.
And alle throuȝ crafft of sorcery   400
The sonne to the daie gaff light,

f. 80ra

The mone and þe sterris to þe nyght,
And euer in thair cours thei went
As planettes done in þe firmament.
And þat simulacre of the sonne,   405
Of wham the temple was bigonne,
Vppon the grounde it stode ful strauȝt
And with his heede the rooff he rauȝt,
Of goolde and perre ful riche withalle,
And in his honde a golden balle   410
In tokene þat Rome was chieff cite
Of alle this worlde vnto se.
But who so wolle the sothe grope,
That time that seint Siluester was *pope*,
He fordid þat riche mamette   415
That so richeli þere was sette,
And distroied that temple of *l*ym and stone
And othir templis ful many oone,
And foundid chirchis many and goode
In the placis there þat the templis stoode,   420
And yaffe ful grete pardoun thereto.
And so hauen oþere popis also,

414 was pope] MS. *partly erased*   417 lym] MS. hym

As pope Boneface the ferth.
While he was pope and dwellid in erth
Of Foca the Cesar he gate one,   425
The grete temple of Pantheone,
And foundid a church of oure lady
And of alle seintis ful rially.
And thus the templis þat were there
With holie men distroied were,   430
For þe pilgrimes þat come to toun
Thai had more deuocioun
To seen þe meruailis in þat stage
Than to fulfillen thaire pilgrimage.
Therefor thoo vanitees thei did cese   435
And holie churche thei made encrese.
Foure [score] and sixti and seven þere be
Parissh churchis in that cite,
But amongis alle þere beth seuen
And her names I shal you neuen.   440
Of thaire pilgrimage and dignite

f. 80rb

Gretter then any oþere thei be.
Seint Petris frist is principalle,
And than seynt Poules wiþout þe walle,
Seint Iohn the Lateranense tofore,   445
And then seint Marie church the more,
Seint Laurence without the clois.
There is a churche of the holie crois,
And seynte Sebestianes also.
Ful moch pardoun is grauntid hem to,   450
But at seint Iohn the Lateranences
There ben þe grettest indulgences.
None hert mai thenke ne tonge rechace
The pardones of þat holie place.
And alle the churchis of that toun   455
And alle thaire grete pardoun
I wolde you reherce with good wille
And I had space to abide þeretille.
But al to longe than shuld we dwelle
And I shuld of þat pardoun telle,   460
And þerefor ferthirmore wol I wende,

437 score] MS. hundrid

And here of Rome I make an eende.
Now go we to þe worþi man
Of whom oure talking frist began.
Forth in his waie nowe wendith he   465
Ouere the grete Grekisshe Se
Into the lande of Hungare,
Vnto Cleperone þat faire cete
And bi the castelle Neyesburghe,
And so to Malleleuile he passeth throuhe   470
Ouere þe ryuer of Dayneby,
A stronge ryuer and a myghty.
The water ther is so vigerous
And so stronge rennynge in his cours
So that his fresshenes holdith he   475
Twenti myle within the see.
Than passith he bi conduyt saf
Vnto the cite of Belgraf,
A stronge riche toun and a goode,
Stondinge ful faire vppon þe floode.   480
There is grete plente of brede and wyne
f. 80ᵛᵃ   And flesshe and fissche boothe good and fyne
And of alle vetailis plenteuous
And of beldinge fulle corious.
Than passeth he bi þe water of Mace   485
Into the lande of Bungrece
And ouer a faire brigge of stone
Ouer the ryuere of Marraone.
And fro that cuntre he gan passe
Into the lande of Pyncerasse.   490
And so vnto Grece he passith thens
Into the cite of Sterens,
To Fynepaie and to Dandrenople.
Than come he to Constantinople,
That is chieff cete of Grece,   495
As alle men knowen that it sees.
And there dwelleth moost þe Emperour
In that cite of grete honour.
And in that cite sikirly
Is a church of seynte Sophy.   500

490 Pyncerace *in margin*

Hit is the fairest churche holde
In alle þe worlde newe or oolde,
With many a relique riche and dere.
Herkeneth nowe and ye shal here.
There is þe holie croys sekirly   505
That Criste for vs vppon gan dy,
And the reede and þe sponge withalle
Wherewith thei yafe hym eyselle and galle.
And oone of the naylys also there ys
And also the cote inconsutilis   510
And halff the croune þat was of thorn.
And that othir halff awaie was born
Vnto the cite of Parys,
In þe Kingis Chapelle there it ys.
And þere is the speres hede so smert   515
That Criste was stonge with to þe hert.
And there was buried, as men wel wist,
Seynt Luke the euangelist,
And eke seint Iohn Grisostome,
And seinte Anne also lieth þere with hem.   520
And some time hit felle in that cite
f. 80vb   That an emperour enterede shuld be,
And thei that the graue make sholde
Thei fonde a table alle of golde,
And vppon the table was written   525
This resoun as ye shulle alle weten:
Iesus Criste shal be borne
To saue mannys soule þat shuld be lorn
And soffre peynes grete and grym;
Stedefastly I trowe on hym.   530
This was accounted a grete meruail,
For bi þat deede men wist wel
Hit was twoo thousande yere biforn
That Criste was of oure lady born.
Bi þe londe of Grece þat I did neuen   535
There is an ile men callith Lenpen,
And in that ile there is a grete mountayne
Towarde the coostis of Macedayne.
The mounte of Olympe hit is toolde,

510 inconsutilis] MS. Inconsultilis   524–5 Tabula Ermes *in margin*

An hie mountaine to beholde.   540
And anoþer mounte is þere also
That is hier than such twoo.
The mounte Achos hit hight in speche.
Aboue þe cloudes it dothe areche,
And vppon the toppe thereof certayn   545
Cometh noþere snowe, wynde, ne rayn.
There nys no foule ne beeste on grounde
That there mai liven any stounde.
The seuen sagis that time were,
As men tellen in cuntre there,   550
And euery yere atte a day isette
Vppon that hille togidir thei mette,
And þere through crafft of philosophy
Thai maden astronomy and gematry
A moneth thei dwellid there to þe eende.   555
And whan thei toke leve home to weende
With the fyngres of thaire honde
Thei written resoun in the sonde.
And atte yeris eende when thei come efft
Thei founde the lettris as thei hem lefft,   560
And thereby wist thei there come none othir
f. 81ra   That her writinge did enpere.
Aristotel and eke Ermes,
Anytenne and Ercules,
Tholome and Ypocras,   565
And Catoun oone of hem he was.
These were the philosophres seuen,
The grettest clerkis vndir heuen.
But for to speke of the Greke,
As Maundevile seith I telle you eke.   570
And thei bilevith as don wee
Vppon the holie trenite,
And that the sonne was sent adoun
To take incarnacioun,
And of a maide þat he was born   575
To saue mannes soule þat was forlorn.
In alle þinge thei bileue thus
Right as oure crede techeth vs,

554 Thai] MS. That   557 With] MS. And with

Saue oo pointe ys nought in thouȝt—
Thai seyn þat Criste died nouȝt.   580
For thei seyn in þat time
That þe Iewes did hym so moch pine
And on the roode wolde hym sloo,
Anone he vanisshid aweie hym froo
And transposed the body of Iudas   585
Into the liknes that hymselff was,
And that bodie thei turmentid on þe tre
And wente fulle wele hit had ben he.
This is the bileue that thei haue,
And wel thei trowen thei shul be saue.   590
But forthe passid this gentil knyght
And through Turky he went ful right
To a cite that men callith Nek.
A kinge that hight Achimalek
Som tyme was foundour of þat toun   595
Bifore Cristis incarnacioun,
And yit euery yere men seen hym oones
In riche apparail for the nones,
For as men of that cuntre tellith
Amonge þe fairie he leueth and dwellith.   600

f. 81rb Than went he forth welle I wote
Bi the porte of Chiuitote,
And bi the brake of seint George went he
Forth vnto Gehene See.
And in þat see, I tel you can,   605
Lyeth seinte Nicholas þat holy man
In a faire chapelle of lyme and stoone,
And there hym secheth many oone,
Men and women lered and lewde,
For many faire meraclis þat there ben shewde.   610
And bi the coostes of that see
Dyuers iles ful many there be.
The first ile that he come too
That was the ile of Siloo,
And in that cuntre wondir thikke   615
Groweth grete plente of mastikke.
Folke in þat cuntre sayn and swere

601 *This line occurs also at the end of f.* 81ra   614 Insula Silo *in margin*

That mastik groweth noowhere but there.
The ile of Pathmos than is next,
There that seynt Iohn the euangelist   620
Made the Apocalips and wrote eche dele,
And holie churche knoweth it wele.
And forth than the knyght went hym
Vnto the cite of Ephesym.
And seint Iohn that I spake of beforn   625
In that cite he was born
And lieth welle faire without the toun
In a hous of religioun.
Foure score nyntene yere and more
Forsothe this holie man leued thore   630
In penaunce and in praiers rife,
And atte last he eendid his life.
In the church he stoode to preche,
The lawe of God the folke to teche.
His graue was made, as ye may here,   635
Atte eende of the hie autere,
And atte eende of his sermoun
In þat graue he leide hym doun.
And to þat graue thei went anoone
And founde þere noþer bloode ne boone   640
f. 81va   And noþinge but manna iwis,
That aungelles mete callid ys.
And euer sith wist noo man
Ne herde telle where he bicam.
And þe seuen sleepers lien in tha[t] toun,   645
As holie churche makith mencioun,
And in a caue fast þere by
In the mounte of Sely
There thei slepten bi themselff
Thre hundrid yere sixti and twelff.   650
Nowe forth his cours þe knyght haþe tane
Vnto the cite of Panterane.
Seint Nicholas þat I nempned beforn
In that cite he was born,
And afftirward bisshop was he   655

645 that] MS. tha, *possibly a genuine scribal form but cf.* 85, 100, 455, 495,
762, 812, 922   648 Sely] MS. *perhaps* Selij

Of þe cite of Miree.
There is also þe ile of Grece.
Of londe it is a wel faire pece
And plenteuous of lifis foode
And welle inhabitid with tovnes goode.　　　　660
There is the ile also of Sopheos.
Of good fisshinge it hath the loos
Of alle the cuntrees þat there be
Bi the coostes of þat see.
Anoþer ile þere is also　　　　665
Men clepeth þe ile of Lango.
Of that ile withouten fail
I shalle you telle a grete meruail.
For the grete clerk Ypocras
Som time kinge þerof he was.　　　　670
He had a doughter that was ful faire,
That of the londe shuld ben his aire,
But hir stepmoodire hir forshope
Vnto a dragoun, as seith the boke,
The most horrible that euer was sene,　　　　675
And in þat shappe euer to bene
Vnto the tyme þat a knyght
On hors bak, bothe stoute and wight,
That boldeli dare to her ride,
And þat the hors dare welle abide　　　　680

f. 81ᵛᵇ　　Til the knyght be light adoun
And take a cosse of that dragoun.
Than shuld the dragoun, as men seyn,
Be turned into a woman ayein.
And vppon a time so hit bifelle,　　　　685
As men in that cuntre done telle,
There come a knyght fro seint Iohnes,
An hardi knyght for the nones,
And boldely toward hir he rode.
The worme was glad and hym abode,　　　　690
But when the hors þat was so wight
Of þat dragoun had a sight
He fledde for feere and wolde naught bide
Til he come to the see side,
And into the see lepe the hors than,　　　　695

And so was lost both hors and man.
Anothir time, as I vndirstonde,
There was a shippe dryven to londe.
The maister shippeman verement
Sawe the castelle and thidir he went. 700
In at the yate he gan hym drawe
Som refresshinge there for to haue.
He clepid and cried with all his myght,
And hym aunswerd noo maner wyght.
So longe he gan to crie and calle, 705
And atte laste þere come into halle.
A woman þere he fonde anone,
So faire sawe he neuer none,
And with a combe of goold reede
The woman sate and kembid her hede. 710
Anone as he lokid her vppon
Sho was so faire of bloode and boon
That leuere he had bi hir haue leie
Than alle the good that euer he seie.
And in his armes he gan hir foolde, 715
Hir haue kist fayn he wolde.
Do wai, she saide, þat mai not be.
Thou woste nat howe it stant with me,
For I am but a daie in the yere
A woman as þou seest nowe here; 720

f. 82ra And tolde hym bothe more and lasse
For þat sho myschapen wasse,
And in what manere that he sholde
Done yf he hir haue wolde.
For sho said yif he myght be 725
In this manere to helpen me,
Of alle this londe thou sholdist bene
Lorde and kinge and I thi quene.
Grete sorowe he made in his entent.
He toke his leve and forth he went, 730
And also hastelich as he myght
He ordeined hym to be a knyght
And araied hym in the best manere.
And comen ayenne þe next yere,
He roode vnto the castel yate. 735

The dragoun he fonde redie þere ate.
Hit was so horrible vppon to se
That for alle the goode in cristiante
He derst noo lenger there abide,
But fast to shippe he gan to ride   740
And put þe shippe fro the londe.
The dragoun come glidinge on þe sonde.
Hit was grete sorowe to see and heere
Howe sho ferde with hevie chere.
He durst noo lenger abide for dreede.   745
Than is next the ile of Roodes,
A faire cuntre and brode is
Sixti myle almooste in length.
Hit is a cuntree of str[ength],
Riche and plenteuous for þe nones,   750
And þere is the hede hous of seint Iohnes,
And þere is a castelle realle fulle riche,
In Engelonde is none hym liche.
In the see than shul men sail
Vnto Cipres withouten fail   755
Bi þe Gulphe of Satelly,
A wel faire cuntre sikerly.
Satelly was a faire citee.
Nowe stondeth þere hous ne tree.
I wille you telle in what wise   760

f. 82rb Hit was distroied or þat I rise.
A yonge man was in that toun,
A burgeis sone of grete renoun.
He loued a maide as his life
And wolde haue had hir to wife.   765
And sone þereaffter hit gan falle
The maide deied as wee shulle alle.
This man went a nyghte priuelie
And toke vp þe cors and laie hir bie,
And when he had done þat synful dede   770
He heled þe corse and forth he yede.
Than come þere a vois and spak hym to
And saide, Man what hastou do?
I commaunde the in alle manere

749 strength] MS. sti   756 Gulphe] MS. Gulple

This nyghte xii. moneth þat thou be here, 775
And loke that it be nought foryeten,
And thou shalt see what þou hast geten.
With careful hert and sorie moode
This yonge man forth his waie yoode.
The xii. monethis eende forgate he nought. 780
Thidir he went with carefulle thouȝt
And opened the graue as he was bede.
And out there fliȝe a brennynge hede
With brennynge eie, brennynge chere,
And alle that cite he sette a fere 785
And brent it clene vnto þe grounde,
That man ne beeste was none founde,
And þat cite through hap and chaunce
Was destroied through such veniaunce.
Therefor me thenkith hit mai be said 790
In holie writte as it is laid,
Ve facienti iniquitatem in confusione multorum
Quorum ciuitas igni succensa est, et cetera.
In Cipres that I nempned beforn
Seint Barnabe there was born, 795
But men callith hym in þat cuntre
Ioseph þe noble Barnabe.
And beestes ther beth in many tovnes
That men callith *papiounes.*
Thai ben fulle swifft and wonder kene 800
And liche to libardis moche thai bene.
There mai no beeste froo ham goone
That thei ne wille take hem anone.
Than saileth men forth in that see
Vnto a welle faire cite, 805
A noble cite without mys,
Porte Tire callid it ys,
And than to Beruth and Sadorneye,
And noble citees thei beth tweye.
And from thens thei gon passe 810
Vnto the cite of Damasse.
There prechid seinte Paule first in þat toun
Sone affter his conuersioun.
And the prophete Ananie alsoo

f. 82va

In that tyme he dwellid thoo,   815
And to his hous seinte Paule went
For God allemyghty thidir hym sent.
Fram Cipres vnto Iherusaleme
Men mowe holde þe salte streme
Til þat thei come to Porte Iaffe,   820
Yif God wille that thei be sauffe.
And forth bi londe than mowe thei goon
And come to Iherusaleme anoon.
But I haue herde of men also
That to Iherusaleme wolden go,   825
At Venise thei haue take the see
And at Acoun londid he.
And who þat shall the see taken
Out of Venise into Acoun
He shalle haue, I take in hande,   830
Of Lumbardis milis twey thousande
And foure score and somat more
Bi the see or he come thore.
And besidis the cite of Acoun
Is þe mounte of Carmelioun.   835
The ferst frere Carmes þat euer were
Thei were bigon and foundid there,
And of þe hille thair name thei neme,
Carmes as men doth clepen heme.
And besidis Carmelioun   840
f. 82ᵛᵇ   Is the Fosse of Menyoun.
Fosse Menyoun is rounde pytte,
Of drie sande fulle is hytte,
An hundrid cubitis hit is ouerright.
The sande is wonder clere and bright.   845
Shippis þat makith þere for hir passage
Takith of that sande for thaire lastage,
For thouȝ men taken thereof today
As moche as men mowe carie away,
Amorowe þere wille be neuertheles   850
But fulle ayen as hit was.
And men suppose þat hit be

831 twey] MS. twenti   841 Menioũ *in margin*   845 sande] MS.
secounde

An issue fram the Graueled Se.
And euer men mowe þere fynde
Comyng vp grete brethe of wynde. 855
And of that sonde men taken sere
Virris and glas faire and clere,
And take any metal and scoure it bright
And laie it in þat sande a nyght,
Hit shal be turned out of his kynde, 860
For clere glas þou shalt it fynde.
And yif þou laidist ayenne that glas
Hit turneth to metalle as hit first was.
Therfor men accountith that sande
The grettest meruail of þat lande, 865
As wee fyndith in holie writte
A resoun that accordith to hitte:
Sicut diuini operis est naturam condere
Ita est et in aliud mutare.
Who þat wille from Acoun take his pas 870
To Iherusalem þat holie plas,
From thens he must to Palestine,
A noble cite and a fyne,
And so in his waie forth to fare
Vnto the cite of Coysare. 875
And his waie than shalle he nym
Vnto the castelle of Pylrym,
And so forth right as any seme
To Iaffe and than to Ihorusaleme.
But who þat is in Engelonde nowe 880
And to Ierusaleme hath made a vowe,
He shal take anothir way
Than I haue spoke of today.
The best waie I wille hym wisse,
For frist he mot goone to Venisse. 885
There shalle he take the brode watres
And londe naught til he come to Acres
Ouer þe brode Grekissh See,
And that is a welle werisom iourne.
And fram Acres than sikirly 890
Beth foure leukes to seint Hely,

877 Pylrym] MS. Pyhym

And than a leuk to þe mount [C]armelle,
And than to Tire I wote ful welle.
Of þe baptist þere is a tothe,
Pilgrimes knoweth þat it is sothe.   895
Than is a leuke vnto a toun
That is þe cite of Peroun,
For Ihesus Criste there restid hym
Bifore þe castelle of Pilrym.
And than a leuk shal he haue   900
Til he come vnto the caue
There Ihesus fram þe Iewes hym hid
When thei hir malice to hym kid.
And three leukis than there be
To Nostre Dame de Marroe.   905
Oure ladi for hir sonnes sake
In þat place hir rest gan take.
Than shal he fynde bi the way
To Cesare but leukis tway,
And þere is ȝitte a marble stoone   910
That Ihesus ete his mete vppon.
And also in þat same toun
Was seint Poule put into prisoun.
And fram Cesare vnto Iapheth
Beth xii. mylis, who þat hem geth.   915
The good holie man Noe
In his life had sonnes thre,
Iapheth, Cam, and eke Sem.
Alle oure linage come of hem,
For when Noes floode gan cese   920
Eche of hem her cuntree chese,
And Iapheth made þat toun thoo
And affter his name callid it soo.
Hit is the eldest toun, men sayn,
Of alle the world wide or playn.   925
The grete geaunt Andromounde,
The grettest of alle þe worlde rounde,
Bi a cheine there tied he stoode
Longe bifore Noes floode.
Yit in þe rooche men mowe see there   930

f. 83rb

892 Carmelle] MS. Armelle

Where the cheines fastned were,
And of his ribbis men mowe þere se
Fourti feete of lengthe is he.
To Iherusaleme than men shal pas,
Two leukis noþer more ne las.   935
At þe north gate þere as men geth
There was seint Stephen stoned to deth.
And in þe myddis of þat cite
A welle fair mynster men mai se.
And in þat mynster is [ywis]   940
The sepulcre of oure lorde Ihesu Crist
Closed in with riche toures
And twelff pilers of grete valoures.
And ouer the sepulcre there above
Opene is the church rove.   945
There neuer tempest, snowe, ne rayn
Commyth into that place certayn.
There atte entre as men goon
Stoden oure ladie and eke seint Iohn
And othir disciplis moo also   950
Whan oure lorde thus spake hem to:
Mulier ecce filius tuus. Deinde dicit discipulo,
Ecce mater tua.
Bi the grete dore in þe mynster there
Three Maries cutten of her here   955
And wepte and cried with loude vois
Tho the Iewes did Criste on the crois.
And in the mynster in þat right partie
There is the mounte of Caluarie.
Seuentene staires beth vp þerto.   960
f. 83ᵛᵃ   And a litille fro thens also
Atte eende of þe hie autere
There stant yitte þe same pilere
That Criste was beten with scourgis kene,
And yitte som droopis of bloode þere bene   965
And a litel thens in þe right hande
Fourtie greces adoun passande
A faire chapelle is in þat place.
The holie cros þere founden was.

940 ywis] MS. þᵉ gift   965 bene] MS. beth sene

Twoo hundrid winter there hit lay   970
Til seinte Helene hit fette away.
And thilk seint Helene, I vndirstonde,
That borne was here in Engelonde,
And king Coel hir fader was
That made Colchester þat faire plas,   975
And kinge Constantine was hir sone
That tyme he was emperour of Rome.
But in þat same place right
There that faire chapel is so diȝte
Oure lorde turned the Samaritane   980
Vnto the right bileue than.
And fast therebi a litille doun
Oure lorde was put into prisoun,
And the chaine is there also
That about his necke was do.   985
The midwarde of þe worlde is þere
Euen bifore the hie autere,
And in þat same place sothely
The noble Ioseph of Armathy
Laide the bodie of oure lorde Ihesus   990
When he toke hym doun of the crois
And wasshed the bodie feete and honde,
And in clene sendalle he it wonde
And laide hym in þat monument
Ful derworthli with good entent.   995
In the north side, ful welle I wote,
Ther lieth seint Chariote
Also hoole soth to say
As he was buried the first day,
And ȝit he hath leide buried thore   1000
viii.ᶜ· wynter and somdelle more.
As ferre fram the mynster, as I trowe,
As a man mai shote with a bowe
Is the grete temple iwys
That temple domini callid it ys.   1005
And kinge Dauyd hit bigan
But it was eendid with Salaman,
And afftirwarde in a stounde
The Caldeis beten it to grounde,

f. 83ᵛᵇ

And hit was made ayen fulle wele   1010
With Ihesu and Zorobabele.
Hit was destroied yitte affter this
With the kinge Antiochus,
And ȝitte ayenne made was he
Of þe kinge Iudas Machabe.   1015
Hit was distroied yitte affter than
With Titus and Vaspacian.
Alle þat there was thei bete adoun
As holie writte maketh mencioun:
Non relinquet[ur] lapis super lapidem.   1020
Of Cristis dethe thai toke veniaunce
And distroied the Iewes with grete distaunce.
And sith had thei nothir londe ne toun
Ne neuer siker habitacioun.
And in that temple beth yates twelff   1025
And four dores beth on the selff.
And in þat temple as men goon
There is a grete roche of stoon,
And vppon þat stoone, sothe it is,
Some time stode *archa federis*   1030
And the seuen chaundelers þereby
And the v. bookes of Moysy.
And vppon þat roche Criste was present,
Seinte Symeon in his armes hym hent
And there through grace of God allemyght   1035
Seynte Symeon had his syght.
When Criste woolde to the puple preche
Vppon that stone he stode to teche.
And vppon a time when he þere stoode
To teche and preche þe puple goode,   1040
The fals Iewes in a rowe
Grete stoones at hym gan throwe,
And whan he sawe the stoones approche
He vanisshid awaie from the roche.
To this mater hit mai be laid   1045
As it is in the gospelle said:
Ihesus autem transciens per medium illorum ibat.
And there besidis is a place

f. 84ra (margin, left of line 1041)

1020 relinquetur] MS. relinquet

There seint Petir in prisoun was,
And the cheines bothe hole and sounde   1050
Wherewith he was feterid and bounde.
Bi the Porte David in Iherusaleme
There lieth the waie vnto Bethleme,
And v. leukes is ham bitwene,
As men sain þat there haue bene.   1055
And in the mydwarde of that way
There is forsothe, as I you say,
A wel faire churche sikerly
Of þe holie prophete seint Hely.
And ferþer more a man shal gone   1060
And come to Campe Floree anone,
And whi hit hight Camp Floree
I shalle you telle the veritee.
There was a maide that shuld be brent
That men callid Maide Florent.   1065
Sho was accusid wrongefully
That a man shuld lie her by.
A grete fire was made in haste
And þe faire maide þerein thei caste,
And through the grace of God allmyght   1070
The fire quenchid anone right.
And alle the woode þat gan to brenne
To reede roosis turned all thenne,
And alle the woode þat brent nouȝt
To white roosis hit was brouȝt.   1075
The first roosis that euer were
In this maner bigonne there.
Bifore þat time was neuer none founde
Growenge roosis vppon the grounde.
This is the enchesoun and welle mai be   1080

f. 84rb

That hit was callid Campe Floree.
And thus oure lorde God omnipotent
Delyuerid that faire innocent.
And there is in Bethleme sikerly
A welle fair churche of oure lady.   1085
A litel crofft there is biforne
There oure lorde Ihesus was borne,
And five strides fro than to stracche

There is yitte the same cracche
Of þe oxe and of the asse   1090
There oure lord ibore was.
Anothir place there is fast by
There that alle the children ly
That Heroudes quellid in his outrage
That weren within twoo yere age.   1095
And seinte Ierome þat a doctoure was
There lieth buried in þat same plas.
Withouten Betheleme a myle or mare
A faire chapelle stondith nowe thare.
There the aungelles tolde þe shipperdis forn 1100
Howe that Ihesus Criste was born.
Thei herde aungelles synge also
Gloria in excelsis deo.
The shepperdis þat kepten þe shepe þere
Symon and Iudee forsoth thei were.   1105
Fro Betheleme who so yede or come
Vnto the valeie of Ebrone
Beth v. leukis longe and fyne.
The foure patriarkis þere thei lyne,
Adam þe first and Abraham,   1110
Isaac and Iacob lieth with ham,
And with hem liggeth her foure wifis
That thei had in her lifis,
Eve þe frist and than Sarra,
Rebecca the third, the fourþe Lya.   1115
A faire church there is iwys,
Of seint Abraham foundid it ys.
An heede also þere is isette
There God and Abraham togidirs mette,
For God hym yaff a welle faire chaunce,   1120
There he confermed his creaunce.
And as I vndirstondinge haue,
Without Iherusaleme þere is a caue,
xii. thousand corseyntis þere buried were,
As men tellen þat dwelleth there.   1125
In the south side of Iherusaleme anone
Men shullen fynde the mount Syone
There þat seint Peter, as seith the boke,

f. 84va

Thries there oure lorde forsoke.
And in þat place, wite ye welle,   1130
Men mowe fynde a faire chapelle,
And in that place his freendes he hade
And his maunde þere he made.
And in þat place he made hir seete
And þere hymselff wosshe hir feete.   1135
And ȝit is þere the same vesselle
Bothe hole and sounde, wite ye welle.
And in þe same place verement
There he had his iugement.
Bitwene þe hille and þe cite   1140
Is the welle of Siloe.
And as men in the gospelle fynde,
A man þat was ibore blynde
Bisought oure lord fulle of myght
That he wolde helpe hym of his sight.   1145
And he bad hym, as I you telle,
He shuld goo wasshe hym in þat welle.
And he did as he hym bad
And anone his sight he had.
And in þat mount, sothe it was,   1150
Oure ladi out of this world gan pas,
And þere aungellis with meri steven
Bere hir vp right to heuen.
Anothir mounte there is ȝete
Men clepeth þe mounte of Olivete.   1155
And in that mounte þat I you neuen
Oure lord God stied to heuen.
And in þat place, wite ȝe welle,
Yit stondith þere a faire chapelle,
And in that chapelle is the stoone   1160
f. 84vb   That his lifft fote stode vppon
When he into heuen styȝe.
Men knoweth it welle that it syȝe,
And of his fote there is the shap
Vppon þe stone þere he did stap.   1165
That oþer stone is in Engelond here
In the abbeie of Westmynstere.

And in þat mounte oure lorde also
His disciplis callid hym to,
And the *Pater Noster* he hym taught   1170
And bad hem to wende straught
Through alle þe worlde for to preche
And þat praier men to teche.
Bytwene þat mounte and þe cite
The vale of Iosaphat is he.   1175
A faire mynster there is iwys,
Oure ladie beried þerein ys.
And in a litille chapelle there by
Is a place men callith Gethsemany.
There the Iewes oure lorde toke   1180
And his disciplis hym forsoke.
And in that tyme oure lorde anone
He smote his honde vppon the stone,
And yitte ben alle þe fyngeris sene
In that stone withouten wene.   1185
And a stones cast fro thenne
There is a chapelle þat men kenne,
In þat place the fadir he praid
And these woordis there he said:
Pater, si fieri potest, transeat a me calix iste.   1190
For drede of deth þere as he sat
Bloode and water there he swat.
Witnesse of men þat there han bene,
The drope[s] of bloode ȝit þere ben sene.
And in þat valeie, as men say,   1195
We shulle be demed a domysday.
And fro Ierusalem to Bethany
Nys but oo leuke certaynly,
And in þat place was the hous
That dwellid in Simon leprous.   1200

f. 85ra   He herborowid gladlie alle and some,
Oure lorde and alle þat wolde come.
And in þat place, I am welle ware,
Oure lorde arered seint Lazare,
Fro dethe to life he did hym haue   1205
That foure daies laie deede in graue.

1194 dropes] MS. drope

C 7739   D

Fro Bethanye to flome Iordane
viii. leukis ben þere than,
There þat seint Iohn þe baptist
Baptised oure lorde Ihesu Crist.   1210
And twei leukes than þere fro
Is þe cite of Iherico.
Wel halff a myle fro þe floode
There is a churche faire and goode
Of seint Iohn, and yit men swere   1215
That þe water þat renneth there
Cometh fro the bodie of seint Iohn,
þere erst bifore was neuer noon.
And wel half a leuke fro Iherico
As men from þe flome done go   1220
There is þe place, as men saies,
There Criste fastid fourtie daies.
And fast besidis that place than
Is the gardeine of Abraham,
And in þe mydward of þat gardyn   1225
A wel faire streme renneth þereyn.
Som time þe water of þat welle
Was as bitter as any galle,
And seint Helie þat holie prophete
Through his praier made it swete.   1230
And many pilgrimes þat waie there geth
Vnto the cite of Nazareth,
For in þat cite þere is a place
There oure ladie bore sho was.
The aungell grette hir þere also   1235
And these wordis seid hir to:
Aue gracia plena, dominus tecum.
Besidis the cite of Iherico
A grete meruaile þere is also.
A stonding water þere is iwys,   1240
f. 85rb   The Deede See callid hit ys,
For hit renneth nat but stant still,
Men clepeth it deede for þat skille.
And þat Deede See ys certainly
Bytwene Litille Ynde and Araby.   1245

Fyve hundrid stadies and [iiii.] score
Hit ys in lengthe and somdel more,
And seven score stadies it is in brede
And somdele more, as I you rede.
Noo creature alive may be   1250
But shalle be persshid in þat see,
And þat is quik there mai no[t], *me* thinke,
Forsothe vndir þat water synke.
But nowe þere the see is so clyme,
Fyve citees there stoode som tyme,   1255
In that cuntree thei stode on rawe,
As I shal hir names shawe.
Sodome, Baldam, and Gomore,
Seboyn þere was and eke Segore.
These v. citees, as I you telle,   1260
For synne thei sonke into helle.
But Looth the goode holie man
In Segor he dwellid than.
He cried to God and mercie craued
And so some of þe toun were saued.   1265
When þe wedir is clere and hote
Yit men mai see þe place of Lothe.
And bi þe coostis of that flome
Appul trees there groweth some,
And who so cleueth an appul atwynne   1270
Blake asshes beth þere withynne.
And take irenne and fethers yfere
And cast hem in þat water clere,
The irenne wil flete and þe fethir synke.
Grete merueil þerof men doone thynke.   1275
But for þe puple ayenst kynde
Diden her synnes, as clerkis fynde,
Ayens kynde in þe same manere
Right so dothe the water his devere.
Omne quod natum est a suo primitiuo trahit originem. 1280
f. 85ᵛᵃ   And yif a man wille witterly
Go to þe mounte of Synay
And seint Katerine for to seke,
A fair pilgrimage it is eke.

        1246 iiii.] MS. .V.   1252 not me] MS. none

And yif he wille passen save, 1285
Save conduite he mote have
Of þe Soudon of Babiloine
Yif he thenke to come againe,
For in Babiloine þe Lesse
There þe Sawdones dwellinge es 1290
In the cite of Cair
That stant vppon a fair riuer,
And Nile þat ryuer cleped it ys,
Oone of þe stremes of paradys.
That ryuer commeth rennynge, as I fynde, 1295
Through þe grete wildirnes of Ynde,
And þere it renneth into þe grounde
So þat noo drope of hym is founde.
And so vndir þe erthe renneth he
An hugie space of þat cuntre, 1300
And than he breketh out ageyn
Vndir Aloth the grete mountayn
And environeth without hope
Alle þe londe of Ethiope.
And so he commeth doun fro than 1305
About þe lande of Morecan,
And so bi Egipte for certain
For in þat lande commeth neuer rain.
Therfor alle men þat there abide
Dwellith alonge vppon þe water side. 1310
And þere bene the mountaines of Gelboe
For of ham was made þis auctorite:
Montes Gelboe nec ros nec pluuia super vos veniat.
And so renneth þat ryuer to Palestaner
And to þe cite of Alisaunder. 1315
Nowe lete we þis and turn ayein
To the londe of Babiloin.
In Babiloine, I telle you welle,
There is þe toure of Babelle.
In þe grete desert hit stant certein 1320
f. 85ᵛᵇ Bitwene Arabie and Macedoyn.
But as men telleth in hir gestes
Dragounes, wormes, and wilde beestes,
Beeres and apes and lyounes kene,

Libardis and wolues so many þere bene   1325
That thou3 men wolde þidir gone
Thei shuld be deede and eten anone.
But som [time], as I telle you can,
In þat londe was a sowdan,
His name was Nembras Galeas,   1330
The frist kinge þat euer was.
Ful riche he was of tresour
And he biganne þat same toure,
That it shuld last to þe firmament,
And was his purpos verement.   1335
And first he lete make þe walle
In manere as I you tel shalle.
Fyve and twenti leukes about
Bigan þe walle withouten dout,
And x. leukis and no lasse   1340
Thei made þe walle of thiknesse.
So longe men wrou3t with alle her myght
That it was brought vnto the heyght
Of sixti stadies and foure mo.
So longe werkmen wrought þereto   1345
That in alle þe worlde founde thei noone
That durst gon vp and worch þereon
Sauff xv. men, as I you telle,
And herkeneth nowe what þere bifelle.
The werkmen went to bedde a nyght   1350
To take hir rest as hit was right,
And on þe morne þei risen echone
And to thair werk thought to gone.
And when euery man come to his stage
Euery man spake dyuers langage,   1355
And God such chaunce amonge hem sent
That noo man wist what oþere ment.
And eche man toke his waie to wende
And so þat werk stoode atte eende.
Now this toure Babel let we ben thore   1360
f. 86ra   And of Synay speke we more.
Atte fote of Synay, I [vndir]take,
There is an hous of monkes blake,

1328 time] MS. m̄en   1363 vndirtake] MS. take

And a pore hous hit is withalle
For hir pocessioun nys but smalle.   1365
But I shal telle you a wondir þinge,
The moost substaunce of her livinge.
There is a daie in someris tide
That alle maner wilde foule ny3 and wide
Of dyuers londis ferre about   1370
That daie thei cometh without dout,
And euery foule than bringeth he
A grene braunche of an olive tree
And atte seint Katerines thei leten hem falle
And homeward a3enne thei fleen alle.   1375
Than cometh the monkis and of hem taken
And of þe braunchis oyle thei maken,
And that thei sellen into euery coost,
And þereof cometh her livinge mooste.
And men mowe stande in Synay   1380
And se the mountes of Hermenay,
And 3if þe wedir faire and clere be
Noes shippe þere men mowe see.
Nowe lesteneth and I shalle you telle
A meracle and a grete meruelle.   1385
Besidis Damasse þat fair cite
Beth v. leukis and stadiis thre
A toune þere is and an abbay
Stondinge bi þe hie way.
Hit is callid in mannys spache   1390
Nostre Dame de Sardinache.
Et est stadium tantum spacium
    quantum Ercules cucurit cum vno anelitu.
Aboue þe hie auter certainly
There is an ymage of oure lady   1395
That some tyme withouten fable
There was peyntid vppon a table,
And afftirwarde in processe
The ymage turnede into flesshe.
And through the grace of God allemyght   1400
Hyt droppeth oyle bothe day and nyght
f. 86rb   Out of the plain tabernacle—

1392 *This quotation is written as one line in* MS.

Hit must be nedis a fair meracle—
And there is a vesselle of marble fyne
That the oile doth droppen ine. 1405
That vesselle is boothe hole and sounde,
Fulle welle with irenne it is ibounde.
And pilgrimes whan thei thidir come
Of þat oile thei hath some
And done cures many and fele 1410
And many sike þei maketh hem hele.
And men sayne þat the oile so clere,
And hit ben kepte vii. yere,
Hit wille turne to flesshe and bloode.
Me thinkith this myracle faire and goode. 1415
Nowe wolle we passe to Cisile
And þereof speken a litil while.
There is an hille, an huge in hight,
That euer brenneth bothe day and nyght;
An hie mountaine it is ywys, 1420
Mounte Ethnica callid it ys,
And alle hit is of clene bremstone.
And vii. issues beth þereone,
And þere smyt out a grete fire
Of diuers colouris wondir shire. 1425
And men of þat cuntre doone telle
That thoo issues beth þe yatis of helle.
And in Cisile there is also
A wondir meracle amonge oþere moo.
A maner of naddres hauen they 1430
That thei assaie her children by,
And bi the naddre thei mowe witen
Yiff the children ben treuli geten.
For yif the childe a bastarde be
The nadre hym stynge sone wil he, 1435
And þereby men mowe witen anone
Wheþer thei ben bastarde or be none.
For yiff þe childe noo bastarde be
Anone the naddre wille from hym fle.
Aspes and basiliscus men hem calle 1440
The naddres in þat cuntree alle,
As seith a vers in þe sawtiere

f. 86va

That accordith welle to þis matere:
Super aspidem et basiliscum ambulabis.
Ayen to Egipte nowe turne we   1445
And speken a while of þat cuntre,
For twaine Egiptes þere ben a rowe,
Bothe þe hie and eke the lowe.
In hie Egipte there is a gete
In the wildirnesse of Damyete,   1450
A wondirful beeste walkinge about,
And men of hym han grete dout.
For fram the navelle dounward than
He hath a shappe as hath a man,
And vpward than, fulle welle I wote,   1455
He hath the shappe right as a gote
With longe hornes, and sharp thei be.
A wondir sight it is to se.
And in þat shap he hath gon ay
And euer shal tille domesday.   1460
And in lowe Egipte in þat cuntre
Ys the cite of Cleophe,
And in þat cite is a temple rounde,
There stant noo fairere on Godes grounde.
And þere thei haue the date iwritten   1465
Wherebi thei mowe welle witen
Of a wondirfulle brid withalle,
And fenixe that bridde men doone calle.
For in all the worlde is there noone
Of that kynde but he allone,   1470
And atte eche v.^{c.} yeeris eende
Thidir cometh that brid fleende.
And the preestes han ful welle vndirnome
And knoweth the time when he wil come,
And euen vppon the hie autiere   1475
Ys made a fire both faire and clere.
Anone cometh than that same brid
And falleth in that fire amyd,
And alle to asshes than is he brent.
And than the wardeynes verement   1480
The asshes into an hepe thei lay

1449 a] MS. .a.   1462 Cleopole *in margin*

And shitteth the dores and gone their way.
And the next daie than affter this
Liche a worme alive he ys.
And þe seconde daie he is ful waxen   1485
And stondeth alle above the asshen.
And at none þe thrid day
He takith his flight and fleethe his way.
And in that Egipte beth gardines
Of diuers frute and eke of vines   1490
That beren frute withouten were
Seven tymes in the yere.
And there thei vsen a wondir crafft
That shalle neuer more be lafft.
Thei bringeth forth chikenes boþe more and lasse   1495
In hote hors donge and eke of asse,
Gees and hennes oolde and yonge
Thei bene so haute in hote donge.
And many ben certainly
Of þat crafft and lyven thereby,   1500
For as many eyren as men ham bere
For as many chekenes thei shal aunswere.
And applis there bene ful fair iwys,
Men calleth hem pomes of paradys.
For who that cleueth an appul atwynne   1505
He shal a faire crois fynde there ynne.
But certainli thei wille nat last
But viii. daies atte moost.
And figge trees ben growinge þere
But neuer a leeffe thai done bere,   1510
And faire figges of Maligge
Vppon the braunchis hangen thikke.
And fast besidis the cite of Chaire
There is a felde bothe wide and faire,
And in that feelde, as men mai see,   1515
There groweth bawme grete plente.
And men of that cuntre seyn and swere
That noo bawme groweth but there.
And the grete bernes that Ioseph made
Ben on the plaine of Politrade.   1520
And foure there ben longe and wyde,

With hie walles on eueri side.
And eche an hous is of grete strength,
v.c· cubites eche is of length,
And an hundrid cubitis of brede.   1525
There that thei stondeth withouten drede
Bitwene Egipte and Auffrik,
In alle þis worlde beth none ham lik.
And there mai noo man come saunz doute
For wilde wormes þat ben þere aboute,   1530
Both snakes, naddres, and lisardes,
Cocadrilles also and eke glistardes,
And meny scorpiounes, as men hem calle,
And cocatrices þe werst of hem alle.
And atte cite of Raphao   1535
A welle faire ryuere commeth þereto,
And as it telleth in the storie
Hit is clepid Sabbatory.
And I wille telle you iwys
Whi Sabbatorie callid it ys,   1540
For cause it stondith stille alway
Saue oonelie on þe sonneday.
That daie fro morne til mydouernone
He renneth as othir watris done,
And eueri nyght hit freseth sore   1545
But on þat nyght neuer more.
And in þe kingedome of [Hermon]ye
Besidis the cite of Portepye
In an oolde forleten castelle
There is a wondir grete meruelle.   1550
Vppon a perche amyd the halle
A faire sperhauke þere sitte withalle,
And a gentil ladie of fayrie
Kepeth that hauke and sytteth hym bye.
And who so euer wille vndirtake   1555
Bi that sperhauke for to wake
Three daies and three nyght
Withouten sleepe, withouten lyght,
And eke without any company,
To goone or sytte but nauȝt ly,   1560

1538 Sabbatori *in margin*   1547 Hermonye] MS. libye *and* libie *in margin*

Withouten mete, withouten drinke,
Whateuer he wille þereaffter thynke
Or what thinge that he wille craue
Of erthelie thinge he shalle haue.
And when thoo three daies ben ygone   1565
The ladi wille com forth anone
And salewe hym fulle curteisly,
And vppon þe benche sytte hym by
And byd hym axe whateuer he wille,
And sho his axinge shalle fulfille,   1570
So that hit be of erthelie thinge,
Els shalle he faile of his askinge.
There was a marchaunte in Venise
That had lost through marchaundise
All þe goode that euer he had,   1575
And sore in dette he was bistad.
Vnto that place he wente and woke
And so moche richesse there he toke
So that he and alle his freendis
Hadden richesse withouten eendis.   1580
And a kynge of Hermony also
Vppon a tyme nought longe igo
Thidir he come withouten dwele
And woke and did his devere wele.
And when three daies were come to eende   1585
The gentil lady to hym gan weende,
And salewed hym fulle gentely
And thankid hym of his curtasy,
And bad hym axe what he wolde craue
Of erthelie thinge, and he shuld haue.   1590
The kinge aunswerid withouten drede
And said: Madame, I haue noo nede
Of goolde ne siluere ne noo riches,
Ne of othire tresoure more ne les,
Ne nothinge els I wille craue   1595
But youre selff I wille haue.
Than said the lady gentil and free:
Nay forsoth, that may nat be,
For ye welle knoweth sekirly
That I am noo woman erthely.   1600

But for thou axest ayenst right
f. 87ᵛᵃ   Thinge that thou haue ne myghte,
And thou seist thou hast no neede
And veleny thou doost me bede,
I putte the nowe in subieccioun   1605
Of the Cane for this enchesoun,
And thine ospringe alle affter the
Til ye come to the nyneth degre.
Awaie sho vanisshid fro hym thore
So that of hire he sawe no more,   1610
And in subieccioun thei ben yette
Of the Cane as shoo ham hete.
And a man þat standith in that cuntray,
Evenne atte hiȝe none of the day,
And turneth hym even eeste right   1615
When the sonne shineth bright,
He shalle see his shadowe abide
Euen affter his right side.
And also in the Liby See
There mai no fisshe livinge be,   1620
Hit is so hote bothe thikke and thynne,
There may noo fisshe abide þereynne.
Mesopotane and also Caldeie
And the reame of Arabye,
Thes londes ben withouten les   1625
Bitwene Tigree and Euffrates.
The kingdome of Medie
And the kingdome of Percie,
These twoo londis ben and many an ile
Bitwene Tigree and the water of Nyle.   1630
The kingedome also of Surrye,
Palestine and Florencie,
These reames ben withouten lees
Bitwene Mediteran and Euffrates.
That Mediteran for certaine   1635
Cometh froo Marrok and Despaine
And holdith his cours forth fro than
Vnto the Grete See Occian.
And also the kingedome of Sichie

1619 Liby] MS. Lumby

Vnto the see of Casperie   1640
Is closed aboute for certaines

f. 87vb With wondir grete and hie mountaynes.
And in the same reame thare
Is the ryuere callid Thamare,
That holdeth his cours sikirly   1645
Vnto the kingedome of Albany.
And in that reame of Albanie
Beth stronge dogges hugie and hie,
Thai beth so stronge without faile
That wilde lyounes þay wille assaile,   1650
And libardes also and othir beestes
Thei wille assaile bothe mooste and leestes.
And three kingdomes there ben also
And other iles many moo
Bitwene the Reede See than   1655
And the Grete See of Occian,
And Arthanie and Bacsirie
And the londe eke of Yberie,
And in these three londis þer be
Of dromedaries grete plente,   1660
And thoo beestis hugie and stronge
Of sixtene cubites thai ben longe.
And that beeste so stronge is he
That he wille bere a toure of tree
And twenty men of armes thereyn   1665
When any bataile shal begyn.
And in that lande of Bakkarie
There men doone grete maistrie;
Wilde beestes and foules also,
And thei mowe ones about hem go,   1670
Thei shulle abide and stonde stille
To take of ham atte hire wille.
And in that lande of Yberye
Is moch crafft of philosophie,
For goolde and siluere thei wille make   1675
Of what metalle men wille hem take.
And in the londe of Ethiope
Cometh moch of this blak sope,

1650 þay] MS. þᵗ

For there it renneth out of the tree,
And trees þere ben grete plente   1680
Bitwene Ethiope and Lybie.

Semenge to a mannys eyȝe
The se is hier and eke the sonde
Than any place of alle the londe,
Sauff a mountaine that hight Ertho   1685
That neuer man mai com to,
For euer hit semeth fast hym by
And euermore he is liche ny.
And in þe londe of Hermony
There ben three mountaynes wondur hye   1690
That is Abissacol and Ararath.
Who that his waie taken hath
From Arthiron þat faire cite
That bi thoo mountes passith he.
The hiest hille there is also   1695
That men callith þe mount of Thano.
Seuen leukis it is of hight
Fro the grounde to þe toppe right,
And ther stant yit Noes shippe
Hoole and sounde yit euery chippe,   1700
Sauff oo boorde that thereon was sette.
An holie monek fro thens hit fette
And in an abbeie it is holde
And for a relik it is tolde.
And nowe shalle I telle you redily   1705
Howe þe monke come thereby.
An holie man he was perfay,
With brede and water he levid ay,
And grete desire he had to seen
Noes shippe yif it myght been.   1710
So vppon a meri time hit felle
With water he fillid his botelle
And brede he toke a quantite,
And forth he went in his iourne.
And when he come amyd the hille   1715
To rest and slepe he had grete wille.
He laide hym doun and rest hym toke,
And when he of his slepe awoke

He laie at his owne abbeie gate.
He roos and went hym in þereate   1720
And fyfftene daies in the church he lay
In praiers and penaunce nyght and day
And praied God to yeue hym grace
That he must come to þat place.
And God hym grauntid without lette,   1725
And so þat table fro thens he fette.
But neuer man bifore þere come
Ne neuer shal til þe daie of dome.
And mochil snowe þere is euere,
But man ne beest cometh þere neuere.   1730
Thre hundrid cubites it is alonge,
And fifftie cubites þe ouergonge,
And thirti cubites it is of hight,
Through the ordinaunce of God almyght.
And hoole it shal stande ay   1735
Euer vnto domesday.
And atte foote of þat mountaine
Is a cite þat men clepeth Daine.
To Noes shipp þere men mai se
So þat þe wedir clere and bright be.   1740
An hugie cite þere is also;
Some time men callid it Thesaurizo,
But nowe oþere wise callid it ys—
Men callith it þe cite of Faxys.
The grettest cite it was yfounde   1745
That was in alle the worlde rounde.
For thirti leukis without doute
Conteyneth the walle there aboute,
And some tyme were woned to be
A thousande churchis in þat cite.   1750
And also withouten þe walle
There is a mount þat men calle
Salemount, as men telle.
Vppon the coppe þere springeth a welle
Of fressh water forcertainly   1755
And all the hille is salt þereby,
And comoun it is to that cite
But to noo men of ferre cuntre.

f. 88rb

And when men wil þere salt craue
Of delyueraunce thei shalle hit haue,   1760
For þere ben euer kepers withouten drede

To delyuere salte as men han nede.
Anothir cite men shul come to
That men there callith it Dago,
And in þat cite it is ifounde   1765
No cristen man mai live no stounde.
There mai none liven in þat cite,
Man ne childe þat cristened be,
But deie anone thei shal iwys,
And no man note wherefor it ys.   1770
A man shalle comen anone than
Vnto þe grete se Corudan,
A grete cite withoute any dout
Of fyffe and twenti leukis about,
A noble toun of grete riches,   1775
And welle inhabitid both more and les.
And in the londe of Iob than
There is a mounte callid Ephan.
There men fyndith manna moch iwys
That aungelles mete callid it ys.   1780
And as men of þat cuntre shewe,
Hit is congeled of þe dewe
In the maner of sugre white
And swete, whoo thereof wol bite.
And there shul men passe ouer a see   1785
Into the londe of Caldee,
And alle the men of that cuntre
With good kerchiefes araied gon he,
With goolde and perles and rich stoones,
Welle apparailid alle for the nones.   1790
And foule women there ben echone,
And blake and barefote alle thei gone,
And short sloppes weren hee
That lastith noo ferthire than to þe knee,
With longe mantellis cutte rounde   1795
And thoo hangen vnto þe grounde,
With blake here alle displette,
And vppon her hedis a chapelette.

Than shul men ouere a grete mounteyn
Into the londe of Amozeyn,   1800
And in that lande, as I telle can,

f. 88vb   Al ben women and naught a man.
Tholopeus som time was þere kinge,
And alle thaire lordis oolde and yonge
Were taken and slaine sekirly   1805
With þe kinge of Sichy.
The women ham batailid and þat anone
And quellid the kinge and his men echone,
And neuer sithens affter than
Wolde thei be sogette to no man.   1810
And þe best werreours ben hee
That men shal in batail se,
Bothe wight and boolde to abiden
And stronge in armoure hors to riden.
But hir paramours nei3 ham bene,   1815
But a ryuer ys ham bitwene,
And when ham lust haue solace of man
Ouer the water thei wille than
And plaie ham there a daie or tway,
And than ayenneward take thaire way.   1820
And yif a woman bere a knave
The fadir shal it kepe and have.
And yif it ben of a woman kynde
The moodir shal it kepe and fynde.
And yif of gentil blood be yt   1825
The lifft brest awaie shal be kyt
For sho shalle hir the better were
Whan sho shal a shelde bere.
And a pore mannys childe, as I you say,
The right pappe shal be cut away   1830
For lettinge, as is þere þe sawe,
What tyme sho shal hir bowe drawe.
And euermore thai chese hir quene
Of the doughtiest þat there bene.
And in the londe of Ethiope   1835
There is a welle, as I hope,

1816 ys] MS. nys   1817 when] MS. whem   1825 of]
MS. sof   1835 Ethiope Alta *in margin*
O 7739   E

So colde þe water is by day
That noo man drinke þereof ne may,
And so hote it is on the nyght
That noo man hit handil myght.   1840
Thaire watres beth hote, trouble, and salt

For þe grete hete þat on ham walt.
And alle þe puple of þat cuntre
But oo foote ne hath he,
And so brode that fote is sikerly   1845
That it couereth alle his body
When þe sonne so hote doth shine,
For with hete is alle her pine.
And next þat londe, than men shul fynde,
Is a londe cleped Litil Ynde.   1850
So colde þe water is þere oueralle
Toward the septemtrionalle
That it congelith, as ye mai here,
Into þe cristal bothe faire and clere;
Adiamaundes the best þat be   1855
Out of þat cristalle growen he.
And that cuntree, as I fynde,
Bi this skille is callid Ynde,
For a ryuer þat renneth thereby
That Ynde is callid certainly.   1860
And in that ryuere of grete strengþe
Bethe eelis of thirtie fete of lengþe,
And othir fisshes grete there bene,
The grettest that any man mai sene.
v. m^{l.} iles habitable   1865
Beth in thoo coostis without fable.
Than shul men passe, without les,
Into þe lande of Ermes.
Of alle þe men of that cuntree
Hir ballokkis hangeth binethe hir knee.   1870
And so hote the sonne is þere alleway
So þat in þe water thei liggeth alle day
From mydmorne til affter the noone,
That the grete hete ben alle idoone.
And þere is an ile nought ferre then   1875

That men callith it Chanaen.
And so grette rattis þer be
As ben doggis in þis cuntre,
And som ben white and som ben blake,
And with grete mastifes men ham take.   1880
Than shul men passe ouer a see
f. 89rb   Into þe lond of Lumbe.
In alle þe wide worlde noowhere
Groweth noo peper but ooneli there
In a forest in a cuntre thare   1885
That men callith it Combare,
An hugie forest bothe wide and stronge,
Of foure and xx^{ti.} iournes longe.
And on þe trees hit renneth vp there
Wilde vynes as though it were,   1890
And such beries beren he
As growen here on an yve tre.
And euery vine þat is there
Three maner of peper thei doon bere.
The white peper hit groweth on hy,   1895
And blake peper than next þereby.
And in the lowe bowes, I trowe,
The longe peper there dothe growe.
And in the sesoun of the yere
When thei shul gadre in fere,   1900
Thai haueth a frute in thaire tounes
That thei callith hem lymounes.
And with the iuys of that frute swete
Thay annoynte ham legges, honde, and fete.
Than wille noo vermen abide ne dwelle   1905
Anone as thei þat iuys may smelle.
Scorpiounes, naddres, and lisardes,
Cocadrilles and foule glistardes,
Of these the forest is fulfillid.
But nere that iuys, men shuld be spellid.   1910
And thus thei gadrid atte her wille
In sesoun of the yere þat longeth þeretylle.
But peper, I wote, hit wolde welle growe
In many cuntrees that men knowe,

1876 Chanãã *in margin*   1888 xx^{ti.}] *written over erasure*

But hit is ordeyned bi clergie   1915
And through the crafft of sorcerie
That thou₃ a man wolde hit nyme
And beren it awaie with hym,
He shal by noo witte þat he can kest
Passen the boundis of þat forest.   1920
Anone he shal than taken be

f. 89ᵛᵃ

And hongid an hie vppon a tree
With a withe on the peper wise,
And so he shal haue his iewise.
There ben three citees in þat staunce   1925
That hir pepir is alle hir sustenaunce,
Seneglaunce and eke Fladrin
And Polimpe next to hym.
Without Polympe vppon the playne
There is a wel faire mountayne,   1930
Mount Polumpe men callith þat hille,
The toun hat Polumpe for þat skille.
And at þe foote of þat mount
A grete meruaile there is to account.
For certaine sothe I you telle,   1935
There springeth out a fair welle.
Bothe day and nyght and euery houre
Hit turneth into dyuers coloure,
And as offt as it chaungith coloure
Hit turneth into dyuers sauoure.   1940
Of alle the spicis that ben out
Hit hath the sauour without dout.
And in some houre, without where,
Who that drinketh of that water clere,
Hit encrecith his life many yeeris,   1945
And who ben sike sone ham heles.
And of alle beestes moost and leeste
An oxe thai honour alle hir meeste.
For enchesoun of hir debonernesse
Eueri man hym honoureth more and lesse.   1950
Therefor thei make thair mamettis than
Halff of oxe and halff of man,
And such maumettis many þere be,

1929 Polumpe *in margin*

And many dyuers in eche a cite,
And wickid spirites ben in hem alle   1955
And aunswere to tham þat wolle to ham calle;
For what thinge þat a man wille wite
He shalle hit haue of þat spirite.
And som men in worship of hem
Hir yonge children thei wille nym   1960
And alle to pecis cutte her flesshe

f. 89vb

That is so tendir and so nesshe,
And cast it to hym in his servise
In hir manere of hir sacrifise.
And som hir owne flesshe wille kyt   1965
And to hir mamettis casten hyt
And seie: Lorde, biholde and se
What penaunce I suffre for the
And haue mercie of me and myne
And saue vs fro the endeles pyne.   1970
Therefor vnto tham mai wel be laide
As in holie writte it is saide:
Repleta est terra ydollis et adorant quod fecerunt digiti sui.
And yif a man bicome þere sike,
Man or woman or childe eke,   1975
One of his freendis than anone
Vnto þe temple he shalle gone
And telle þe preest more and lesse
Of alle that mannys sikenesse.
And than with grete deuocioun   1980
Bifore thaire god thei knele doun,
And when thei han longe leye
Bifore hir god hym to preye,
Hir god shal telle ham anone
Whethir that he shalle deie or none.   1985
And hit so be that he shalle lyf,
Anone aunswere he shal hym yif
And telle what medicine thei shal take
Therewith þe sike man hoole to make.
And hit be so that he deie shalle,   1990
Thei gete of hym none aunswere in alle,
And than hamward thei wende anone
As fast as thei mowe than gone.

And than thei maken an hugie fere
Of drie woode brennynge clere 1995
And cast hym euen amyd then
And alle to poudir thai hym bren.
And with hym brent shal be his wyffe
Yif sho no childe haue alyffe,
And yif sho any childe than haue 2000
Sho mai liven and be saue. . . . .

f. 90ra And maketh of hem her lardere,
But a childe that is tendir and fatte
Anone forth right thei eeten thatte.
Anothir see men mowe passe thane 2005
And come vnto the lande of Iane,
And of alle the worlde certainly
Hit is the richest of spicery.
And in that londe there groweth a tree
And of hym commeth grete plente. 2010
Brasile men callith it euerychone,
But kynde brasile it is noone;
But hit is a brasile good ynowe
Bothe in bodie and eke in bowe,
And as welle yeueth his coloure, 2015
But it is more gretter of sauoure.
For alle the canelle that men sene
Is of the rynde of thoo treene,
And alle the notmygges that ye se
That is the frute of þe same tre. 2020
And the macis beth huskis of hyt
And in þe huskis the notemygge syt,
And so thei wexen in the same manere
Right as done the philberdis here.
And oþere spicis þere beth feele 2025
More than I can nempne wele,
As gynger, cloves, and galingale,
Gilofres, bayes, and setuale,
Quibibus and graynes of paradis,
And also alkenade and lycoris. 2030
And of alle lifelood there is grete wone,

2001 MS. *has the catchwords of the first line of the next quire,* Or els with hir,
of which only one bifolium is extant

Sauff wyne and ale is there none.
But of hir spicis and of hir water
Thei make ham drinke neuere þe later,
That wyne and ale men wil forsake 2035
And to that licoure thai wold take.
And men shulle com affter than
Into þe kingedome of Pathan,
An hugie reame and a myche,
And welle inhabitid sikirliche 2040
And plenteuous of alle good

That longeth vnto mannys foode.
And in that londe, wite ye wele,
There wexen trees many and fele.
Of some cometh breede and som wyne 2045
And some commeth hony and som venyme.
Of these trees I shal you telle
Grete meruailis yif ye wil dwelle.
First þere ben trees many and fele
That bereth floure and eke good mele. 2050
Now takith hede and ye shalle here,
I shal telle you in what manere.
Thei taken a vessel clene and net
And vndir the trees thei done hem sette.
Than shal the rynde perisshid be 2055
In two placis othir in three.
Than commeth a licour, wite ye wele,
And renneth into þat same vessele,
And with the sonne sekirly
Hit congeleth and wexeth dry. 2060
And when it is harde and dried also
In fair trowes thai wolle it do,
And stampe it and make it smalle
And into faire floure it commeth alle.
Therof is brede þat thei shul ete 2065
As goode as þouȝ it were of whete.
The licour that thei wyne of make
In the same maner thei it take
Of a tree that is his kynde
And tonned it vp til it be fynde, 2070

2038 Pathēne *in margin*

And than thei drinken that licour
For it is wyne of goode sauour.
And yit there is anothir tree
That bereth hony fulle grete plente,
And into vessellis it renneth in   2075
Right as the licour of brede and wyn.
And out of trees þere commith venym
And there ayens is noo medicyim,
And what man it taken haue
There is noo þinge þat mai hym saue   2080
But with a drinke þat made shal be
With the iuys of þe same tree.
And anothir ile þere is beside
That men callith Calopide,
And þerein is a stondinge see   2085
And neuer more renneth he
But stondith stille euermoo,
And none yssue commeth þerefroo.
And fyfftie leukis it is longe
And tuelff leukis þe ouergonge.   2090
And what þinge falleth in that see,
Quik or deede whethir it be,
Anone it synketh doun to grounde
And neuer affter shalle it be founde.
And bi the bankis of þat see   2095
Reedis ther growith grete plente.
Thabies men callith thoo reedes stronge,
Of thirty fethemes thai ben longe.
And of thoo reedis men done take
And shippes and hous þereof thei make.   2100
And atte rootes doun in the grounde
Precious stoones there ben ifounde.
For whoo that bereth a stone of thoo
Dredeles alle though he nakid goo,
There shal none egge toole hym dere   2105
Whilis þat stone on hym he bere.
And þerefor withouten fail
When thei fighten in batail,
With her shafftis men ham sloon

f. 90ᵛᵃ

2098 fethemes] MS. femethes

For othir wepenes drede thei noon.   2110
And three stones thei had some time þere
Moost vertues þat euer yit were,
And yif ye wille a while dwelle
Of hir vertue I shal you telle.
Men shuld take that water clere   2115
And make it hote vppon the fere,
And cast the water vppon the stoone,
And take that water ayenne anone
And þerewith wasshen a mannys wounde;
Anone he shulde be hoole and sounde.   2120
There were three geauntis in Auffrik—

f. 90ᵛᵇ   In alle þe worlde were none ham lik,
Gebal, Amon, and Amalek.
The stoones froo thens thei let fett
And in the worlde whereuere thei cam   2125
The stoones with ham euer thei nam,
And atte last thei were slayne
In Yrlonde vppon an high mountayne,
And so the stoones bilefften there
Vppon the mounte of Carloere.   2130
And afftirwarde longe tyme
Vter Pendragon and Merlyne
Thoo stoones froo thens they fette
And here in Engelond thei ham sette
Vppon the plaine of Salisbury,   2135
A noble toune and eke a mery,
And in þe same maner thei stondith there
As þei first in Irlonde were.
Ovir a see than shul men passe
Vnto þe ile of Calomasse.   2140
And in þat londe nys neuer more sene
That a kinge shalle wedde a quene,
But as many women he shal haue
As hymself vouchith saue,
For eueri daie þere cometh newe   2145
And eueri daie some remewe.
For he shal neuere sikirly
But oo nyght lie a woman by,
And grete meruail it is to wite

So many children as he doth gete.   2150
And in that ile is a ryuere,
The fairest I knowe fer or nere,
And fisshe of euery diuers kinde
That men shul in the see fynde
Eueri yere three daies in a rewe   2155
In þat ryuer hit dothe hym shewe,
And stille abidith in þat stede
Til eche man take of hym nede,
And whan eche man hath his parte inome
Thai swymmen forth and oþere doth come.   2160
And men saie þat it is þe fisshes doynge. . . . .

f. 91ra   That bereth applis grete plente,
And who þat cleueth an appul atwyn
A litille beest he fyndith thereyn.
To a litille lombe liche it ys   2165
Of bloode and bone and eke of flessh
And welle shapen atte folle
In al thinge saufe it hath noo wolle,
And men and women þere meest and leest
Eten of þat frute so with þat beest.   2170
And vines þer groweth in that londe
That bereth cloustris, I take in honde,
There is no man þat dwellith there
That mai oone of þe cloustris bere,
For euery grape is as mannys heede.   2175
Such vines þere beth bothe white and reede,
And with the grapis of oo vine
Thei mowe make a pipe of wine.
Anothir lande is next þereby
That men callith it Caspery.   2180
The kinge Alisaundre the conquerour
That of alle conquest bare the flour,
In his time þere he roode
Throuȝ alle the worlde longe and broode.
Tho two and twenti kingis there,   2185
That of þe Iewes lynage were
That weren of Goth and Magothes kynde,
And alle hir hostes, as wee fynde,

2151 Charkaise *in margin*   2161 MS. *lacks the next four leaves*

Anon to þe mounte of Caspery
He droofe ham alle throuȝ maistry.   2190
And whan he had chasid hem so
That he myȝte nat com hem to,
Vppon his knees he sette hym doun
Hertelich with good deuocioun
And praied God with alle his myȝte   2195
And to grete penaunce he hym hiȝte
So þat he wolde sende hym myght and grace
That thei shulde neuer passe that place.
And þere the myȝte of God was kyd
And a wondir meruaile þere betyd.   2200
The mountaines departid hem anone

f. 91rb   And a depe valeie þere was ful sone,
And anone the Gewes alle
Into þat valeie thei gonne falle.
And there thei ben closid without doute   2205
With hie hilles ham alle aboute,
That thei shulle thens neuer come
Into the hie day of dome.
And a place bifore þe kynge
Thei lefft þere a litille entringe,   2210
And Alisaundre shette þat anone
With stronge walle of lyme and stone,
And throuȝ þe grace of God allemyght
The mounte ouerheeled hem anone right.
And also in that othir side   2215
A litil space he lefft that tide
And bifore that is a stondinge see
And foure myle of brede ys he,
And stille euermore he stondith so
For þere cometh noo wateres þereto.   2220
And þere the quene of Amozein
Hir londe ys ham oueragayn,
And sho with strength holdith ham in
That thei may nat thens wyn.
And so thei shul abide þere ay   2225
Til þat it ben domysday.
And yit thei haue a prophecie,

2189 Anon] MS. And in   2193 hym] MS. ham

And that thei bileueth sikirlie,
That atte last a foxe shalle come
Into þat cuntre þere to wone,   2230
And throuȝ the mountayne his hole make
And thei shalle founden hym to take.
And thei shalle pursewe hym so swythe
That to his hole thei shalle hym drife.
Than shul thei come that hoole about   2235
And fonde for to drive hym out,
And affter hym shul thei dige ilome
So that to the yatis thai shul come.
And when thei han the yates founde
Than shalle thei breke hem in a stounde.   2240
And this [is] thaire bileve alleway

And thus thei bilevith nyghte and day,
And than thei beleueth, bothe more and lasse,
Throuh alle the worlde that thei shal passe
And to hir bileve turne alle mankynde.   2245
This is thaire prophecie that thay fynde,
And þat this shalle accorde to hyt
That thai fyndeth in holie wryt:
Et fiet vnum ovile et vnus pastor.
And than shulle men come certainly   2250
Into þe londe of Bakkary.
And of grete trees that londe ys fulle
And grete plente thei bereth wolle;
That wolle is goode and faire booth
And þereof thei make hir clooth.   2255
And yif ye wille abide a throwe
I shal telle alle howe it doth growe.
Twey manere of wolle thei dothe bere
Alle the trees that beth there.
The worst wolle, I telle the,   2260
Hit groweth without vppon the tre.
As ravenne growith in an oke here
So groweth it in the same manere.
And of grete buries thoo trees ben fulle
As grete as is a mannys sculle.   2265
And when þe beries ripe be

2241 is] MS. *omits*   2251 Bakkarie *in margin*   2262 here] MS. ther'

Into foure quarteres than cleuen he.
Than is euery berie also fulle
As it may hange of fyne wolle.
Here in Englonde beth many pepleren   2270
That smalle many beries beren.
And better cotoune is nawhere
Than thoo grene beries bere.
And good ensaumple ye may se
Accordinge to that othir degre,   2275
For God made euery thinge in his kynde
As clerkis in thaire bookis fynde:
Producat terra lignum fructiferum vnumquodque
Secundum genus suum.
And then shal men passe ouere a see   2280
That is a ful longe iourne

f. 91vb   And come than into Ynde.
The frist lande þat thei shal fynde
There Preter Iohn is emperoure;
He is a lorde of grete honoure,   2285
Save the Grete Cane verement
The grettest vndir þe firmament.
That is wide and wondir longe,
Foure monethis iourne þe ouergonge.
Fyve thousand iles habitable   2290
There longith to Ynde without fable.
Thre score crouned kynges and twelff
Ben tributaries to hymselff,
And vndir hym echone han he
Othir kinges twoo or thre.   2295
Seven kinges beth with hym alleway
Hym to serve bothe nyght and day.
The patriark of seynt Thomas
Allewaie is with hym in his plas,
And twelff archebisshoppis also   2300
Beth dwellinge with hym euermoo.
And fourtie bisshoppes of lower degre
In his cuntraie allewaie thei be.
An hundrid dukes, as I you telle,
And foure hundrid erles with hym dwelle,   2305
And so oone and othire for to accounte

Thirti thousand thei amounte.
And Erropheroun, as I fynde,
That is the chief toune of Ynde,
And Londene is a faire cite   2310
Nought the tenthe parte as goode as he.
Hit is the thrid or els the ferthe
The grettest cite aboue this erthe.
And foure and fourty mile about
The walles ben withouten dout   2315
And voide place within ys noone
So moch as an hous mai stonde vppone.
And amyd the cite þere is a mounte,
Twelff a myle about it is to accounte,
And alle that is a castelle riche   2320
In alle þe worlde is none hym liche. . . . .

f. 92ʳᵃ   And of thoo deede bodies in þei caste.
And in that othir side is a pytte
An ful of water stondith hitte,
That is as blak as any gete   2325
And brenninge fire þereouer ful grete,
And therbi stant that foule visage.
This is a well perilous passage,
His eiȝen clastrenne and gliden about
And smoke of fire þere renneth out.   2330
The hardiest man in alle myddille erde
To gone þerebi must ben afferde.
And men of þat cuntre seyn and telle
That it is accountid a parcelle of hell.
Thai tellith also that who þat hath grace   2335
Harmeles to wende through that place,
That he shal neuer þereaffter, thai seyn,
Come in purgatorie ne in othire peyn.
The knyght was þere tho hymselff
And had with hym fellawes twelff,   2340
And clene of synne thai lete ham shrive
And alle thaire rightis thei token blive.
With stedefast hope and goode entent
They neme the passage and forth thei went.
And throuȝ the grace of Goddis sonde   2345

2321 MS. *lacks the next leaf*   2335 Thai] MS. That

The knyght passid the perilous stronde,
And sevenne of his fellawis alsoo,
And fyve lafft þere for eueremoo;
And thankid God with alle her myght.
And thus to God than seid the knyght: 2350
Transiuimus per ignem et aquam et eduxisti
nos in refrigerium, et cetera.
There is an ile men calleth Ruspo,
But that ile mai noo man to go,
For yif a man wold thidir gone   2355
He shulde be slaine and eeten anone.
For in that ile beth geauntis stronge,
Of thirti fote the leste is longe,
And som of fourtie and som of fyffty.
Of stature thei ben hugie and myghty,   2360
And man or beeste what thei mowe geten
Anone alle rawe thei wille ham freten.

f. 92rb

And othir clothis haue thei none
But wrappid in skynnes euerychone.
And a depe see is ham alle about,   2365
But thens come thei neuer out.
Anothir ile þere is than
That men callith it Crasseran.
And smale trees ful many þere be
That bereth of cotoun grete plente,   2370
And groweth in the same manere
As dooth the mos of þe trees here.
But hit is longe, white, and smale,
But liche vnto cadasse it is ale,
And hit semeth when it is growe   2375
As though the trees were ful of snowe.
And there beth also in that cuntre
The queintist beestis þat a man may se,
That ben as mochil as is an hors
And is a beeste of welle grete fors,   2380
For more burthein he wil bere
Than twenti hors, I dare welle swere.
And *gerfans* men done ham calle.
He hath a nek both longe and smalle,

2346 stronde] MS. stronge

And twenti cubites he is saunz doute   2385
Of lengthe when he strecchith hym oute;
And when he wille he may certayn
Into his bodie put it agayn.
A chameliouns also there beth fele
Of þe mochilnes of a cheuerele.   2390
A wondirful beeste forsothe is he
And moost dyuers as a man may se,
For euery day in certain houres
He chaungith into seven coloures,
And he livith nauȝt bi mete and drinke.   2395
This is a wondir thinge, me thenke,
And euere he is both fatte and fayre,
And yit he levith but by the eyre.
And foure elementis also there bene
That alle the worlde done sustene.   2400
The ayre ys oone and water and erth
And than the fire that is the ferth.
Without these elementis may noþing be
That euer God made in cristiante.

f. 92va   And foure thingis livith bi these foure euere   2405
That eetenne ne drinken done thai neuere,
These crekettis and these molles echone
And þe hiringe [and] the gamalioune.
And þe crikette bi the fire he leueth,
And the molle bi the erthe cleueth,   2410
The heringe bi the watir faire,
And the gamalioun bi the aire.
Quatuor ex puris vitam ducunt elementis
Camalioun, talpa, maris allec, et salamandra.
And anothir ile þere is beside   2415
That men calleth hit Barelide.
And huge forestis þereon bene
And grete plente of cipres trene,
For the cipres is plenteuous there
As okis in Engelonde beth here.   2420
And in thoo forestis beth addris stronge,
Of vi. score fete þei ben longe,

2395 drinke] MS. drinketh   2396 thenke] MS. thenketh   2408 and]
MS. of

And comounlich addren thore
In grete cavis thei lif euermore;
But hit be oones or twies a yere   2425
When the sonne is hottest and moost clere
About the forest in that sesoun
Men dare nat walke for þat enchesoun.
And there ben many of wilde swine
That ben as grete as any kyne.   2430
And when a boore is þere fulle woxe
He is as grete as is an oxe.
And the folk of þe cuntre thore
Of ham thei ben afferde ful sore,
Fore more perilous thei ben iholde   2435
Than ben the addres manyfoolde.
Anothire ile ys naught ferre then
That men clepeth it Orchepen.
And in þat londe is euer grete hete
And many cedrus þere groweth grete,   2440
For cedre is the hiest tree
That in the worlde growinge mai be.
And queinte beestis also ben there
And ben shape lich moch a bere,

f. 92vb   But his hede is liche a bore   2445
With longe tuskis sitting bifore.
Vppon sixe leggis he goth ful stronge
With grete clawes sharpe and longe.
A longe taile he hath as a lioun,
The coloure of hym is dusket broun.   2450
And anothir ile þere is iwys
That Exedrath icallid it ys.
Grete angur thei haue and tene
With myse þat there bene,
And grete thei ben, hugie and fatte,   2455
Thei ben more gretter than any catte.
Thei done the folk mochil woo and noy,
For mochil of thaire corne thai distroy,
And lien in the grounde so depe also
That þere mai noo man come ham to.   2460
And than þere ben oþere iles twey,

2436 Orchipenne *in margin*

Sinosople and also Dragmey.
And of alle the puple in cristiante
The best lyuers I trowe thei be;
For loue and charite and eeke pees   2465
Is euermore þere withouten lees,
And mekelich thei serueth God almyȝte
In penaunce and praier daie and nyȝte.
And plente thei haue of alle goode
That longith to cristen mannys foode.   2470
When Alisaundre the conquerour
That of alle þe world bare the flour
With his hooste þere forth gan ride
In the cuntrees ham beside,
He herde welle telle of her doynge,   2475
Of hir penaunce and of her livynge.
Of ham the kinge was fulle blithe
And thankid God fulle many a sithe,
And yit messangeris to ham he sent
For to wite of thaire entent   2480
And whethir thai woolde her londis yeelde
Or els thei wolde holde the feelde.
And thei sent ham this aunswere.
Godis seruauntis thei seid þei were,
f. 93ʳᵃ   And redie thei were for Cristis sake   2485
Yif that thei shulde the deth to take,
And alle that thei hadden loude or stille
Thei bad hym take it atte his wille.
The kinge was welle apaid theremyd
And no manere harme ham dyd,   2490
And thankid God with hert free,
And vppon this resoune than thouȝt he:
Iudicium sine misericordia illi qui non facit misericordiam.
And yit þere is anoþere cuntre
And ful goode cristen men þere be.   2495
That cuntree is callid Anguilande,
For in an angle it doth stande
Bitwene þe Graueled See thare
And the ryuer of Ronnemare,
A plenteuous lande of al thinge   2500
That appendith to mannes levinge,

And of olive trees beth none nowhere
So grete plente as is there.
And such langage as done we
Right such thei spekith in þat cuntre.   2505
Anothir ile þere is certeine
That men callith it Pikteine.
And the puple of the cuntree thore
Thei worche noo werke neuer more,
Nothir thei werk noþer thei swynke   2510
Ne neuer thei etenne ne neuer thei drinke,
But eeuerybodie in that londe
Bereth an appulle in his honde,
And wheresoeuer that thei dwelle
To that appul alwaie thei smelle.   2515
For such a giffte God hath ham yeuen
That bi the smelle thereof thei leuen,
And yif thei shuld that smelle forgone
Thai shulde be deede and þat anone.
And noble cristen men ben he   2520
And spekith Englisshe as don we,
And out of Saxsone her langage come
Right as we of ham it nome.
Here of Engist and eke of Horn
In Saxone were tho bretheren born,   2525
And here thei were grete lordis,

f. 93rb   As holie writte þerto accordes:
Nemo propheta acceptus est in patria sua.
And the ile of Dendros, as I vnderstond,
That is than þe next lond.   2530
With flesshe and fisshe thei leueth mooste
That nothir is sodenne rawe ne rooste,
But howe thei done in what manere
I shal you telle with good chere.
Hit is a wondir hie cuntre,   2535
Oone of the hext þat in erth mai be,
So moche hete þere is alleway
That thei mai nat wel come out a day,
But a nyȝte thei gone about hir mete
Fisshe or flesshe what thei mai gete.   2540

2527 Dondros *in margin*

And when thei shul eeten hit
Flesshe or fisshe thei wille it kitte
Into thynne leshes alle for the nones
And leie it than vppon the stoones,
And than þere so with grete hete   2545
Hit shal be broilid and than ihete.
And throuȝ the myddil of that londe thare
Renneth the ryuer of Rennomare,
As moch fisshe thereof thei haue
As hem nedith or vouchsaue.   2550
And byyonde that ryuere on þat oþere side
There is a wildirnesse boþe large and wide,
An huge wildirnesse and a stronge,
Fyfftene daies iournees longe.
That place men calleth Eufronere.   2555
And twoo trees thei haue stondinge þere
Of the moone and of the sonne
Sith the world was frist bigonne,
And euer grene shal ben alwaie
Vnto the terme of domesdaie.   2560
And the grettest trees thei beth iholde
In alle this worlde yonge or oolde
And hugiest in hie that thei stonde thore;
And fulle of frute thei ben eueremore,
But what manere of frute hit ys   2565
There is no man can telle iwys.
But who that myght þereof geten
And a quantite þereof myght eeten,

f. 93va   He shuld liven in good life
A foure hundrid yere or fife.   2570
And kinge Alisaundre þere gan abide
For he myght noo ferthir ride,
For tho twoo trees in certeine
Bade hym for to turne ageine;
For Godis wille forsoth hit nas   2575
That he shuld noo ferthir pas
For that place is nere hande
The eende of the worlde, I vndirstande.
And so thei toolde hym certainly
Daie and tyme when he shuld dy.   2580

He takith his bridelle and ayen roode
And no lengere þere he ne abode
But went into Greke there he was kinge
And þere he toke his last eendinge.
And nyne conquerours þere hath bene;   2585
I wille ham rekenne alle bidene,
For three were iewes and thre sarasens
And othir thre were cristiens.
The iewes were Dauid and Iosue
And the thrid was Iudas Machabe.   2590
The sarasenes were Alisaundre and Ectare
And þe thrid Iulius the grete cesare.
And thoo three cristenne was kinge Charles certain
And Arthoure and Godfray of Bolain.
And these were the nyne conquerours   2595
That of conquest bere honours.
And anothir ile forsoth is þere than
That men calleth it Traprophan.
And in þat cuntree without were
There ben twoo someris euery yere   2600
And twai wyntris beth ham biforn,
And twies a yere they repe her corn.
And euery tyme of the yere there
Hir trees beth floured and frute bere.
In someris tyme men þere se may   2605
The sonne shine bothe nyght and day,
And comeli folk so *ar th*ay alle
And noble cristen puple withalle.

And of othir two iles speke I wille,
One þat hat Orrille and þat oþere Argille,   2610
That ben þe richest vndir grounde
That in alle þe worlde ben founde.
For al thair mynes vndir moolde
Beth of siluer and of goolde,
And that þe fynest that men hath   2615
Out take the land of Engelath,
For Engelath ys the fynest awhere
And moch berille men fyndith there.
And anothire ile yitte þere is oone

2590 the] MS. thre   2607 ar thay alle] MS. as it may falle

That men callith it Eufronone.　　　　　2620
And in þat londe þere is certaine
A wondir grete hie mountaine
And þat is alle, as I you ensure,
Of clene goolde fyne and pure.
And thikke þere it groweth oueralle　　　2625
Of grete braunchis of coralle,
And wondir hugie trees þere bene
As grete and hie as men mowe sene
Ferres, cedrus, and eke cipres,
Alle that londe fulle it ys.　　　　　　2630
And in thoo trees, wite ye wele,
Gripes there ben bredde fulle fele,
And that bridde ys so mochil of myȝte
That he wille bere an armed knyȝte.
And griffouns þere ben grete plente,　　　2635
And none oþere foules but he.
An hugie ampten þere ben withalle,
And pissemeris som doth hem calle.
Thei ben as grete as a grehounde
And depe thei liggen in þe grounde.　　　2640
What for the foules and what for hem
In that londe dare come noo men
That he ne shulde be deuourid anone;
Therfor wille noo man thidir gone.
And þat londe withouten doute　　　　　2645
The Reede See goth hit alle aboute.
An the Graueled See þere metiþe with hym,
That is an hugie se and grym,

f. 94ra

Bothe depe, broode, and perilous.
Men callith it Mere Arenous,　　　　　2650
And so hit mai be callid wele
For smale white sonde is euery dele,
For al men hens vnto Ynde
A drope of water þere shuld nauȝt fynde;
And ebbeth and floweth in þe same manere　2655
Riȝt as done þe sees here.
There was neuere man ȝit þat couth make
Shippe ne vesselle þat see to take,

2647–8 Mare Arenosum *in margin*

Nethir man so hardie in cristiante
That durst wende into that see. 2660
And hit strecchith, as we fynde,
Bi the coostes and iles of Ynde,
And offte tymes bi þat see stronde
Men fyndith goode fisshes vppon the sonde
And large fisshis bothe longe and grete 2665
And as goode fisshe as man mai eete.
And grete trees þere ben of allaes,
Men fyndeth þere many withouten lees
That groweth nowhere iwisse,
But oonelich in paradis. 2670
As men tellith in that cuntre,
Paradis is biyonde þat see.
And the londe of derkenes is þere also
And paradis enioyneth thereto.
But for to speken of paradis, 2675
Noo man can telle what it ys.
But thei telleth that many man thore
Affter the tyme þat thei deede wore
The spritis of ham haue come ayayne,
Some fro ioie and som fro payne, 2680
And som fro payne and some fro blisse,
And tolde hir freendis howe it ys;
And oþerwise telle noo man can
For þere come neuer noo livinge man.
But as men of þat cuntre sayn 2685
Hit stondeth vppon a welle faire playn,
And þat it is the hiest grounde
That is in alle the worlde so rounde.
For thai telleth that Noes floode
f. 94rb   Neuere vppon þat grounde stoode. 2690
Hit is so hie, bi mennes speche,
That almoost it dothe areche
Vnto the cercle of the moone,
And thus men tellith þat þere wone,
And extendith hym fulle couth 2695
Out of the north vnto þe south
With an hie stonen walle,

2664 sonde] MS. see sonde

And growen with moos hit is alle;
But man alife is there none
That knoweth the maner of þat stoone.   2700
And in the mydward, as men telle,
There is a welle faire springenge welle,
And in foure parties also
Foure streemes renneth þerefro,
Phison and Tigre without les   2705
And Gion also and Eufrates.
Of these foure stremes certainly
Cometh alle the watres vndir the sky.
And fulle of trees þat euere beth grene
Of alle manere kyndes þere bene,   2710
And briddis syngynge in that stede ay,
And nyghte ys noone þere but eueremore day,
Alle maner of merth and mynstralcy.
Without ioie and blis and melody
None hert may thenke ne tonge telle   2715
What ioie thei haueth þat there doth dwelle.
And in the north side there is also
A londe ioynaunt euen þereto
That is þe londe of derkenes.
That is a place of grete distres   2720
And purgatorie men telleth hit ys.
Of paynes þer is neuere moo lys
To tham that in that woo abidinge bene
Til thei of synne be purgid clene.
Noone hert may thenke ne tonge telle   2725
What payne thei suffren þat there dwelle.
And in paradis there is a gate
For soules to come in þereate,
And þat is fulle of brenninge fyre
Eueremore brennynge hote and clere,   2730

f. 94va And throu3 þat fire the soules shulle pas
Out of purgatorie both more and las.
And when thei throu3 þat fire shalle wende
Thei wene her paynes ben atte an eende,
But harder payne thai shulle haue thore   2735
Than euer had thai before.
For when thei felen that fire so hote

The soules had leuere, God wote,
To lete that blis and turne ayenne
Than for to suffre that brennynge peyne.　　2740
But, blessid be God, he mai welle say
That so ferforth is in his way
In paine and woo no lenger to abide.
And þat is alle in þe north side:
Ab aquilone pandetur omne malum, et cetera.　　2745
But for to lete nowe this doynge
And speke more of othir thinge,
Of iles about the coostis of Ynde
I mai nat haue alle in my mynde.
And toward the south þe knyght gan drawe　　2750
Moo meruailes to see and haue,
So þat he come for certayne
Into the kingedome of Casseyne,
That is a noble londe and a riche.
In that cuntre but fewe hym liche　　2755
For it is plenteuous of alle thinge
That fallith to mannes levinge.
And thilk coostes beth in the eeste,
Right as we ben here in the weste.
And when somere is in þis cuntre here　　2760
Than haue thei her winter there;
And when wynter dothe here abide
Than haue thei her someris tide;
And when longe daies here be
Than ben þei short in þat cuntre.　　2765
A riche kingedome is than withalle
And Ribooth men done it calle,
And wel inhabitid londe is he
With many a noble rich cite
And plenteuous of alle goode　　2770

That appendith to mannys foode.
And when a man of that cuntre
Wexeth sike and deede shal be,
Than shul his freendis alle and some
Gadren togidir and to hym come　　2775
Into his blisse alle the route,
And sytten doun alle hym aboute

And gynne to wepe alle at ones
And make foule noise alle for þe nones,
For thei wille make so hiduous a bere　　　　　2780
That half a myle *m*e mai hit here.
And so thei sytten in that doloure
Welle þe mountaunce of an houre.
Than shulle thei drinke alle aboute
Noble wine withouten doute,　　　　　　　　2785
And than thei wille begynne to synge
Euery man affter his konnynge.
Than shal the eire or els his wife
Vnto the temple wende fulle blife
To hir preeste þat is thare,　　　　　　　　2790
For to haue a redie answare
Whethir that he shalle die or none.
To praie his god the preeste shal goone,
And than with good deuocioun
Bifore hym thei shul knele adoun.　　　　　2795
And yif it be so that he shal lif
Than wille her god aunswere yif
To telle ham with what medicine
That he shal recouer welle a fine.
And ȝif it be so þat he deie shalle　　　　　2800
He wille none aunswere yeve at alle.
Alle quik than thei wille hym nyme
And vppon a bere fast bynden hyme,
And vppon a mountaine he shal be bore,
And euer þe preste shal goon bifore　　　　2805
And in his hande haue a sharpe knyfe,
And alle men folowe hym blife
And crien and wepen with hiduous chere
The foulest noise that a man mai here.
And vppon that hille withouten lette　　　　2810
The beere thei shul adoune sette,
f. 95ʳᵃ　　And þe preeste to hym shal gone
And cutte of his heede anone
And layne it in a charger faire
And take it hym that shal ben his aire,　　　2815
And home than shal that hede be sent

2781 me] MS. ne

And ben sodene anone verement.
Than shal the preeste his wombe slytte
And alle the bodie into peces kytte
And pare the flesshe alle fro the bones.   2820
Than cast he the pecis hym about
Also ferre as he mai ham rout,
And in euery side he shal ham slinge,
And euer he shal this songe synge:
Subuenite sancti dei occurrite angeli domini.   2825
Than cometh foules fast fleenge
That knoweth the maner of þat doynge
And etenne that flesshe eueri dele,
For thei knowe the custome wele.
Than shalle the preeste and euerychone   2830
Gone home vnto hir mete anone,
And þe sone þere abide shal he
Til alle the flesshe clene etenne be.
Than gothe he home without lette
And fyndith ham al hir mete,   2835
And seith to ham with mylde steuen
Howe aungelles bere his fadris soule to heuen.
And in a chaire he shal be sette
And þat hede bifore hym fette,
And euery man þereof a moselle [s]hal haue   2840
And hymself þe boones shalle gnawe.
And affter of the braine panne
A coppe he shal doo make hym thanne,
And while he leueth þereof to drinke
For vppon his fadir he shal thinke.   2845
And than shul men in a litil while
Come in to anoþer ile.
Of corne and ris grete plente
There is growinge in þat cuntre,
Spicis and wyne and alle goode   2850
That longeth vnto mannys foode.
And he that is lorde of þat londe
He is ful grete, I vndirstonde,
And ȝitte I telle you without lesinge
That he is nothir prince ne kinge,   2855

f. 95rb

2840 shal] MS. hal   2849–50 Sepharage *in margin*

Duke ne erle ne baroun,
And yitte he is a lorde of grete renoun.
Three hundrid thousand lodehors of corne
And eke of ris cometh hym biforne
Euery a yere all for his rent,   2860
That shal neuer ben affter sent
But redeli brou3t to euery stage
That he receiueth for his truage.
And fifftie damiselles he hath eueremore
In housolde dwellinge with hym thore   2865
And of the fairist that mai be founde
Goynge vppon Godis grounde.
Thoo shulle hym serve ny3te and day
Richelich vnto his pay.
And to his mete when he is sette   2870
The damyselles his mete shul fette
And sette his messe by and by
And serven hym ful rialy.
And eueremore atte hir commynge
A curious songe thei shal synge   2875
That men wolde leten hir mete be
For to haue that swete melode,
For as I telle you sikirly,
Hit passeth alle manere of mynstralcy.
And richeli araied thei ben for the nones   2880
With goolde and perre and precious stones,
And eueri daie without lesynge
Dyuers in sight is her clothinge.
And oone of ham his mete shal kytte
And some shalle in his mouthe hit pytte,   2885
For hymself handeleth noo þinge
Of that thei done bifore hym bringe;
But his hondis eueremore
Beth vppon þe table hym before,
For his naylis beth so longe   2890
That with his hondis he may nat fonge,
For euery naile of that man
I dare welle say ys a large span,
f. 95va   And in þat lande halde it ys
For a grete gentilnes,   2895

For whos nailis lengest þere be
Mooste gentil than holde is he.
Than shul men come into a londe
That Tipus men callith, I vndirstonde,
And Tipiscenes þat folke men calle.   2900
Brode shoilinge fete thai haueth alle.
In Engelonde groweth no better wolle
Than þere wexeth vppon her solle,
Bothe white, reede, blak, and blewe,
Of many maner dyuers hewe.   2905
And longe beerdis haueth alle he
That hangeth adoune binethe her kne,
And I dare welle avowe this,
A large yerde of brede it ys.
And women also han brode fete   2910
And alle gone wrapped in a shete
With a knotte aboue hir croun,
And alle about ham hit hangeth doun.
And when a man in that cuntre
Falleth sike and deede shal be,   2915
Anone al quik he shal be slawe
And euery lymme from oþere ben drawe,
And his wife shal haue his skynne
To make a garnement to gone inne.
And yif a wife ben deede thore   2920
Than shalle the husbonde hir skynne were,
And the flesshe and the boones alsoo
His freendis shul ete it or thei goo.
Anothir lande is there than
That men callith Sapheran,   2925
For sapheronne groweth in that cuntre
Wondir thicke and grete plente.
For I dare wel seine hit sikerliche,
In noo londe of þe worlde so myche
So moche þere wexeth in that fryth   2930
That men thekke theire houses therewith
With þe gras, as I you telle,
And the sapheron þei doth selle.
But to speke of þat gaderinge
I shalle telle you a wondir thinge.   2935

f. 95vb

When it is gaderid without lette
In bagges of letheris thei done it sette,
And lete it stonde and gone hir way
And commeth noo more þere þat day.
And chapmen of that cuntre   2940
With asses and mules thidir commeth he
And hir payment þere thai doun leie
And take the bagges and gone hir weie.
And yif the paymente faile any thynge
Thai shul neuer thens hit bringe,   2945
For alle the bagges ben made fulle right
Accordinge of a certeine wight
That noone of ham is more than oþere,
Though a man shulde bie hit of his broþere.

COMMENTARY

In this Commentary the anonymous author of *Mandeville's Travels* is styled 'Mandeville' and the author of the Metrical Version is styled the author without further qualification. References to interpolations are to matter which, unless otherwise stated, is not found in other versions of the book.

Other versions of *Mandeville's Travels* are cited by the names adopted in Appendix B of this edition. Page and line references, expressed in arabic numerals, are to the latest editions of the versions cited in that appendix. The Continental Version is printed by M. Letts, *Mandeville's Travels. Texts and Translations*, Hakluyt Society, 2nd series, cii (1953). The Insular Version, printed by G. F. Warner with the Egerton Version, is cited by the siglum W, and the Harley Version printed in Appendix A by the siglum H. Free-standing arabic numerals which are not dates refer to lines of the Metrical Version.

Classical works are cited in the editions of the Loeb Classical Library, and the references in round brackets which follow the citation are to the relevant volumes and pages. The Golden Legend is referred to in the translation of Caxton, printed in the Temple Classics edition (1900).

The *Oxford English Dictionary* and the *Middle English Dictionary* (Ann Arbor, 1952—in progress) are cited as *O.E.D.* and *M.E.D.* respectively. References to J.-P. Migne, *Patrologiae Cursus Completus . . . Series Latina* and *Series Graeca*, are cited as Migne, *P.L.* and Migne, *P.G.* respectively. The works of Vincent of Beauvais are printed in *Bibliotheca Mundi*, vols. i and iv (Douai, 1654). Bartholomaeus, *De Proprietatibus Rerum*, is quoted in the translation by Trevisa extant in British Museum MS. Additional 27944, the base manuscript of *On the Properties of Things* (Clarendon Press, forthcoming).

1–14 This general introduction, like the reference to **Brute** in 109, shows a familiarity with ME. romance and suggests that the author may have been a professional story-teller. Cf. Bodleian MS. Laud 595, f. 1 (printed in *The Thornton Romances*, p. xvii) and *Pricke of Conscience* ll. 1–8.

18 Sir Iohn Mavndevile is an entirely fictitious character. See the Bodley Version, note to 147/13. And the references to **his auncestres** and **his kynne** are interpolated by the author. For a detailed listing of historical members of various families of Mandeville of medieval England see Mrs. J. W. Bennett, *The Rediscovery of Sir John Mandeville* (1954), pp. 181–216.

36 The major abridgements which the author makes in þis talkinge

80   COMMENTARY

concern the Sultan of Cairo, Prester John, and the Great Khan, who are
all described at length in the Harley and other versions. A similar process
of redaction is discernible in the Bodley Version and the stanzaic frag-
ment. Comparison of these and other redactions and epitomes of *Mande-
ville's Travels* made in England which are concerned with practical
information about the Holy Land demonstrates the wide appeal of the book
to all classes. See notes to 2001 and 2284 below.

37–8 nauȝt/offt The rhyme may be assonantal or even perfect, though
a form *noft* is not recorded. In the latter case the pronunciation of **nauȝt** has
been affected by the development of [x] to [f], cf. ME. *doffter* 'daughter'
and mod. E. *laughter* and forms cited by R. Jordan, *Handbuch der mittel-
englischen Grammatik* (2nd. ed., 1934), p. 176.

47–51 For the origin of this date of departure, 29 September 1322, see
Bodley Version, note to 3/11. The date is variously corrupted in the
Defective and Egerton Versions and in individual manuscripts of other
versions, and the relevant leaf of the Harley Version is lost.

53 The reference to Dover and the Channel crossing is interpolated. The
author may have been aware of various royal decrees dating from 1332
which restricted to Dover the port of departure from the realm. Cf. *Piers
Plowman* B iv. 131 and the note to l. 128 in the edition of W. W. Skeat
(1886), ii. 59.

67 The longer interpolation describing Rome which the author is about
to begin ultimately derives, like almost all medieval accounts, from the
twelfth-century *Mirabilia Urbis Romae*. It has no obvious link with
Mandeville's Travels where, apart from one brief reference and an inter-
polated story of 'Mandeville's' visit to the Pope in some English versions
(see the Bodley Version, note to 146/7), there is no mention of Rome. But
it is possible that the manuscript of *Mandeville's Travels* used by the
author also contained a copy of the *Mirabilia Urbis Romae*.

The standard edition of the work is C. L. Ulrichs, *Codex Urbis Romae
Topographicus* (1871), which also contains five Latin recensions made
before 1415. A very good English rendering with commentary is F. M.
Nichols, *The Marvels of Rome* (1889). Much useful matter is given by
H. Jordan, *Topographie der Stadt Rom in Alterthum* (1871), and by
R. Valentini and A. Zucchelti, *Codice topographico della Citta di Roma*
(1946). G. Parthey, *Mirabilia Romae* (1869), is also useful.

Among other accounts of Rome by Englishmen written within 100 years
of the Metrical Version are Higden's *Polychronicon* (ed. C. Babington,
Rolls Series, 1865), i. 206–52; Capgrave's *þe Solace of Pilgrimes* (ed.
C. A. Mills, 1911); William Brewyn's Latin description, partly translated
by C. D. Woodruff as *A XVth Century Guide-Book to the Principal
Churches of Rome* (1933); *The Stacyons of Rome* in *Political, Religious, and
Love Poems*, ed. F. J. Furnivall, E.E.T.S., o.s. 15 (1866). Capgrave visited
Rome *c.* 1450, and Brewyn wrote his book in 1477.

It is not clear what recension of the *Mirabilia Urbis Romae* the author used nor from what **croniclis** he derived the supplementary information given in 80–110 and elsewhere. There is a general correspondence between the Metrical Version at these points and Capgrave's *þe Solace of Pilgrimes* and *Chronicle of England* (ed. F. C. Hingeston, Rolls Series, 1858), and it seems possible that both men followed identical sources.

83–4 This date appears to be scribally corrupted, cf. notes to 152 and 162 below. Capgrave, *þe Solace of Pilgrimes*, pp. 4–5, dates the foundation of Rome at 3,282 years after the beginning of the world and 454 years after the destruction of Troy.

107–18 The **seuen kingis** are named in the *Mirabilia Urbis Romae* (Nichols, pp. 2–4) as the successive rulers of cities by the Tiber before the coming of Aeneas, cf. Varro, *De Lingua Latina* v. 41–6 (i. 38–42), and Livy i. 3 (i. 14–16), and are listed before the names of the tribes who first peopled Rome at the request of Romulus, cf. Capgrave, op. cit., p. 6. The author has confused the two references. He has also suppressed the detail, found in all chronicles and other derivative accounts of Rome, that 454 years elapsed between the siege of Troy and the founding of Rome; made Romulus and Remus the **sones** of Aeneas; and interpolated a reference to **Brute**, the eponymous founder of Britain, who is frequently mentioned at the beginning of ME. historical romances. Each of these changes seems deliberate.

The **Sabanense, Abbanense, Scalane, Spolitane,** and **Campanie** are the peoples of the Sabines, Alba Longa, Tuscany, Spolitium, and Campania. The scribally confused **Camarence Calanem** denotes 'Camaria' and Lucania. Cf. *Mirabilia Urbis Romae* (Nichols, p. 5); Varro, loc. cit.; Livy 1. 3–33 (i. 14–118); Pliny, *Historia Naturalis* iii. 5 (ii. 30–56); Procopius xii. 12 (iv. 252).

120–7 The references to the kings of Judah are found in almost all English chronicles, e.g. Capgrave, *Chronicle of England*, p. 44.

131 the Grete See The name, which is applied variously to the Mediterranean (as here) and the Black Sea, originated in Asia Minor where the small Sea of Marmara suggested the idea of the **Grete See**. The phrase is, however, also used of the Great Ocean Sea; see the Bodley Version, note to 101/5.

145 as þe boke sais, perhaps the recension of the *Mirabilia Urbis Romae* used by the author. Cf. Nicholas, pp. 2–4. But a precise meaning for so common a metrical tag (cf. 326, 674, etc.) cannot be pressed. Cf. J. P. Oakden, *Alliterative Poetry in Middle English. A Survey of the Traditions* (1935), pp. 387–8.

152 fourtie undoubtedly a scribal error but probably one already present in the author's source, cf. **eighte and tene** 162. All other medieval accounts of Rome give the better (though still exaggerated) 'xxii. myle' as the circuit of Rome's walls (e.g. Capgrave, p. 7), an estimate which is apparently based on a misreading of Pliny iii. 5 (ii. 50).

159 Both the *Mirabilia Urbis Romae* (Nichols, p. 6) and Capgrave, p. 8, state that there are 361 **toures** in Rome, not 348. Cf. note to 152 above.

162 eighte and tene MS. *eighte and twenti* There can be no doubt that the manuscript is corrupt here; the author lists eighteen gates, cf. the *Mirabilia Urbis Romae* (Nichols, pp. 6–9) and Capgrave, pp. 7–12, which provide similar, though not identical descriptions.

With the exception of the *Porta Ardeatina* and the *Porta Salaria*, the author mentions all the gates in the Aurelian Wall as well as two in the Servian Wall, **Porte Collecte** and **Porte Campanie**, and **Porte Castelle Sancte Angeli**, the entrance to the former mausoleum of Hadrian on the west bank of the Tiber. See A. A. M. van der Heyden and H. H. Scullard, *Atlas of the Classical World* (1959), p. 145, map 56, and cf. William of Malmesbury, *De Gestis Regum Anglorum* iv. 352 (ed. W. Stubbs, Rolls Series, 1889, ii. 404–8).

167 Sepulcre Remy Cf. Capgrave, p. 8: *on þe rith hand of þis ʒate* (i.e. *Porta Capena*) *stant a grete sware hille ny ioyned onto þe wal, mad al of fre ston, grete benethin and smal abouyn, hier þan ony tour, in whech Remus is byried as þei sey þere.*

169 Domine quo vadis, in the Chapel of Relics of s. Sebastiano fuori (otherwise s. Sebastiano ad catacumbas), marks the spot where, according to legend, Jesus appeared to St. Peter when he was about to leave Rome in despair. A piece of white marble bearing the crude impression of a human foot is still venerated there as a relic. Cf. note to 1166 below; and the *Stacyons of Rome*, p. 122, ll. 252–63; Capgrave, p. 162 nn. 1 and 2.

172 The legend that before his banishment to Patmos St. John was miraculously preserved after being immersed in a cauldron of boiling oil is first told by Tertullian, *De Praescriptione Haereticorum* xxxvi. 3 (Corpus Christianorum, Series Latina, *Tertulliani Opera*, 1954, i. 216–17). And the exile is first recorded in connection with the persecution of Domitian by Eusebius, *Historia Ecclesiastica* iii. 18 (i. 234). The traditional siting of the immersion in boiling oil before the *Porta Latina* is widely recorded in English sources, cf. Capgrave, p. 9; C. Horstmann, *The Early South English Legendary*, E.E.T.S., o.s. 87 (1887), p. 404; T. Erbe, *Mirk's Festial*, E.E.T.S., e.s. 96 (1905), pp. 31–2; E. H. Weatherly, *Speculum Sacerdotale*, E.E.T.S., 200 (1935), p. 11. The tradition is at least as old as the fifth century when the church of s. Giovanni a Porta Latina was founded by Gelasius I (492–6); see Capgrave, p. 145 n. 2.

178 Porte Lucane þe more This curious and unique designation is probably a corrupted reference to the classical *Porta Labicana* (the modern Porta Maggiore), which is otherwise unnamed by the author. But Capgrave, p. 11, mentions *Lucane þe poete* while describing the *Porta Salaria*, also unnamed by the author, and it is possible (though less likely) that the reference is to this latter gate.

181 Porte Collecte, otherwise unknown and probably a corruption of the *Porta Collina* in the Servian Wall.

183 Porte Petri The classical *Porta Aurelia* leading to the *Pons Aelius* was called *Porta sancti Petri in Adriano* in medieval Rome. See note to 207 below.

185 Porte Viridaun, i.e. the modern Porta Angelica. The *viridarium* 'garden' lay behind the Vatican Palace. See Nichols, p. 9 n. 17.

188–91 The *Mirabilia Urbis Romae* (Nichols, p. 6) numbers 49 **castellis** and 6,900 **barbicans,** and there can be little doubt that the numbers given here are scribally corrupted. Cf. notes to 152, 159, and 162 above.

193 archeris The word is not recorded in *O.E.D.* or in *M.E.D.* Its meaning seems in the context to be 'embrasures', i.e. defensive positions for archers, but its origin lies in a misunderstood reference in the *Mirabilia Urbis Romae* (Nichols, p. 6, Ulrichs, p. 92) to the arches of the *portus xii* in the Aurelian Wall; unless it is merely a scribal error.

195 the golden arche of seint Alexi was, according to the popular legend recorded by Capgrave, p. 18, *rered in worchip of Alisaundre, not grete Alisaundre kyng of Macedony but of on Alisaundre emperour of Rome*; properly, the gilt-covered imperial *arcus Arcadii Honorii et Theodosii,* which fell down in the reign of Urban V (1362–70).

198–200 The **seven lanternes** and the **seuen chaundelers of Moysy** refer to the same bas-relief on the imperial *arcus Titi*, erected by Domitian in honour of the captor of Jerusalem, where the spoils of the city are depicted, including the golden seven-branched menorah taken from the Temple of Jerusalem and deposited by Vespasian in the *Templum Pacis.* According to Procopius iii. 5 and iv. 9 (ii. 46 and 280), the menorah was taken to Carthage by the Vandal Genseric in 455 and, after its capture by Belisarius, sent to Constantinople.

201 The imperial *arcus Severi* was mistakenly associated with **Iulii Cesaris** in the Middle Ages by a misunderstanding of the still visible inscription IMP. CAES.

203 The *arcus Claudii* adjoined a column commemorating Antoninus Pius and thus was mistakenly called the arch of **Antonyne.**

205 Capgrave, pp. 12–13, lists nine bridges but says that only five were standing at the time of his visit to Rome *c.* 1450. The author, however, is probably following a corrupt copy of the *Mirabilia Urbis Romae* (Nichols, pp. 24–5), which also lists nine bridges, in his reference to **seuen brigges.** His false creation of a bridge of **Fabian** (see note to 208 below) is probably due to a misreading of his source.

207 the castel brigge of seinte Aungelle, i.e. the *Pons Aelius,* built by Hadrian to lead to his mausoleum. Cf. note to 183 above.

208 Iewes brigge The *Pons Fabricius* was sometimes called the *Pons Iudeorum* because of its proximity to the ghetto. The name **Fabian,** otherwise unknown in connection with Rome's bridges, is a scribal corruption of *Fabricius* and does not denote a separate bridge.

210 Gracian The *Pons Cestius* was restored by Quintus Aurelius Symmachus in A.D. 370 and thereafter known as the *Pons Gratiani* after the reigning emperor.

212 Valerianus brigge The *Pons Aurelius* (otherwise the *Pons Antonius*) was restored by Valentianus in A.D. 366 and renamed in his honour. **Valerianus** is a scribal distortion of *Valentinus*, possibly in the author's source.

213 the senatoures brigge, i.e. the *Pons Aemilius*, the first stone bridge across the Tiber, built in 179 B.C. and destroyed by floods in the sixteenth century.

216 seuen MS. *eiʒte* Scribal error, cf. notes to 152, 159, 162, and 188. The names of the Seven Hills of Rome enclosed by the Servian Wall are as variable as those of the Cinque Ports. See S. B. Platner, *A Topographical Dictionary of Ancient Rome* (revised by T. Ashby, 1929), s.v. *Septimontium*. And cf. Capgrave, p. 13: *seuene famouse hillis wer sumtyme rehersid of Rome, and þe names of hem haue be so ofte chaunged þat it is ful hard for to write þe treuth of hem.*

219 mounte Tanelle Called by Capgrave *mons canalis* and elsewhere (Bodley MS. Laud 203, f. 147) *mons cavalleus*, the name appears to be corrupted from *mons Quirinalis* which is falsely identified with the *Aventinus mons* in the *Mirabilia Urbis Romae* (Nichols, p. 16, Ulrichs, p. 93). The reference is to the pseudo-Aventine, a spur of the main hill, where the body of St. Alexis lay in the ancient church of St. Boniface. Cf. Capgrave, p. 15 n. 1.

220 mounte Stephan in Soleo, a scribally distorted reference to the church of s. Stefano rotondo *in celio monte*, i.e. the classical *Caelius mons*.

221 seint Marie mount The church of s. Maria Maggiore on the classical *Esquilinus mons* popularly gave its name to the entire hill on which it was built. The confusion of this hill and that associated with the **grete clerke Virgille** (properly the *Viminalis mons*, cf. Nichols, p. 17) is probably scribal, and MS. *is* has therefore been replaced by **and**.

224 The medieval reputation of Virgil, as thickly overgrown with legend as that of Alexander the Great, is admirably discussed by D. Comparetti, *Vergil in the Middle Ages* (translated by E. F. M. Benecke, 1895, revised edition, Florence, 1946), esp. pp. 239–376, and by J. W. Spargo, *Virgil the Necromancer* (1934). The story here ascribed to Virgil was originally related of the magician Heliodorus, who escaped from a Sicilian prison in the eighth century by drawing a picture of a ship on a wall and transforming the image into a real ship. According to a thirteenth-century interpolation in the *Mirabilia Urbis Romae*, Virgil escaped the penalties of insulting a matron by plunging into a tub of water and so magically swimming to Naples. Cf. Comparetti, pp. 329 and 350, Nichols, p. 17 n. 32, Hawes, *The Pastime of Pleasure*, ll. 3626–729.

227 The list of the **twenti paleicis** corresponds to that given by Cap-
grave, pp. 16–18, and the *Mirabilia Urbis Romae* (Nichols, pp. 19–22).
Like them, it identifies as **paleicis** ruins and monuments, such as the
mausoleum of **Adriane** 246 and the baths of **Olimpias** 265, but it is
more scribally corrupt than any other similar account.

229 **the grete paleis** The ruins of the imperial palaces on the Palatine
were collectively known as the *palatium maius* (Ulrichs, p. 93) in the
Middle Ages. MS. *grete* is retained although it may well be a scribal
corruption of *greter*, both here and at 223.

232 **the paleis of Surrie**, i.e. *palatium Susurrianum*, identified in the
Mirabilia Urbis Romae as *modo ecclesia sancte crucis*, cf. 233.

234 **Romulus** MS. *Remus* Cf. the *Mirabilia Urbis Romae*: *palatium
Romulianum . . . vbi sunt due edes Pietatis et Concordie, vbi posuit Romulus
statuam suam auream dicens, Non cadet donec virgo pariet* (Ulrichs, p. 93).

239 With varying detail this prophecy is widely recorded, e.g. Alexander
Neckham, *De Naturis Rerum* clxxiv (ed. T. Wright, Rolls Series, 1863,
p. 310), but its ultimate source appears to be the *Mirabilia Urbis Romae*
(Nichols, pp. 20–1, 136). Both Neckham and Capgrave, pp. 27–8, ascribe
the prophecy to Virgil, and Capgrave attempts a laboured explanation
of Christian prophecy by a pagan which has an obvious source in the
paradoxes of classical oracles.

250 The popular belief that Nero slew himself on the site of the fifteenth-
century s. Maria del Popolo is still current. But the reference here derives
from an interpolation in the *Mirabilia Urbis Romae* (see Nichols, pp. 21–2
n. 41) and duplicates the earlier reference to **Neroes paleis Lateranense**
(otherwise **a paleis faire ynowe**, i.e. the *palatium Neronis*) in 231. But
cf. Capgrave, p. 163 n. 3.

251 **þe hospitalle of seinte sperite** Cf. the *Stacyons of Rome* (ed.
cit., p. 170, ll. 818–21) and Rossetti's note on p. xli: 'the Hospital of
Santo Spirito, near St. Peter's, in connection with the church of Santo
Spirito in Sassia, is the chief hospital in Rome'.

259 The **hors and man of bras** are well attested. Benjamin of Tudela
(translated by T. Wright, *Early Travels in Palestine*, 1848, p. 68; cf.
Nichols, p. 156), writing in 1160, reports that the gilt equestrian statue
near St. John Lateran was of Constantine. Higden, *Polychronicon* i. 25
(i. 228), refers to the brass statue *quem peregrini Theodicum vocant, vulgus
Constantinum, sed clerici curie Marcum seu Quintum Curtium appellant.*
And a legendary account of its origin appears in the *Mirabilia Urbis
Romae* (Nichols, pp. 42–5) and Capgrave, pp. 31–3. In fact, the statue
was of bronze in commemoration of Marcus Aurelius. Cf. Nichols,
p. 42 n. 97.

264 **ad micam auream** The reference to the *palatium Domitiani in
transtiberim ad micam auream* is derived from the *Mirabilia Urbis Romae*

(Ulrichs, p. 116), but the exact location and relevance of *mica aurea* 'golden grain' is obscure. Nichols, p. 22 n. 43, suggests a site distinguished by the presence of yellow sand, cf. the modern *Montorio*. See Platner, p. 341.

270 Scala Celi The church of s. Maria Scala Coeli was named in commemoration of a vision of St. Bernard (d. 1153) who saw a soul ascend from purgatory by virtue of his prayer, according to a posthumous legend first recorded in the *Vita Prima* vii. 2 (Migne, *P.L.* clxxxv. 416–17). However, no classical monument to **Veneris** is known at this site and the whole reference is suspect, cf. Capgrave, p. 17, *the paleys of Uenus was fast by þat place whech þei clepe Scola Grecorum*, where *Uenus* may reflect an earlier corruption of *Remus*. But it seems more likely that **Scala Celi** is itself corrupted from *Scola Graeca* (cf. the marginal rubric *Scala Greca* in the MS.), and that an uncorrupted reference to **Veneris** is to the *templum Veneris et Romae*.

271 Camille, i.e. Camillus the conqueror of Veii who founded the *templum concordiae et pacis* (**the paleis of Camille**) in 367 B.C. The temple was splendidly rebuilt by Augustus. Cf. 236 and note to 234; Capgrave, p. 17; and Nichols, p. 97 n. 7. The church of **seinte Anthony** is only recorded on this site in the *Mirabilia Urbis Romae* tradition.

274 helle The legend of the *locus qui dicitur infernus* is briefly mentioned in the *Mirabilia Urbis Romae* (Nichols, pp. 97–8), and was possibly inspired by the great vaults of the Palatine ruins. The name is preserved in the name of the church of s. Maria *Libera nos a poenis inferni*. Cf. a similar interpretation of Mt. Etna as an entry to Hell in 1420–7 above.

275 An informative account of the **holie churcheyerdis** of Rome is given in the *Catholic Encyclopaedia* iii. 510–18. Before 900 the ancient crypts had been emptied and the bodies of the martyrs reinterred in Roman churches, and consequently this list is a conflation of the names of the pre-Constantine catacombs and of later churches. Cf. the *Mirabilia Urbis Romae* (Nichols, pp. 26–9, and Ulrichs, p. 95); Capgrave, pp. 20–1; William of Malmesbury, *De Gestis Regum Anglorum* iv. 352 (loc. cit.). The stories of some of the martyrs buried at Rome are related in the Golden Legend (iii. 176–88); and see *Itineraria et alia Geographica*, Corp. Christ., Ser. Lat. (1965) clxxv. 299–301, clxxvi. 638–9.

277 The phrase **and Pancras hole** is undoubtedly corrupt, cf. *cimiterium Calepodii ad sanctum Pancratium* (Ulrichs, p. 95) and Capgrave, p. 20, *cimiterium kalepodii is at seynt Pancras in Transtibir*. The cemeteries of Calepodius and St. Pancratius adjoined each other on the Via Aurelia, and confusingly near at hand lay the *cimiterium Praetextati iuxta portam Appiam ad sanctum Pancratium*.

278 þe Girole, i.e. the circus of Caligula, popularly known as *girolus* 'ring'. **seint Agace** is apparently a garbled reference to St. Agapitus, once buried in the cemetery of Praetextatus on the Via Appia and, according to Brewyn, p. 66, reinterred in s. Maria in Trastevere.

283 Concorde is possibly a corrupted reference to the church of ss. Gordian and Epimachus, but it occurs also in Capgrave, p. 20, and most probably was present in the author's source. The corruption possibly arose by association with the more familiar *templum pacis et concordie* or with the sepulchre of Concordia, the nurse of St. Trifena, mentioned by William of Malmesbury (ii. 406). Alternatively, **Concorde** may be corrupted from *Iordanorum*, itself a corrupted form of *Germanorum*, and refer to the *cimiterium Germanorum* on the Via Salaria Nova named in honour of the sons of St. Felicitas.

286 The **holie churcheȝerde** between the two bay-trees near the mausoleum of St. Helena on the Via Labianca was named after ss. Peter and Marcellinus, who suffered under Diocletian. The body of St. Helena was reinterred in the Basilica Laterana by Anastasius IV (d. 1154), and her sarcophagus may be seen in the Vatican Museum. The story of the saints' martyrdom is told in detail by Capgrave, pp. 113–14, and cf. the Golden Legend (iii. 176–88).

leepres is not recorded in *O.E.D.* and (unless it is a corrupt form of *cipres* 'cypress tree') its meaning is 'bay-trees'; cf. the phrase *ad duas lauros ad Helenam* describing the cemetery in the *Mirabilia Urbis Romae* (Ulrichs, p. 95). In the MS. margin is a corrector's mark.

287 The corrupt reference to **Seynt Sabines and seinte Vrsus** is apparently to the *cimiterium ursi pileati ad sanctam Bivianam* (Ulrichs, p. 95) where the church of s. Bibiana, founded by Pope Simplicius *c.* 467, stood near the statue of a hatted bear. See Capgrave, p. 20 n. 4.

288 The cemetery near s. Lorenzo fuori le mura was the *ager Veranus*, otherwise known as the cemetery of St. Cyriaca.

289 seint Petris Wille, properly the *fons sancti Petri*, occupied the site on the Via Nomentana where St. Peter was popularly supposed to have baptized his converts. The form **Wille**, 'well', is due to the scribe's fondness for eye-rhymes, rather than a south-western dialect form.

290 Seint Eracene, a very garbled reference to the *cimiterium Cucumeris* which is listed at this point in the *Mirabilia Urbis Romae* (Nichols, p. 28, Ulrichs, p. 95).

291 The church of **Seint Saturnine** stood until the reign of Nicholas IV (1287–92) on the Via Salaria by the *cimiterium Trasonis*. See Capgrave, p. 21 n. 1.

293 The phrase **Seinte Heremite þe Domicelle** obscures the reference to ss. Nereus (otherwise and corruptly, Hermes) and Domitilla, martyred by the consul Memmius Rufus and buried on the Via Ardentina. See Capgrave, pp. 21, 148–9.

295 The names of the **templis** are, like those of the **paleicis** mentioned earlier, exceedingly corrupt and in many cases can be identified only by reference to the *Mirabilia Urbis Romae* (Nichols, pp. 82–6, Ulrichs, pp. 107–12). The emended **nynetene** (MS. *nyne*) is justified if a dual reference to the three temples mentioned in 367–8 is accepted.

299 Florre and **Pheby** denote the *templum Flora* and the *templum Febris* near the *thermae Alexandrinae* and, according to Capgrave, p. 25, *now dedicat on to Our Lady and þe opir onto seyn Iame*, now the churches of s. Maria Traspontina and s. Giacomo di Scossacavalli.

300 þe temple of Virgily, i.e. the classical *aedes Bellona* (Nichols, p. 83, Ulrichs, p. 107). The stages by which *Bellona* was corrupted to **Virgily** defy palaeographic reconstruction.

302 Newe Rome An inscription, probably dating from the political revival of Rome in the twelfth century and found only in the *Mirabilia Urbis Romae*, was carved on the *conca Parionis*: *Roma vetusta fui sed nunc noua Roma vocabor. Eruta ruderibus culmen ad alta fero.* But the identity of the *conca Parionis* (which the author refers to as **Temple Enee**) is uncertain; it may have been an ancient fountain. Cf. Nichols, p. 83 nn. 6 and 7.

303 temple Appoline, i.e. an oracle to Apollo in the *templum Gnei Pompeii.* Cf. *Mirabilia Urbis Romae* (Ulrichs, p. 107): *monumentum vero illius quod dicitur maioretum decenter ornatum fuit oraculum Apollinis.*

304 temple Neron, i.e. the *secretarium Neronis*, an imperial chancery. Capgrave, p. 26, tells a gruesome legend of *these houses* [which] *comounly wer called her sory secretaries.* The site, however, is not known. The medieval church of St. Ursus, mentioned in the *Mirabilia Urbis Romae* and by Capgrave as standing on the site, is not listed by Brewyn. Cf. Nichols, p. 84 n. 8.

305 temple Marci is a corrupt reference to the *Campus Martius*, cf. Capgrave, p. 26, *a feld fast by Martis Temple*, where stood the temple of Mars. The details of the consular elections which follow are partly obscured by the word **councel** which is probably a corrupt form of an earlier *consuls*, cf. *Mirabilia Urbis Romae* (Nichols, p. 84, Ulrichs, p. 107). But Capgrave explains the word *consules whech is as mech to sey as wise men of councell*, and the form in the Metrical Version may be a deliberate simplification by the author.

311 Numie MS. *Ninine* The author or a scribe has apparently 'normalized' the spelling to echo the biblical Nineveh, cf. MS. *Ninene* 367 above and H 175/39. The classical *aedes Numa* was also and perhaps more widely known as the *aedes Vesta*, which the author mentions as a separate monument **temple Veste** in 313 and **temple of þe west** in 368. Capgrave, p. 21, identifies this as the *place whech is cleped now sancta Maria de penis inferni*: see note to 274 above.

314 seint Kirias The ancient monastery of ss. Cyriac and Nicholas was absorbed before **1400** in the convent of s. Marta near the Collegio Romano. Cf. Nichols, p. 21 n. 40, and Capgrave, p. 28.

315 the golden castelle, i.e. the Circus Flaminius, called *castellum aureum* in the *Mirabilia Urbis Romae* (Nichols, p. 86, Ulrichs, p. 108) which speaks of it *in monasterio dominae Rosae*. This is now s. Caterina ai Funari. But the identity of **Dame Rose** is mysterious. The reference may be to the Blessed Virgin Mary as Our Lady of the Rose, or to some lost association of a woman and roses (cf. note to 1061 below), or to something now corrupted beyond recovery, perhaps *domus rose* (cf. the crenellated London mansion of Sir John Poultney). See Capgrave, p. 28 n. 1.

318 The Pantheon was the most famous of all Roman temples, and the sumptuous description which follows, while clearly inspired by the medieval reverence for precious stones, reflects the veneration of anti-quity. However, despite the claim advanced in 326, the catalogue of stones is not found in any known recension of the *Mirabilia Urbis Romae*, and it seems possible that it was interpolated by the author. Its source may have been the description of the new Jerusalem in Revelation 21: 19–20. Cf. the Golden Legend (vi. 94–5); *The Awntyrs of Arthure* 391–6; *The Book of the Howlat* 339–45; *Cleanness* 1468–72; *The Parlement of Thre Ages* 120–9; *The Siege of Jerusalem* 1245–64; *Piers Plowman* B ii. 8–14; *Mum and the Sothsegger* i. 35–48.

325–35 The scribal forms of the names of many of the stones are note-worthy: *beches, crapotines, coteices, dianes, vermidore, peritotes, reflambines, ligoyns* are not recorded in *O.E.D.*; and *beches, coteices, vermidore* are not recorded in other medieval sources, such as Bartholomaeus *De Proprie-tatibus Rerum* xvi; *English Medieval Lapidaries*, ed. J. Evans and M. Ser-jeantson, E.E.T.S. 190 (1932); Isidore, *Etymologiae* (ed. W. Lindsay, 1911). See J. Evans, *Magical Jewels of the Middle Ages . . .* (1922).

crapotines, cf. *Promptorium Parvulorum* s.v. *crepawnde or crapawnde, precyous stone, smaragdus*. The stone was believed to be produced in the head of a toad. Cf. Bartholomaeus xvi. 59.

dianes, black gems streaked with red. Cf. *O.E.D.* s.v. *dionise*, and *English Medieval Lapidaries*, p. 85.

peritotes, recorded in *English Medieval Lapidaries*, p. 118, *periot is a stone þat is lyȝt grene*. Cf. OF. *peridoz*, and *penitotes* in *Cleanness* 1472.

ligoyns, stones believed to be formed from the urine of the lynx. Cf. *O.E.D.* s.v. *ligure*.

vermidore probably denotes rubies or similar deep-red stones < OF. *vermeil dor*. Cf. *O.E.D.* s.v. *vermeil*. The OF. *Sidrac* lists a *termidor*.

reflambines are possibly carbuncles (Late Latin *reflammanda*), believed to reflect intense light and so described by 'Mandeville' as illuminating the chamber of the Great Khan (W 117/42). Cf. *flaumbeande gemmes* in *Cleanness* 1468 and *reflambine* in the OF. *Sidrac*. The immediate repetition of the reference in **carbuncles** 332 may be due to the author's misunder-standing of the word in his source and is exactly paralleled in 2027–8.

337 men þat it knewe Capgrave, p. 27, echoes this vague authority, *a temple whech þei sey as of ricchesse was worth þe þrid part of þe world of gold, siluyr, perle, and precious stones*, cf. Nichols, p. 87. Line 339 reads awkwardly and may be the relic of three earlier lines which gave the sense of Capgrave's sentence.

341 The richly adorned **god that was thair maumetee**, which is described with fanciful detail in the *Stacyons of Rome*, p. 169, was an Etruscan statue of Jupiter of terracotta set in the central chamber of the cella.

350 The legend of the *salvatio Romae*, miraculous bells hanging in a marvellous palace which was the hub of the Roman empire, is told in the *Mirabilia Urbis Romae* (Nichols, p. 47, Ulrichs, p. 179); it is at least as old as the eighth century, being recorded by Cosmas of Jerusalem, *Commentaria in carmina sancti Gregorii* (Migne, *P.G.* xxxviii. 546) and the pseudo-Bede, *De Septem Mundi Miraculis* (ed. J. A. Giles, *Venerabilis Bedae Opera*, 1843, iv. 10). Both Alexander Neckham, p. 310, and Capgrave, p. 27, link the device to Virgil, cf. a similar account of a miraculous mirror related by Gower, *Confessio Amantis* v. 2031–67 (ed. G. C. Macaulay, E.E.T.S., e.s. 82, 1901, ii. 3). See Comparetti, pp. 298–9.

360 The Pantheon was consecrated as **Seinte Maries the Rotounde** by Boniface IV in 608. Cf. 423–7 above, Capgrave, pp. 157–8, and Matthew Paris, *Chronica Maiora* s.a. 609 (ed. F. Madden, Rolls Series, 1866, i. 263), and Lydgate, *Fall of Princes* ii. 4495–4551.

363 Cf. the *Stacyons of Rome*, p. 169, ll. 768–70:

> vppon his hed a covert of brasse,
> to Seynt Petyr blowen it was
> with a wynde of hell, I trowe.

Such legends of a satanic removal of roofs and church steeples are commonplace, e.g. in the *Speculum Sacerdotale*, but this one is particularly detailed, cf. Brewyn, p. 34. Its origin lies partly in the plundering of the Pantheon by Constans II in 663 and partly in a confusion of names (see Rossetti's note in *Political, Religious, and Love Poems*, p. xl; Nichols, p. 82 n. 3; Brewyn, p. 34 n. 5).

371 Legends of **Iulius Cesare** are widely reported in English sources, e.g. Capgrave's *Chronicle of England*, p. 57, and the *Anonymous Short English Metrical Chronicle* (ed. E. Zettl, E.E.T.S. 196, 1934, pp. 10–11, cf. p. 18), but his association with **the Petir Pens** is notable. *The Serpent of Division* (ed. H. N. MacCracken, 1911, p. 51), doubtfully attributed to Lydgate, repeats the common story that the tribute exacted from Cassibellanus was *þre þowsande pownde eueriche ȝere*, but other medieval writers variously attribute to Ine, Offa II, and Æthelwulf the origin of this voluntary payment of alms, first recorded in the legal code of Athelstan II (ed. F. Liebermann, *Die Gesetze der Angelsachsen*, 1898–1916, i. 130–1) and probably instituted before Alfred. Cf. W. E. Lunt, *Financial Relations of the Papacy with England to 1327* (1939), pp. 3–14.

377–8 The small **temple of Iovis**, i.e. the *aedes Iuppiter Feretrius* allegedly dedicated by Romulus, was one of many erected on the Capitoline, among which were the **Temple Ercules**, i.e. the *aedes Hercules Victor* in the forum Boarium, and the neighbouring **temple Ofilis**, i.e. the monument to Hercules Olivarius. But Julius Caesar was assassinated in the *curia* below the great *aedes Iuppiter Optimus Maximus Capitolinus*; the *Mirabilia Urbis Romae* (Nichols, p. 90) is itself confused at this point.

382 Seinte Maries church þe more cannot refer to s. Maria Maggiore, which stands on the Esquiline, cf. note to 221 above and Nichols, pp. 121–2. The distortion was probably made by the author for the convenience of rhyme. The *Mirabilia Urbis Romae* (Nichols, p. 90) refers merely to s. Maria, almost certainly s. Maria in Ara Coeli, built on the shrine dedicated to Virgo Caelestis and described by Capgrave, pp. 39–42, as *standyng on a hille fast by þe capitolle*.

385 Colise The name refers to the Coliseum, but the description which follows properly belongs to the near-by *templum solis*. In later copies of the *Mirabilia Urbis Romae* the original *ante Coliseum fuit templum solis* has lost its vital preposition (Ulrichs, pp. 110, 136), and the mistake was copied into the recension used by the author.

405 The **simulacre of the sonne** was probably the statue of 'Samson' before the Lateran, described by Benjamin of Tudela, p. 68, and in detail by Higden, *Polychronicon* i. 25 (i. 232), who mistakenly associates it with the Colossus of Rhodes. In all recensions of the *Mirabilia Urbis Romae* the statue is placed inside the temple.

414 According to the *Mirabilia Urbis Romae* (Nichols, p. 64), the destructions of Silvester I (314–35) during the reign of Constantine spared the head and hands of the idol which were deposited before the Lateran. Cf. Capgrave, p. 36 n. 1. The head and a hand holding an orb, i.e. the **golden balle**, probably belonged to a statue of Domitian and are preserved in the palazzo dei Conservatori.

437 score MS. *hundrid* An earlier *iiii.ˣˣ·* has been misread as *iiii.ᶜ·* Cf. the *Stacyons of Rome*, p. 143, ll. 17–18:

> In Rome I shall ȝou steuene
> And honþred kyrkes fowrty and seuen.

439 The Seven Churches of Pilgrimage, named in 443–9, are described in detail by Capgrave and Brewyn.

448 The church of s. Croce in Gerusalemme, founded by Constantine, contains a portion of the True Cross brought by St. Helena from Jerusalem, cf. 233. See Capgrave, p. 76 n. 1, and Brewyn, pp. 52–7.

451 seint Iohn the Lateranences, built on the site of the classical *domus Laterana* (cf. 231) and first known as the Basilica of the Redeemer, was the diocesan church of the Bishop of Rome, allegedly granted by Constantine to Silvester I as his episcopal residence. It was severely damaged by fire in 1307 and 1361, and on the return from Avignon in 1377 Gregory XI took up residence in the palace of the Vatican. The church of s. Giovanni Laterano, however, has retained its supremacy as *omnium ecclesiarum urbis et orbis mater et capud*.

466 the grete Grekisshe Se The reference is interpolated by the author. In all other versions 'Mandeville' follows the overland route to Constantinople taken by Peter the Hermit and described by Albert of Aix, *Historia Hierosolimitana* (printed in *Recueil des Historiens des Croisades* iv, 1879). A map of the journey is given by S. Runciman, *A History of the Crusades* (1951–4) i. 143, and the towns along the route are identified in the Bodley Version, p. 150, and the Egerton Version, pp. 157–8.

469–70 Neyesburghe and **Malleleuile** are unique forms, cf. *Neselburgh* and *Malleuillam* H 149/24 and *Neiseburgh* and *la Male Ville* W 4/28. Both places are mentioned by Albert of Aix, pp. 290, 274.

479–84 This description of **Belgraf** is interpolated by the author, cf. note to 661 below. It is historically accurate. Belgrade, made the capital of Serbia in 1403, owed its importance to its dominating position on the Danube.

485 þe water of Mace, apparently a distorted reference to the Danube which W 4/30 describes as flowing *parmy Trachie*, cf. H 149/28, even though this reference precedes the mention of Belgrade in all other versions.

500 seynte Sophy, dedicated by Justinian in 538 to Ἁγιά Σοφία, is described by William of Boldensele, *Itinerarius* (ed. C. L. Grotefend, *Die Edelherren von Boldensele*, 1885, p. 30): *ecclesia sanctae Sophiae, id est Sapientiae, quae Christus est*. For the dependence of *Mandeville's Travels* on this account see the Egerton Version, pp. 158–9, where the confusing history of the various relics is admirably summarized.

515 the speres hede is not mentioned by Boldensele. According to the *Gesta Francorum* (ed. R. Hill, 1962, pp. 59–60), the Holy Lance of the Crucifixion was found during the siege of Antioch in 1098. It was among the holy relics presented by Baldwin II to St. Louis in 1239 and 1241 and deposited in **þe Kingis Chapelle**, i.e. Sainte-Chapelle. Aware of the association of the relic with both cities but not of this translation, 'Mandeville' claims to have seen two spear-heads, one at Constantinople and another at Paris, cf. H 151/42, and the author's **þere** is thus (perhaps deliberately) ambiguous.

518–20 Neither **Seynt Luke** nor **seinte Anne** are mentioned by Boldensele (p. 30) among the *plures alias sanctorum reliquias venerandas* at Constantinople; indeed, he later (p. 55) refers to the early twelfth-century church of St. Anne at Jerusalem *sepulchraque Ioachim et beatae Annae, parentum eius, in quadam cripta subterranea ostenduntur*. But 'Mandeville' knew of another tradition of the translation of St. Anne by St. Helena, cf. W 44/41, which may have been linked with the church of St. Anne dedicated by Justinian—cf. Procopius, *De Aedificiis* i. 3 (vii. 40)—at Constantinople.

521 This legend is first reported by Oliverius Scholasticus, *Historia Damiatina* xlii (ed. J. G. von Eckhart, *Corpus Historicum Medii Aevi*, 1723, ii. 1447):

> nam in longaevis Thraciae muris homo quidam fodiens invenit lapideam archam, quam cum expurgasset et apperuisset invenit mortuum iacentem et litteras conglutinatas archae continentis haec:
> Christus nascetur de Maria Virgine et in eum credo.
> Sub Constantino et Hirena imperatoribus, o sol,
> iterum me videbis.

The transformation of *homo quidam* to **an emperour** and of *lapideam archam* to **a table alle of gold**, like the identification of the corpse with the mythical Hermes Trismegistos in other versions (cf. W 9/40), is not found in the Golden Legend, and 'Mandeville' may have been responsible for these changes. But see B. Smalley, *English Friars and Antiquity in the Early Fourteenth Century* (1960), pp. 119–20, who reports the mention of a golden tablet bearing the prophecy in Plato's tomb by William Wheatley in 1309 and John Ridevall, both learned friars.

549 This reference to the **seuen sagis**, like their names which follow (563–6), is interpolated by the author; in all other versions of *Mandeville's Travels* and its source at this point, Vincent of Beauvais, *Speculum Naturale* vi. 21 (i. 382–3), the philosophers on Mount Olympus are anonymous. The names of the classical Seven Sages are variously recorded in medieval sources, e.g. Capgrave, *Chronicle of England*, p. 48, and þe *Solace of Pilgrimes*, p. 44; but there also existed a completely distinct tradition of more widely known names, e.g. K. Brunner, *The Seven Sages of Rome*, E.E.T.S. 191 (1933), and C. F. Bühler, *The Dicts and Sayings of the Philosophers*, E.E.T.S. 211 (1941).

Six of the names given here are identifiable as Aristotle, Hermes Trismegistos, Heraclides, Ptolemy, Hippocrates, and Dionysius Cato, but **Anytenne** is puzzling. It may perhaps refer to the Greek Antenor through a mistaken association with **Ercules**; or it may be a corruption of *Lentyllous*, the third of the 'Seven Sages of Rome', cf. L.-F. Flutre, *Table des noms propres avec toutes leurs variantes figurant dans les Romans du Moyen Âge* (Poitiers, 1962); or it may denote Avicenna (d. 1037).

569 At this point 'Mandeville' does indeed **speke of the Greke**, accurately describing their Orthodox beliefs which he found in Jacques de Vitry, *Historia Hierosolimitana* (ed. J. Bongars, *Gesta Dei per Francos*, Hanover, 1611, pp. 1089–91). But the author has suppressed this account, and substituted a brief extract from the description of the Mohammedans which 'Mandeville' copied into his chapter on the Saracens from William of Tripoli, *De Statu Saracenorum* xliii (ed. H. G. Prutz, *Kulturgeschichte der Kreuzzüge*, 1883, pp. 594–5). Cf. H, pp. 154, 171 below.

594 This legend of **Achimalek**, which does not occur elsewhere in English sources, may have been transmitted orally by the Crusaders after the capture of Nicaea in 1097 and recorded in a lost romance of Alexander. Lysimachus, one of the inheritors of the Alexandrine empire, renamed the city in honour of his wife after he had defeated and killed its ·founder Antigonus in 302 B.C. His legendary annual reappearance may be linked with the story of his savage death related by Vincent of Beauvais, *Speculum Historiale* iv. 46 (iv. 129). Cf. Higden, *Polychronicon* iii. 28 (iii. 448–50), and G. Cary, *The Medieval Alexander* (1956), p. 114. A similar legend, relating the founding of Patras by Antipatros, another heir of Alexander, is reported by Benjamin of Tudela (p. 71) and derives ultimately from Josephus Gorionides (in part trans. E. A. Wallis Budge, *The Life and Exploits of Alexander the Great*, 1896, ii. 403–25).

602 the porte of Chiuitote, on the south coast of the Gulf of Nicomedia, was a fortified camp, which Alexius prepared for the use of his English mercenaries, in the neighbourhood of Helenopolis. It had considerable importance for the Crusaders as the terminal of the ferry from Aegiali. See Runciman i. 128–9, 152.

603 the brake of seint George, i.e. the Bosphorus. The name is explained by William of Tyre, *Historia Rerum in Partibus Transmarinis Gestarum* xxxvi (translated by Caxton in 1481 as *Godeffroy of Boloyne*, E.E.T.S., E.S. 64, 1893, p. 73):

> This braas or arme . . . it is sayde that it is mooste paysible and easyer than the see is. Nyghe therto stondeth Constantinople, whiche is lyke a tryangle. The first syde is bytwene the porte and this arme. Ther standeth a chirche of Seynt George, of whiche that see is named the Braas of Seynt George.

604 The **Gehene See** is obviously the Aegean Sea, where St. Nicholas was originally buried at Myra, in Lycia. But the form **Gehene** is curious. The Continental Version, p. 239, and W 11/30 both read *la meer* without further qualification, and of the versions of *Mandeville's Travels* made in England only the Defective Version and the derivative Egerton Version describe the sea more precisely as *þe Grekes see*. As the Metrical Version has apparently no connection with either of these English versions, the more precise reference is probably interpolated by the author. However, the absence of a definite article is metrically and syntactically puzzling, and the form **Gehene** may therefore be a scribally distorted relic of an earlier *þe Egeum* or some similar phrase; unless the extreme shortness of this line is in some way due to the comparative length of the previous line, an earlier scribe having falsely divided the lines.

606 seinte Nicholas was translated from Myra to Bari by Italian merchants in 1087, and his relics are still preserved in the church of s. Nicola where an oily substance, *manna di san Nicola*, is reverenced. But 'Mandeville' was unaware of the translation, and the author's interpolated reference to the **faire chapelle** underlines the grossness of the error.

614–19 The descriptions of the isles of **Siloo** and **Pathmos** are copied from Boldensele (p. 32); see the Egerton Version, notes on pp. 162–3, where both **mastikke** 616 and **manna** 641 are explained. The details of the saint's age and the 'manna' in his tomb are added from the Golden Legend (ii. 174), where the story of the empty tomb ultimately derives from the sixth-century pseudo-Abdias (ed. J. A. Fabricius, *Codex Apocryphus Novi Testamenti*, Hamburg, 1703, ii. 589). 'Manna' is similarly associated with the tomb of St. Andrew in the Golden Legend (ii. 104–5).

645 þe seuen sleepers are not mentioned by 'Mandeville', but their cave on **the mounte of Sely**, Mount Anchilos near Ephesus, was frequently visited by Christian travellers until the Turkish conquest in the fourteenth century. The legend, recorded by Jacob of Sarug (d. 521) and St. Gregory of Tours, circulated widely, e.g. the Golden Legend (iv. 120–7) and Higden i. 26 (i. 264–6).

657 þe ile of Grece, i.e. Crete. See p. xii above. 'Mandeville' does not describe the island, and the details given in 658–60 are interpolated by the author. Cf. notes to 479–84, 661.

661 Sopheos, i.e. Cos, a variant name for **þe ile of Lango** mentioned immediately afterwards and not, as in all versions of *Mandeville's Travels*, a separate island. The detail of the **good fisshinge** is interpolated by the author.

668 a grete meruail The immediate source of the legend is not known, but Aelian xvi. 39 (iii. 316) tells of a monstrous snake on the island of Cos, which is clearly connected with the story here. Cos was a centre of the cult of Aesculapius, the god of medicine, whose emblem is a serpent-entwined rod, and the **grete clerk Ypocras** (Hippocrates, the physician of Cos) had a son or grandson named Draco. Some of these details are discernible in the local legend reported by Fabri, *Evagatorium in Terrae Sanctae, Arabiae, et Egypti Peregrinationem* (ed. C. D. Hassler, 1849, iii. 267), when he visited Cos in 1483, and see G. Huet, 'La Légende de la fille d'Hippocrate à Cos', *Bibliothèque de l'École des chartes* lxxix (1918), pp. 45–59.

The legend has been strongly influenced by classical and medieval myth. The theme of *le fier baiser* is a commonplace of romance; see R. S. Loomis, 'The Fier Baiser in *Mandeville's Travels*, Arthurian romance and Irish saga', *Studi Medievali* xvii (1951), pp. 104–13, and S. Eisner, *A Tale of Wonder* (1957), pp. 121–34. And the details of the reflection in the mirror (suppressed by the author, cf. H 156/13), the combing of the hair 710, and the mute changeling who can speak only in human form are paralleled in Ovid, *Metamorphoses*.

The version told by the author differs in two major particulars from that told by 'Mandeville'. The former makes the enchanted damsel resume her natural shape **a daie in the yere** 719 and makes the enchantress **hir stepmoodire** 673 instead of the goddess Diana, as in other versions of *Mandeville's Travels*. It is possible that the author had in mind Kemp Owyne or an English version of the associated *Hiamðers ok Olvers saga*, which both tell of a changeling and a wicked stepmother, though the enchantment of a beautiful woman by her envious stepmother is a common theme of medieval romance, e.g. Dame Ragnell in *The Weddynge of Sir Gawen*, ll. 692–6. On the metaphorical usage of 'step-mother' see *O.E.D.* s.v.

673–4 forshope/boke An assonantal rhyme common in Lydgate, and cf. Chaucer, *Troilus* ii. 884/6 *sike/endite*, and 2233–4 below *swythe/drife*.

687 The reference to the **knyght fro seint Iohnes** (cf. note to 751 below), which is common to all versions of *Mandeville's Travels*, probably dates from the fourteenth century when the order fell into disrepute after their seizure of the Byzantine island of Rhodes in 1308. Elsewhere, in a passage omitted by the author from the tale of the sparrowhawk (1547–1612), 'Mandeville' tells of an avaricious Knight Templar, whose order was suppressed in 1308.

691 the hors, cf. W 12/45 *le chiual*. All other English versions (but no extant Insular manuscript) give a reading derived from a corrupt variant *le chiualer*.

696 All extant manuscripts of Subgroups A and B of the Insular Version read *et ensi fuist perduz le chiualer* W 13/23. But the phrase **both hors and man** is otherwise paralleled in the Cotton Version 17/7, H 156/9, and two manuscripts of Subgroup C of the Insular Version (MSS. Palais des Arts, Lyon 28, f. 10 and Bürgerbibliothek, Bern 58, f. 7), and in the Continental Version, and undoubtedly derives from an original *le chiualer et le chiual*. When it occurs elsewhere in ME. (e.g. Malory), the phrase has a strong overtone of completeness, cf. 'lock, stock, and barrel'.

709 of goold reede, a detail interpolated by the author. The phrase is common in ME. verse, e.g. *Havelok*, l. 47, and derives from the older alliterative tradition, cf. **mydille erde** 2331 and note.

732 This ordination into a secular order, as distinct from elevation by accolade, would normally have been a lengthy process, cf. E. J. King, *The Knights Hospitallers in the Holy Land* (1931); but in all other versions of *Mandeville's Travels* the knight adventurer is made to return on the morrow. The author speaks more realistically of þe next yere, though this change is necessitated primarily by the interpolation of 719 above. See note to 668 above.

751 the hede hous of seint Iohnes After the abandonment of Tortosa in 1291 and the subsequent extinction of the kingdom of Jerusalem (during which campaign the Order was almost annihilated) the Knights Hospitallers were re-established first in Cyprus, then in 1309 in Rhodes under the leadership of Grand Master Foulques de Villaret. See A. S. Atiya, *The Crusade in the Later Middle Ages* (1938), pp. 286–90; J. Riley-Smith, *The Knights of St. John in Jerusalem and Cyprus* (1967). Even before the withdrawal from Jerusalem the Order fell into popularly picaresque but unjustified disrepute. See the Anglo-Norman satire *Le Ordre de Bel Eyse* (T. Wright, *Political Songs of England*, Camden Soc. vi. 140) and the songs

of the troubadour Peire Cardinal, which both attack the pride and ostenta-
tion of the knights, and cf. the popular misconception of *la légion étrangère*.

The interpolated reference to **a castelle realle fulle riche** is to the
great castle of Filermo, betrayed to the Knights Hospitallers on 11 Novem-
ber 1306, which lies west of the city of Rhodes.

758 Satelly, the medieval Satalia near the modern Adalia, suffered many
vicissitudes and many conquerors after its capture by the Seljuks in 1207,
but it was never entirely destroyed. The precise and misleading association
of the town with a legend generally diffused along the southern shores of
Asia Minor was probably present in the source used by 'Mandeville'.
The legend may owe something to the severe storms of the region.
St. Helena was reputed to have stilled the violent waters forever by
throwing into them a golden nail of the True Cross, but Saewulf (ed.
T. Wright, op. cit., p. 49) reported his escape from near shipwreck in the
gulf in 1102, and later medieval travellers experienced similar storms.

The immediate source of this version of the legend, which ultimately
derives from the classical myth of Medusa and the Gorgon's head, has not
been traced. But there are many similar accounts in the later Middle Ages,
and the story was probably widely diffused as a result of the Crusades.
Cf. John of Brompton, *Chronicon* (ed. R. Twysden, *Historiae Anglicanae
Scriptores X*, 1652, cols. 1216–17); Roger of Hoveden, *Chronica* (ed.
W. Stubbs, Rolls Series, iii, 1871, p. 158); Benedict of Peterborough
(ed. Stubbs, op. cit. ii. 195); Gervase of Tilbury, *Otia Imperialia* (ed.
F. Liebrecht, 1856, p. 11); Walter Map, *De Nugis Curialium* (ed.
T. Wright, Camden Society, 1st series, l, 1850, p. 177). The theme of
necrophily is part of the story of Callimachus and Drusiana of Ephesus
told by the pseudo-Abdias (ii. 547), where the crime is avenged by a
serpent, cf. note to 783 below. And the theme of *la laide semblance*, thrown
by Merlin into the Gulf of Satalia, is part of the Arthurian cycle; see *Le
Livre d'Artus*, ed. O. Sommer (1913), p. 150. See the Egerton Version,
note to 14/6.

775 xii. moneth W 14/31 gives the better reading of *ix. mois*, cf. H
157/10. But the alteration, repeated at 780, occurs independently in the
Bodley Version 21/29 (cf. its Latin source) and possibly represents a
popular belief about unnatural gestation.

783 a brennynge hede A similar detail occurs in the legend of the
monstrous serpent of Cos related by Aelian, loc. cit., the death of which
involves widespread destruction. See note to 668 above.

792–3 This interpolated quotation does not occur in Vulgate.

795 Seint Barnabe, cf. W 14/41 *seint Barnabe*, i.e. the saint mentioned
by Boldensele (p. 34) whose account of Cyprus 'Mandeville' copies. But
in the Harley and Egerton Versions the reference is omitted, and in the
Defective Version it is corrupted to *seynt Bernard*. Lines 796–7, inter-
polated by the author, echo the authority of Acts 4: 36: *cognominatus est
Barnabas ab apostolis, quod est interpretatum filius consolationis, levites,
Cyprius genere.*

C 7739   H

799 papiounes, i.e. hunting leopards. See the Bodley Version, note to 23/19.

829 Acoun Acre was the principal port of entry for pilgrims to the Holy Land during the Frankish occupation. Cf. the account by Benjamin of Tudela (p. 81) in 1163.

831 Lumbardis milis Elsewhere, in a passage omitted in the Metrical Version, 'Mandeville' states that these are identical with English miles; *miles de Lumbardye ou de nostre pais qi sont auxi petites. Ces ne sont mie lieues de Gascoigne ne de Prouince ne Dalemaigne, ou il y ad grandes lieues* W 58/33.

    twey MS. *twenti* Cf. H 157/24 *bis mille* and W 16/31 *mm. . . . lieues.*

841 the Fosse of Menyoun, an area of vitreous sand at the mouth of the Belus near Ptolemais (later Acre), is described by Josephus, *De Bello Judaico* ii. 10 (ii. 396), and Pliny v. 17 (ii. 278). The latter account is repeated by Vincent of Beauvais, *Speculum Naturale* vii. 77 (i. 474). Josephus explains the name of the fosse by reference to the near-by tomb of Memnon, the son of Tithonus and Eos, killed by Achilles. 'Mandeville' derived the story from Jacques de Vitry (p. 1166).

853 the Graueled See See note to 2647 below.

868 This interpolated quotation does not occur in the Vulgate.

877 the castelle of Pylrym The great Templar fortress of Château Pèlerin at Athlit, thirteen miles north of Caesarea, was one of the strongest and most famous of crusader castles. It was evacuated in 1291 and subsequently dismantled by the Saracens. Although its ruins are still visible, this reference is anachronistic, like much else in 'Mandeville's' account of the Holy Land. In medieval England the fortress was known as 'the Pilgrims' Castle'. See T. S. Boase, *Castles and Churches of the Crusading Kingdom* (1967), pp. 61–3.

889 For a contemporary verse account of the discomforts of medieval sailing see *Men may leue alle gamys That saylen to seynt Iamys* (ed. F. J. Furnivall, *The Stacions of Rome*, E.E.T.S., o.s. 25, 1867, pp. 37–40). A graphic description of the dangers and discomforts of a four-month voyage from Jaffa to Venice in 1506 is given in the anonymous *Pylgrymage of Sir Richard Guylforde* (ed. H. Ellis, Camden Society, 1st series, li, 1851, pp. 56–78).

890–909 The coastal road southwards from Acre passes by Haifa, Mount Carmel, and Château Pèlerin before reaching Caesarea, and the itinerary given here is accurate except for the misleading reference to Tire.

891 seint Hely, the site of Elijah's meeting with the priests of Baal on Mount Carmel (1 Kings 18: 19), mentioned by Boldensele, op. cit., p. 35. In 1163 the shrine was visited by Benjamin of Tudela who reports (p. 81): 'Under the mountain [i.e. Carmel] are many Jewish sepulchres, and near the summit is the cavern of Elijah, upon whom be peace. The Christians have built a place of worship near this site, which they call St. Elias.'

893 Tire, a distortion of the reference to the *Scala Thiri* (e.g. H 157/37), i.e. 'the Ladder of Tyre', the name given in 1 Maccabees 11: 59 to the road which climbs the steep headland Ras en Nakurah between Acre and Tyre. Cf. Josephus, loc. cit. 'Mandeville' is responsible for the geographical confusion which places this road south of Acre.

894 a tothe The reference is interpolated by the author. But teeth were the most common of holy relics; William Brewyn (op. cit., pp. 25, 60) reports one of St. Peter and another of St. Paul. Robert Langton (ed. E. M. Blackie, 1924) lists numerous teeth and other personal relics of various saints throughout Europe in 1522.

897 Peroun At this point the only town mentioned by 'Mandeville' in the vicinity of Mount Carmel is *Saffra* (e.g. H 157/33), the modern Seffurich, which is immediately followed by a reference to the *riuulus paruus qui Beleoun dicitur*, i.e. the Belus mentioned in the note to 841 above. The form **Peroun** is in no way explicable as a corruption of *Saffra* but it could be a distortion of *paruus* or *Beloun*. See above, p. xiii.

905 Nostre Dame de Marroe is not mentioned by 'Mandeville' by name, but he does refer to *vna pulcra ecclesia sancte Marie vbi morabatur vii annis quando fugit de terra Iude* H 158/29, following Boldensele, p. 39. The author may have found the name in another source, but it appears corrupt, possibly from an earlier *nostra domina Maria*.

926 Andromounde 'Mandeville' confused the monster with Andromeda, whose tale is told by Ovid, *Metamorphoses* iv (i. 226), and by Vincent of Beauvais, *Speculum Naturale* xvii. 100 (i. 1300). See the Egerton Version, note to 16/1.

942-8 These details of the Church of the Holy Sepulchre are interpolated by the author and appear to refer to the marble casing which surrounded the Rock of Calvary during the Frankish occupation. See W. Harvey, *The Church of the Holy Sepulchre, Jerusalem* (1935).

954 Bi the grete dore This detail is interpolated by the author. 'Mandeville' associates the hair-rending of St. Mary Magdalen, Mary Cleophas, and Mary the Egyptian with the *chaustel qad a noun Bethanye* W 48/37, cf. H 169/19.

972 seint Helene Legends associating St. Helena with England are discussed in detail in Capgrave, *þe Solace of Pilgrimes*, p. 126 n. 1.

975 Colchester in the Middle Ages is briefly described by J. R. Green, *Town Life in the Fifteenth Century* (1894), i. 14–15.

986 The midwarde of þe worlde was traditionally placed in Jerusalem on the authority of the Septuagint version of Psalm 74: 12: ὁ θεὸς βασιλεὺς ἡμῶν πρὸ αἰῶνος εἰργάσατο σωτηρίαν ἐν μέσῳ τῆς γῆς. In garbled form

'Mandeville' quotes this in other versions (e.g. W 39/33), probably from Peter Comestor, *Historia Scholastica* (Migne, *P.L.* cxcviii. 1634) or a derivative. But the exact centre seems to have varied. See the Egerton Version, note to 40/6. More imaginatively, the Tartars believed that the centre of the world was indicated by the navel of the Great Khan enthroned in the great palace near Peking; see note to 2308 below, and cf. the stone ὀμφαλός still to be seen at Delphi, and the derivative Marian legend.

997 Chariote The form of this name is close to that of the saint (*Karicoti* H 165/23 and *Karitot* W 38/25) whose church is mentioned by 'Mandeville' two miles south of Bethlehem. But despite this similarity the reference is probably interpolated. The author may refer to the Orthodox Convent of St. Charalampos which stands just north of the chapel of St. Helena, although there is no tradition of his bodily preservation. A less likely but possible identification is the monastery of St. Saba which, as Saewulf reports (p. 44), originally lay three miles west of the Church of the Holy Sepulchre but was abandoned for a site within the walls after a Saracen attack.

1009–13 These references to the destruction of the Temple by the Chaldeans in 587 B.C. and by Antiochus Epiphanes in 168 B.C. and to the restorations of Jeshua and Zerubbabel are interpolated by the author. But they are found in most of the chronicles; e.g. Capgrave (pp. 47–8).

1020 The quotation from Matthew 24: 2 is interpolated by the author.

1030 archa federis, i.e. the Latin designation of the Ark of the Covenant (Exodus 25: 10–22). The phrase is probably a stylistic flourish by the author.

1031 the seuen chaundelers, i.e. the golden menorah with seven branches and seven lamps. Cf. note to 198–200 above.

1034 Seinte Symeon, the holy and devout Jew who took the infant Jesus in his arms in the Temple and spoke the words known as the *Nunc dimittis* (Luke 2: 25–32). But the belief that Simeon was originally blind and miraculously cured was based on a misunderstanding of the Evangelist's words: *et responsum acceperat a spiritu sancto, non visurum se mortem nisi prius videret Christum domini . . . Nunc dimittis seruum tuum, domine, secundum verbum tuum in pace, quia viderunt oculi mei salutare tuum.*

1047 Luke 4: 30.

1049 The story of **seint Petir in prisoun** is told in detail by Capgrave, *þe Solace of Pilgrimes*, p. 96.

1061 Campe Floree Names similar to this (e.g. *champ flori*, cf. *campus floridus* H 164/31, *Chaump Flory* W 35/45) are found in French and Latin itineraries, variously describing the site of Elijah's ascent to Heaven and the Garden of Gethsemane. Although the source of the legend in *Mandeville's Travels* is unknown, the story is related, in much fuller detail, in a French Life of the Blessed Virgin dated 1323 (Fitzwilliam Museum MS.

20, ff. 1–3: see M. R. James, *A Descriptive Catalogue of the Manuscripts in the Fitzwilliam Museum*, 1895, pp. 31–2) where the miracle of the *champ flori* is told of Abraham's daughter by his second wife, Cetura; and the legend also occurs in Arabic sources. See E. Montégut, *Heures de lecture d'un critique* (1891), p. 278, and cf. the ME. *Pistill of Susan*. The origin of the story may lie in the *plantatio rosae in Iericho*, a place noted for its fertility by Josephus iv. 8. 3 (iii. 135), which is a possible source of the annual blessing of the Golden Rose. Roses are commonly the emblem of Christ's passion, cf. A. W. Pollard, *English Miracle Plays* (1890), p. xlvii, and are also associated with the Virgin Mary (e.g. Lydgate, *The Life of Our Lady*). Cf. the sermon *Maria in Purificatione Rosa* (1629) by Maximilianus Sandaeus, echoes of which in Crashaw and Herrick are cited by J. B. Leishman, *The Art of Marvell's Poetry* (1966), p. 47.

For analogous medieval stories of the divine saving of women see *The Man of Law's Tale*, ll. 669–79, and the parallels cited by Skeat; *Speculum Sacerdotale*, pp. 180–1; the legend of Cunegonde and the Emperor Henry III told in the Golden Legend (vii. 130). And a somewhat similar legend concerning the miraculous saving from the stake of Gelgehe, the daughter of Aelfiud and the niece of Brendin, is told in the Irish version of the life of Furseus; see T. Wright, *St. Patrick's Purgatory* (1844), p. 13. A close parallel where a treatise by St. Dominic against heresy is thrown into the fire but does not burn is related in the Golden Legend (iv. 174–5).

These parallels and the detail of the punishment by burning (which is specifically European, e.g. the doom against Guinevere, cf. the later Hebrew practice of stoning) suggest that the legend of the innocent maid, at least in the version copied by 'Mandeville', was of western origin.

1085 of oure lady, a detail supplied by the author. In the context of the *chaump flory* 'Mandeville' describes an unnamed *mult belle esglise* W 35/43 on the site where Christ was born.

1105 Traditionally the three shepherds are not named; e.g. H. Deimling, *The Chester Plays*, E.E.T.S., E.S. 62 (1892), p. 132; R. E. Parker, *The Life of St. Anne*, E.E.T.S., 174 (1927), p. 28; *Speculum Sacerdotale*, p. 6. But occasionally they are given names, e.g. *Maunfras*, *Boosras*, and *Moyse* in K. S. Block, *Ludus Coventriae*, E.E.T.S., E.S. 120 (1917), pp. 146–7. The names **Symon** and **Iudee**, oddly without a third, do not occur elsewhere in this context in English sources.

1116 a faire church is mentioned by 'Mandeville' in the immediate vicinity of the graves of the patriarchs (H 164/9 and W 34/35) but it is not associated with Abraham. The author has confounded this reference with the later mention of *la meson Abraham* W 34/40 'the house of our father Abraham', visited by Benjamin of Tudela, p. 86; see the Egerton Version, note to 34/17.

1118 heede The meaning is clearly a monument or head-stone of some kind, influenced by a developed sense of *caput* in Late Latin, but the word is not otherwise recorded in this sense. 'Mandeville' does not refer to this metting between God and Abraham (Genesis 17: 1).

1123 a caue, i.e. the *carnarium leonis*, the place where twelve thousand Christians, killed in battle against Chosroes II (d. 628) near Jerusalem, were miraculously interred by a lion. The legend (cf. W 47/27 and H 168/33) is a commonplace of medieval itineraries, e.g. Thietmar, *Peregrinatio*, ed. J. C. M. Laurent (1857), p. 27.

1141 the welle of Siloe, the Pool of Siloam (John 9: 7), situated at the extreme south-west of the city and joined by underground conduit to the Spring Gihon (1 Kings 1: 33).

1151 The Assumption of the Blessed Virgin Mary, three days after her earthly death (see 1177 above), is reported by 'Mandeville', probably from the full account in the Golden Legend (iv. 260).

1164 When Arculf visited the church on Mount Olivet in A.D. 700 he was shown the imprint of Our Lord's foot miraculously preserved in dust (p. 5). The invention of the stone relic, a more durable monument still shown to pilgrims, probably occurred after 1102 since it is not reported by Saewulf who mentions all such items, and before *c.* 1250 when it is reported by the pseudo-Odoric (ed. J. C. M. Laurent, *Peregrinatores Medii Aevi Quatuor*, 1864, p. 151). A similar impression (allegedly of the foot of the angel seen by St. Gregory on the summit of Hadrian's tomb) is still to be seen in Rome. Cf. note to 169 above.

1166 That oþer stone of white marble was one of the most venerated of the Westminster Relics. It is first reported by Matthew Paris, *Chronica Maiora s.a.* 1249 (v. 81), cf. the Westminster abstract:

> Dominus rex [i.e. Henry III] in lapide marmoreo vestigium pedis Christi ascendentis in caelum, quod receperat a fratribus Praedicatoribus de Terra Sancta venientibus, ecclesiae contulit Westmonasterii in hoc anno.

It is last reported in a list of relics [Westminster Abbey Muniments 9485] dated November 1520, and was presumably lost after the dissolution in 1540. The impression was as famous as the ring in the Abbey, given to St. John in the guise of a pilgrim by Edward the Confessor and miraculously restored (Golden Legend ii. 176), and this interpolated reference by the author can have no local significance in determining the origin of the Metrical Version.

1182–5 The relic is well attested from the twelfth century, but it is not known from what account 'Mandeville' derived his reference. See the Egerton Version, note to 47/7.

1190 Matthew 26: 39: *Pater mi, si possibile est, transeat a me calix iste.* The slightly variant form of the quotation used by the author is common to all versions of *Mandeville's Travels*.

1214 a churche faire and goode Of seint Iohn is described by 'Mandeville' (cf. W 51/37, H 170/29), but the reference to the **water þat renneth there** is interpolated by the author. It is not found in the account of St. John the Baptist given in the Golden Legend (v. 67–78).

1224 the gardeine of Abraham, mentioned by Theodoric (p. 72) and Boldensele (p. 65) as the site of Abraham's dwelling (Genesis 12: 8), and identified in the Egerton Version, note to 49/9, as a jebel about three miles north-west of Jericho.

1241 The Deede See For the sources of this description see the Bodley Version, note to 61/16, and the Egerton Version, note to 50/4.

1246 stadies, cf. *stadies* W 50/32 and *stadia* H 170/8, denoting measures of length (600 Roman feet) approximately equal to an English furlong. The word is used for 'furlong' without qualification by Chaucer, *Boethius* iv, and by Bartholomaeus xix. 129 (*the stadium is the ei3teþ part of a myle*, f. 332ʳᵇ) and less precisely by William Worcestre, *Itineraries* (ed. J. H. Harvey, 1969, p. 181). The author's knowledge of the precise meaning of the word is perhaps attested by its use in 1392, but the expression of distance here is ambiguous and possibly corrupt, cf. W *diiiiˣˣ.* and H *dᶜ. et lxxx stadia* (which is certainly corrupt), and MS. *v. score* is accordingly emended.

1248 seven score, cf. *cl.* W 50/32 and H 170/9. No extant manuscript reads *cxl.* at this point, but emendation is metrically impossible and, if a liberal interpretation is given to **somdele more** in the next line, probably unnecessary.

1254 clyme The form is not recorded in *O.E.D.* or *M.E.D.*, and the meaning 'still, clear, calm' assigned in the Glossary is tentative. The form may be due to metathesis or, at least in part, to the scribe's fondness for exact eye-rhymes, e.g. an earlier *cleine* 'clean' being reshaped to correspond to *tyme*, cf. note to 2078 below; or it may be dialectal.

1258 Baldam, i.e. Admah. The initial *B-* is probably a distortion of an earlier *A-*, confusion between them being common in English *textura libraria* hands; e.g. the Bodley Version 5/9 and 5/25. The intrusive *B-* cannot be a relic of an earlier OF. prepositional prefix *D-* because W 50/39 is syntactically clear at this point: *en cel mer fondirent les v. cites par irour de Dieu, cest assauoir Sodome et Gomorre, Aldama, Seboym, et Segor.* Cf. H 170/22–3.

1267 þe place of Lothe, i.e. Zoar, unless the author is deliberately distorting his source for greater vividness. 'Mandeville' (e.g. H 170/26) merely claims that the walls of the town are visible in good weather.

1280 The quotation is interpolated from an unidentified source.

1283 seint Katerine With this reference to the sepulchre of St. Catherine of Alexandria on Mount Sinai (see the Egerton Version, note to 31/9) the author reverts to an earlier part of his source where 'Mandeville' describes the route from Cairo to Jerusalem.

1289 Babiloine þe Lesse, i.e. Cairo. See the Bodley Version, note to 25/18.

1302 Aloth The ultimate source of most medieval accounts of the Nile is Pliny v. 9–10 (ii. 252–64), who describes its emergence from an underground course *alio lacu maiore* (ii. 256), and the name **Aloth** may derive from a corruption of this phrase. The reference seems to be independent of the tradition which locates the source of the Nile near a fabulous Mount Atlas; e.g. Honorius of Autun, *Imago Mundi* i. 10 (Migne, *P.L.* clxxii. 123), *Nilus iuxta montem Athlantem surgens*, and Higden, *Polychronicon* i. 16 (i. 132), *non procul ab Atlantico monte*.

1313 2 Samuel 1: 21.

1330 Nembras Galeas, apparently a corruption of the Latin *Nembrot gigas* (e.g. H 160/23). Nimrod, the idolator and builder of the Tower of Babel, is twice briefly mentioned by 'Mandeville' (W 21/35 and 109/31), and these details of the building of the tower are interpolated. A similar account is interpolated into the Harley Version by the translator: *vnum verbum inserere quod in Maundeville non vidi sed in cronicis repperi* H 160/21; and it is possible that the author is not himself responsible for this interpolation in the Metrical Version. For a learned note on the legend see G. V. Smithers, *Kyng Alisaunder*, E.E.T.S. 237 (1957), pp. 155–6, and cf. the account in the *Cursor Mundi*, ed. R. Morris, E.E.T.S., o.s. 57 (1874), part 1, pp. 134–9.

1362 Atte fote of Synay The monastery of black monks on Mount Sinai contained in 1217, according to Thietmar, *Peregrinatio* (ed. J. C. M. Laurent, op. cit., p. 46), an inexhaustible jar of oil given by the martyr whose relics lay in the sepulchre. The oil was customarily given to distinguished pilgrims, and the story of the **wilde foule** told here is a variation of Thietmar's explanation of the monastic supply of oil. Its origin, however, is unknown.

1380–3 'Mandeville' makes no such claim but much later in the book, in a passage following the tale of the sparrowhawk (see 1739–40 above), he states that Noah's ark is on Mount Ararat and *la veoit homme de loinz quant il est cler temps* W 74/44, cf. H 174/11. The author has apparently distorted his source to achieve a greater sensationalism. Cf. note to 1267 above.

1391 Nostre Dame de Sardinache, otherwise the church of *Nostre Dame de la Roche* at Saidenaya, about twelve miles north of Damascus, was visited and described by all medieval pilgrim authors, e.g. Boldensele, p. 76, Jacques de Vitry, p. 1126, Thietmar, p. 14. The miraculous picture of the Blessed Virgin Mary, said to have been painted by St. Luke and to consist half of stone and half of flesh, is still an object of local superstition. The exudation of oil, which is well attested, may possibly be connected with the ancient Hebrew practice of anointing stone pillars. See the Egerton Version, note to 61/5.

1406–7 Cf. W 61/34 *vn vesseal de marbre par dessoz la table bien lie et bendez de feer pur resceiure loile qi degoute*. The relevant leaf in the Harley Version is lost.

1427 þe yatis of helle Originally *chymenes denfern* 'chimneys of Hell'
W 29/32, the phrase was corrupted by independent scribes to *chemyns
denfern*, which ultimately gave this English 'translation' as well as *vie
inferni* H 163/4. The corruption occurs in all manuscripts of Subgroup B
and four manuscripts of Subgroup A of the Insular Version; see p. xii
above. However, Mt. Etna was commonly described as an entry to Hell,
as the author notes, and the phrase here and elsewhere may not be
entirely due to an earlier copying error.

1429 A wondir meracle, reported by Pliny vii. 2 (ii. 514) and Aelian
i. 57 (i. 76) of the North African tribe of the *Psylli*. But in the Golden
Legend (iv. 30), which is possibly the source of the account in *Mande-
ville's Travels*, it is related of the people of Malta, descendants of those
who sheltered the shipwrecked Paul after his miraculous preservation
from the snake (Acts 28). The reasons which prompted 'Mandeville' to
locate the legend in Sicily are not clear. The origin of the story appears
to be a distorted account of some ancient practice of exposing unwanted
babies.

1440–2 This sentence, interpolated by the author, is apparently sug-
gested by the quotation from Psalm 90: 13 which follows it.

1451 A wondirful beeste The ultimate source of this story of the
monstrous prodigy is St. Jerome, *Vita sancti Pauli* (Migne, *P.L.* xxiii. 23)
where it is related of St. Anthony. But in the Golden Legend (ii. 206),
whence it passed into *Mandeville's Travels*, it is told of St. Paul the
Hermit. The legend is widely reported, e.g. Matthew Paris, *s.a.* 407
(i. 176), the *Prose Life of Alexander*, ed. J. S. Westlake, E.E.T.S., o.s.
143 (1911), p. 109, Isidore xi. 3. 21.

1458 Unlike St. Jerome who states that a similar monster was once
brought alive to Alexandria, 'Mandeville' claims that the head and horns
of this monster are displayed *a Alexandre pur le meruaille* W 24/45, cf.
H 161/17. The author has rectified this confusion, possibly on the
authority of the abstract of St. Jerome incorporated in Gervase of
Tilbury, p. 7.

1462 Cleophe, i.e. Heliopolis. The form is due to an earlier corruption
of *E-* to *C-*; such corruption is common in English *textura libraria* hands
of the fifteenth century, cf. note to 1258 above. See p. xii above.

1468 fenixe The legend of the Phoenix is related by Pliny x. 2 (iii.
292–4) and by Aelian vi. 58 (ii. 78–80), the latter following Herodotus ii.
73 (i. 359) and specifically linking the bird with Heliopolis. The legend
was widely reported, e.g. Alexander of Neckham, *De Naturis Rerum* xxxiv
(pp. 84–7) quotes Solinus, Ovid, and Claudianus; and like much else in
Mandeville's Travels it features in the Alexander cycle, e.g. the *Prose Life
of Alexander*, pp. 93–4. 'Mandeville' probably followed the account of the
Phoenix derived from the *Physiologus*, although this is omitted in the
Latin and English texts of the work printed in *An Old English Miscellany*,

ed. R. Morris, E.E.T.S., o.s. 49 (1872). Cf. M. R. James, *The Peterborough Psalter and Bestiary*, Roxburghe Club (1928).

1493 a wondir crafft, reported by Boldensele (p. 42) and almost all other medieval travellers. See the Egerton Version, note to 25/18.

1504 pomes of paradys, i.e. fruit of the plantain. See the Bodley Version, note to 37/8, and the Egerton Version, note to 25/29.

1511 figges of Maligge, i.e. the figs of Pharan (otherwise Arabia Deserta, cf. Genesis 21: 21) mentioned by Thietmar (p. 52) and Jacques de Vitry (p. 1099), the source of the account in *Mandeville's Travels*, as *ficus Pharaonis*, otherwise *ficus sycomorus*. This fruit is also described by Pliny xiii. 14 (iv. 130–2), Isidore xvii. 7. 17, and Vincent of Beauvais, *Speculum Naturale* xiv. 29 (i. 1034); but the substitution of **Maligge** (presumably the classical Malaca, later Malaga) is unique. The nonsense of 1509, common to all versions of *Mandeville's Travels*, is ultimately due to a misunderstanding of Pliny, *pomum fert non ramis sed caudice ipso*.

1514 a felde Sometimes identified with the *Ager Damascenus*, the field of 'balsam' is described by almost all medieval pilgrims, e.g. Boldensele (p. 51) and Simon Symeonis, *Itinerarium* (ed. M. Esposito, 1960, p. 80), and by Vincent of Beauvais, *Speculum Naturale* xiii. 84 and 99 (i. 1000 and 1008). The **bawme**, described by Burchard as *gleba rubea . . . quasi pro specie carissime venditur*, is identified in the Egerton Version, note to 34/27, as 'a reddish dust-like powder obtained from a shrub (*Mallotus Philippinensis*) growing in Arabia, India, and other eastern countries'.

1519 the grete bernes that Ioseph made This popular identification of the pyramids, first recorded by Bernard the Wise in A.D. 867 (ed. T. Wright, op. cit., p. 24), is discredited by Boldensele (p. 44). 'Mandeville' dismisses the argument that they are graves, however: *si ces estoient tombes, elles ne fuissent mie voide par dedeins* W 27/34.

1520 Politrade This name does not occur elsewhere and may possibly have been invented by the author. Cf. note to 2084. 'Mandeville' and his sources (e.g. Boldensele, p. 42) merely locate the pyramids *inter Aegyptum et Africam*, cf. 1527 above.

1521 foure, apparently a scribal error, cf. W 27/30 *les ii. sunt merueillousement grantz*, and H 161/35 *duo supereminent altitudine*.

1530–4 This catalogue of serpents is interpolated by the author; 'Mandeville' merely refers to *pleinz de serpents* W 27/31, cf. H 161/38.

glistardes The form is not recorded in *O.E.D.* or *M.E.D.*, and the meaning 'toads' assigned in the Glossary is tentative. It may derive either from OE. *glisnian* 'to shine, glitter' or from the Latin *gliscere* 'to swell up, rise up'; in either case the attribute could equally apply to the speckled adder. The OF. suffix *-ard* is usually found in words of romance origin.

1538 Sabbatory This account is derived from Jacques de Vitry (p. 1098), cf. Josephus, *De Bello Judaico* vii. 5 (iii. 534); Pliny says the river *ceases* to flow on the Sabbath. It has been identified with an intermittent spring about twenty miles north-east of 'Arka (the Archas of the crusaders), a few miles north of Tripoli; see the Egerton Version, note to 61/20. Its literary name is properly *riuus Sabbaticus*.

1547 Hermonye MS. *Libye* The emendation, undoubtedly right on textual comparison (cf. *Hermenie* W 73/41 and *Armeniam* H 173/4), is difficult to justify palaeographically. In some *textura libraria* hands (and in this manuscript) the vertical downstroke of *h* is identical in form with *l*, and an initial confusion may have caused a later radical reformation of the word.

1549 an oolde forleten castelle In Odoric, *Relatio* (ed. H. Yule, *Cathay and the Way Thither*, Hakluyt Society, 2nd series, xxxiii, 1915, pp. 98–9; and A. Van Den Wyngaert, *Sinica Franciscana*, vol. 1 (1929), p. 414) this castle is called Zegana, near Trebizond in Greater Armenia, and is associated with a story about partridges. The castle is perhaps one reported by Clavijo in 1406 (ed. C. R. Markham, Hakluyt Society, 1st series, xxvi, 1859, p. 65) and cf. Marco Polo (ed. H. Yule, *The Book of Ser Marco Polo*, revised by H. Cordier, 1913, i. 46). In all versions of *Mandeville's Travels* the castle is unnamed and sited in Lesser Armenia near the coastal town of **Portepye** (cf. *Persipee* W 73/42 and *Percipie* H 173/7), perhaps modern Porto di Plas; and the story of the partridges is replaced by the legend of the sparrowhawk.

The source of the legend is unknown, but it recurs, independently and more fully, in the French romance of *Melusine*, written by Jean d'Arras after 1387, where the **gentil ladie of fayrie** 1553 is named Melior; a ME. translation is edited by A. K. Donald, E.E.T.S., e.s. 68 (1895), see pp. 15–16, 364–8. But Jean d'Arras does not mention the **marchaunte in Venise** 1573, and it seems certain that 'Mandeville' merged two accounts of the legend; in all other versions he gives an alternative time limit, e.g. H 173/10 *vii. diebus et vii. noctibus* (*et quidam dicunt iii. diebus et iii. noctibus*), cf. 1557, which perhaps argues two distinct versions of the legend unless an earlier *in vii.* has been misread as *iii. vii.* The author's suppression of this alternative time limit may have been due to his knowledge of falconry. The traditional method of taming a wild hawk is to keep it awake continuously until it falls asleep from sheer exhaustion on the falconer's wrist, which generally takes three days and nights.

The kingdom of Cilician Armenia finally succumbed to the Mongols in 1307 after the murder of Leon IV by the emir Bilarghu; see K. M. Setton, *A History of the Crusades* (1962), ii. 630–59. As the Christian kingdom of Trebizond in Greater Armenia preserved its independence until its absorption into the Ottoman empire in 1462, the fable of the sparrowhawk clearly refers to Cilician Armenia, and developed in its present form between 1307 and *c.* 1357 (the date of the composition of *Mandeville's Travels*). Cf. a reference to the *heyres of Lusynen* in the ME. *Melusine* (p. 367) and the description of the vanquishers of the Lusignan dynasty by 'Mandeville' as *sarazins* 'pagans' W 74/31. But the reference to **the Cane** 1606 is supplied by the author.

However, the sparrowhawk is much associated with legend, and the story is unlikely to have been invented in the fourteenth century. Cf. Gervase of Tilbury (p. 26) and the Egerton Version, note to 73/17.

1572 In all other versions of *Mandeville's Travels* the penalty of not watching the allotted time is stated; *sil dort il est perdu, qe homme ne le verra mais* W 74/35, a reference to imprisonment in the land of faery made more explicit in the ME. *Melusine.*

1573 a marchaunte of Venise, an alteration by the author, reflecting the importance of Venetian trade in the fifteenth century. 'Mandeville' describes him merely as *le filz dun poure homme* W 74/31, cf. H 173/29. The author omits a similar tale of *vn chiualer de Temple* which follows in all other versions of *Mandeville's Travels.*

1613 that cuntray In other versions of *Mandeville's Travels* (W 72/41, cf. H 172/32) this claim is made falsely of *Libie.* It ultimately derives from a reference by Herodotus iv. 42 (ii. 240) to the upper reaches of the Nile, which he styles Upper Libya, a vast and ill-defined region in classical geography.

1619 Liby MS. *Lumby* The initial *L* is unusually formed, but a similar shape appears in **Londene** 2310. There can be no doubt of the original reading, cf. *Libie* W 72/42 and *Libicum* H 172/34 where 'Mandeville' explains that the **Liby See** extends from the columns of Hercules to Egypt (cf. Herodotus, loc. cit.); a scribe has misread *Liby* 'Libyan' as *Lumby* 'Lombard'.

1632 Florencie, cf. *Phenicie* W 72/32 and *Finecia* (MS. *ffinecia*) H 172/13, i.e. Phoenicia. The corrupt scribal form arose from a confusion between an initial *ff-* and *fl-*, a common source of error in manuscripts of the period.

1644 the ryuere callid Thamare, i.e. the Don, is not placed by 'Mandeville' in Scythia, cf. W 72/35 and H 172/19. The author has perhaps deliberately simplified his source.

1647 Albanie This kingdom on the Caspian Sea derived its name from the white hair of its inhabitants, according to Isidore xiv. 3. 34 and Vincent of Beauvais, *Speculum Historiale* i. 69 (iv. 26), who report the **dogges hugie and hie.** Cf. Trevisa's translation of Higden's *Polychronicon* (i. 145): *þe houndes of þat londe beeþ so greete, so grym, and stronge þat þey proweþ boles and sleeþ lyouns*; Pliny vii. 2 (ii. 514); *Kyng Alisaunder,* note to l. 7945; and Gervase of Tilbury, p. 10.

1657 Arthanie, i.e. the classical Hyrcania, a region south-east of the Caspian Sea. The form is corrupt, cf. *Hircanie* W 72/37 and *Hircania* H 172/25, and distorted by an earlier confusion of initial capitals. Cf. notes to 1258, 1462, and 1619 above.

   Bacsirie, i.e. the classical Bactria by the upper reaches of the Oxus, one of the northernmost desert provinces of the Persian and Alexandrine empires. Cf. *Bactrie* W 72/37 and *Bactira* H 172/25.

1658 Yberie, i.e. the classical Hiberia, lying south-west of the Caspian Sea between the marches of Greater Armenia and Caucasian Albania, and described by Pliny vi. 10–11 (ii. 356–8), Isidore xiv. 3. 36, cf. Higden, *Polychronicon* i. 8 (i. 56).

1660 dromedaries, properly elephants, the account of which is placed out of context by the author. In all other versions of *Mandeville's Travels* it occurs just after the description of the giant reeds (see 2096 above, and W 95/42). The use of the term **dromedaries** is curious, cf. the ME. *olifauntz*. The beast is described by Isidore xii. 2. 14, Vincent of Beauvais, *Speculum Naturale* xix. 38 (i. 1403), Jacques de Vitry (p. 1101), and Brunetto Latini, *Li Livres dou Tresor* (ed. P. Chabaille, 1863, p. 243).

1673–6 This reference to the alchemists of **Yberye** is interpolated by the author.

1678 blak sope, otherwise known as *sapo saracenica*, the coarser-grained substance, cf. black salt, and the finer *whyte castell sope* mentioned in the *Libelle of Englyshe Polycye*, l. 55. It is mentioned in *John Arderne's Treatises* (ed. D'Arcy Power, E.E.T.S., o.s. 139, 1910, p. 118). But 'Mandeville' nowhere describes so homely a product, and if a Latin source for the Metrical Version is accepted, it seems most likely that *sapo* has been corrupted from an earlier *sapa* 'wine' or *sapor* 'smell', both of which are associated by 'Mandeville' with wonderful trees. Cf. 2045–50 above.

1682–4 This distorted reference to the appearance of a sea horizon is reported by Brunetto Latini (p. 169) and it is doubtful whether 'Mandeville' or the author understood the meaning.

1685 Ertho, unnamed by 'Mandeville' (W 72/41) and possibly identical with the fabulous Mount Atlas, cf. note to 1302 above, sited in or near the Earthly Paradise and so inaccessible to man (as explained in W 151/20). The name is possibly invented by the author, cf. notes to 1520 and 2084 *infra*. It does not seem to have any relation to *ly mount Cochaz qi est la plus haute de mounde* W 126/27, i.e. Mount Caucasus.

1687–8 This sentence, interpolated by the author, reads oddly and is possibly corrupt; the sense requires some final phrase like *nou3t ny*, instead of **liche ny**. But no satisfactory emendation suggests itself.

1691 Abissacol, ultimately the *Sarbisacalo*, va. *Solissaculo*, reported by Odoric (Yule, p. 101, Van Den Wyngaert, p. 416), otherwise called *Sabissa Collosasseis* by medieval travellers, i.e. Hassan-kala, a mountain about twenty-four miles east of **Arthiron**, i.e. Erzerum.

1696 Thano is quoted by 'Mandeville' as a variant Hebrew name for Mount Ararat (W 74/44). The author has treated it as a third mountain, cf. **three** 1690. The name has no obvious source unless it be a corruption of *Kuh-i-Nuh* 'Noah's mountain', the Persian name for Ararat. See the Egerton Version, note to 74/23.

1703–4 The **relik** is still venerated in the cathedral of Etchmiadzin, about thirty miles north of Ararat, but the monastery of St. James was destroyed by an earthquake in 1840. The story is briefly reported by William of Rubruck (ed. W. W. Rockhill, Hakluyt Society, 2nd series, iv, 1900, pp. 269–70; and Van Den Wyngaert, p. 323). In Armenian sources the monk is identified with St. James, archbishop of Nisibis. See F. Parrot, *Reise zum Ararat* (1834), i. 134, trans. W. D. Cooley (1845), pp. 150–1. In 1969 an expedition reported the discovery of a wooden artefact, perhaps 4,000 years old, in the frozen lake at the top of Ararat.

1711–14 Interpolated by the author. The whole story is considerably enlarged from the brief details given by 'Mandeville' (W 75/28–33, H 174/20–6) and possibly appealed to the author's professional skill.

1718–24 'Mandeville' says merely that on waking the monk found himself at the foot of the mountain, but adds that an angel appeared in answer to his prayer, a detail omitted by the author. None of these details are recorded by William of Rubruck whose account 'Mandeville' probably read (if at all) at second hand, e.g. in Roger Bacon's *Opus Maius* (ed. J. H. Bridges, 1900, i. 356–76).

1731–4 These measurements of the relik are interpolated by the author.

1738 Daine 'Mandeville' mentions two adjacent cities, Dovin (W 75/30 *Dayne* H 174/28 *Delasayne*) and Ani, the capital of Greater Armenia and about sixty miles north-west of Ararat (not, as the author claims, **atte foote of þat mountaine**), and almost totally destroyed by earthquake in 1319. 'Mandeville's' account is similar to that of William of Rubruck (Rockhill, p. 273, Van Den Wyngaert, p. 325) who visited Ani in 1253.

1742 Thesaurizo, i.e. Tabriz, described by Odoric (Yule, pp. 102–4, Van Den Wyngaert, p. 417). In all other versions of *Mandeville's Travels* the **thousande churchis** 1750 are included in the description of Ani, where they are reported by William of Rubruck (Rockhill, p. 273, Van Den Wyngaert, pp. 325–6). Cf. W 75/30, H 174/29.

1753 Salemount The hill of salt is described by Odoric (Yule, p. 104, Van Den Wyngaert, p. 418), but it is not named by him or 'Mandeville'; cf. *montaigne de siel* W 75/37 and *mons salis* H 174/36. The author's invention of the name appears to have been inspired by Latin, rather than French, forms. See p. xiii above, and cf. Pliny xxxi. 39–42 (viii. 422–34).

1764 Dago The reference, as well as the form, is much corrupted in all versions of *Mandeville's Travels*, cf. *et lappellent ils la char Dabago* W 75/45 and *ibi vocant homines carnes Dabago* H 175/10. Ultimately the derivation appears to be the Persian *chau baghi* 'four gardens, palace', a term which was specifically applied to the royal gardens of Isphahan; cf. F. Steingass, *A Comprehensive Persian–English Dictionary* (1930), p. 148 s.v. *bāgh*. Although no extant manuscript of Odoric gives the reference, it seems most likely that it was found in the text followed by 'Mandeville'.

1772 Corudan, i.e. the medieval Camara and the modern Kinara, near the site of the ancient Persepolis, destroyed by Alexander the Great. The ruins were visited by Odoric (Yule, p. 108, Van Den Wyngaert, p. 420). The form **Corudan** is corrupt, cf. *Cornaa* W 76/28 and *Cornaam* H 175/14. Earlier, in a passage omitted by the author, 'Mandeville' described Mahomet as prince of *Corodane* W 70/41, i.e. Khorasan (medieval Persia), but this coincidence cannot have affected the form here.

1777 the londe of Iob reflects a corrupted reference in the text of Odoric used by 'Mandeville', cf. Marco Polo (Yule, pp. 109, 281–2, Van Den Wyngaert, p. 420). Odoric describes *Huz* in the mountains of Kurdistan as a rich cattle-bearing country, and a later scribe has interpreted this as a reference to the wealth of the patriarch (Job 42: 12). But in other versions of *Mandeville's Travels* (W 76/29) Job is identified with Jobab, the son of Zerah of Bozrah (Genesis 36: 33), an identification which ultimately derives from Isidore, *De ortu et obitu patrum* xxiv (Migne, *P.L.* lxxxiii. 136).

1778 Ephan, apparently a gross scribal corruption, cf. *Theman* W 76/29 and *Temar* H 175/22, where the reference is to the royal city (not the **mounte**) of *Cassan*, visited and described by Odoric (Yule, p. 106, Van Den Wyngaert, p. 149) who reports the presence of manna. Its description, however, in all versions of *Mandeville's Travels* derives from Vincent of Beauvais, *Speculum Naturale* iv. 84 (i. 285), where it is possibly to be identified with the calamus reed, sometimes used in the preparation of sugar. See J. I. Miller, *The Spice Trade of the Roman Empire* (1969), pp. 92–4.

1786 the londe of Caldee, i.e. Baghdad, the inhabitants of which are described by Odoric (Yule, p. 110, Van Den Wyngaert, p. 421).

1800 the londe of Amozeyn, traditionally sited at the eastern end of the Black Sea adjoining Scythia. Although the Amazons figure prominently in the Alexander cycle, the source of this account in *Mandeville's Travels* is unknown; see A. Bovenschen, 'Untersuchungen über Johann von Mandeville und die Quellen seiner Reisebeschreibung', *Zeitschrift der Gesellschaft für Erdkunde zu Berlin* (1888), pp. 278–81. But the reference to **Tholopeus** 1803 is undoubtedly derived from Vincent of Beauvais, *Speculum Historiale* i. 96 (iv. 36), who names the king *Scolopitus*, cf. *Colopeus* W 77/44 and footnote 16.

1815 hir paramours, named *Sauromatae Gynaecocratumenoe* by Pliny vi. 6 (ii. 350), live across the water which separates the mainland from the promontory of the Amazons in all other versions of *Mandeville's Travels* (cf. W 78/34 and H 176/31). The author reduces the sea to a **ryuer.** Cf. 2217–22 above.

1835 Ethiope, i.e. Arabia. Cf. Isidore, *Etymologiae* xiv. 5. 16. The story of the miraculous well is derived from Vincent of Beauvais, *Speculum Naturale* xxii. 15 (i. 2410), and has many literary parallels; see the Egerton Version, note to 78/15. Trevisa (*Polychronicon* i. 161) gives a very similar translation: *Also among þe opere peple Garamantes is a welle al day so colde þat no man may þerof drynke, and al ny3t so hote þat no man may it touche.*

1844 This account of the *sciapodae* is derived from Vincent of Beauvais, *Speculum Historiale* i. 93 (iv. 34). Cf. Pliny vii. 2 (ii. 520) and the Egerton Version, note to 78/22.

1850 Litil Ynde is generally represented on medieval maps as an area extending from Arabia to the Indus delta. See G. H. T. Kimble, *Geography in the Middle Ages* (1938), and the Egerton Version, note to 79/1.

1855 Adiamaundes 'Mandeville' derives his description of the diamond from Vincent of Beauvais, *Speculum Naturale* viii. 40 (i. 514), but there are many similar accounts, e.g. Isidore xvi. 13. 2; Bartholomaeus xvi. 8 (f. 196vb); and cf. Latini i. 5 (p. 186); Marbodus, *Liber de gemmis* (Migne, *P.L.* lxxi. 1739). Of the description in his original the author preserves merely one reference.

1862 Pliny vi. 26 (ii. 412) reports *hydri marini* of thirty feet, and as **eelis** these creatures are variously placed in derivative accounts in the Indus and the Ganges. See the Egerton Version, note to 81/5.

1868 þe lande of Ermes, i.e. Hormuz in the Persian Gulf, an ancient and medieval mart described by Odoric (Yule, p. 112, Van Den Wyngaert, p. 422). Formerly Armuza, it remained an important entrepôt of Indian trade until the seventeenth century.

1876 Chanaen, i.e. Thana on the island of Salsette, about twenty miles north-east of Bombay. An important medieval trading centre, it was visited by Marco Polo (loc. cit. ii, pp. 395–6) and Odoric (Yule, pp. 114–15, Van Den Wyngaert, p. 422); 'Mandeville' follows the latter's account. The reference to the colours of the dogs in 1879 is interpolated by the author. See the Egerton Version, note to 82/7.

1882 Lumbe corresponds to the *Polumbum* of Odoric (Yule, p. 129, Van Den Wyngaert, p. 440) and the *Coilum* of Marco Polo (ii. 363), i.e. the medieval Kaulam and the modern Quilon on the Malabar coast. The account of the Pepper Forest is mainly derived from Odoric; Vincent of Beauvais, *Speculum Naturale* xiv. 64 (i. 1051), refers to the white and the black peppers only, cf. 1894–8, and the Egerton Version, note to 83/17, and Bartholomaeus xvii. 131 (f. 242va).

1888 foure and xx$^{ti.}$, so manuscripts of Subgroup B of the Insular Version (W 83/39 and footnote 18) and its affiliates. Manuscripts of Subgroup A read *xviii*.

1902 lymounes Odoric (Yule, p. 171, Van Den Wyngaert, p. 454) speaks of the use of lemon juice as protection against leeches in his description of Adam's Lake in Ceylon. 'Mandeville' adapts the reference to the Pepper Forest and repeats it in its proper context (W 84/36 and

98/39). The author, however, has considerably enlarged the brief description in his source.

1912–24 These details are interpolated by the author, probably to heighten the sense of mystery surrounding the Pepper Forest. 'Mandeville' tells a somewhat similar story of the apple-smelling pygmies which the author repeats in its context (2512–19 above).

1925 three citees In all versions of *Mandeville's Travels* and in Odoric (Yule, pp. 133–4, Van Den Wyngaert, p. 439) only two cities are mentioned, i.e. **Seneglaunce and eke Fladrin**, which are identified as Cranganor, the seat of an old Malabar principality, and Bandinanah near Calcutta by H. Cordier, in *Marco Polo*, loc. cit. **Polimpe** is merely a variant form of **Lumbe**; see note to 1882 above and W 84/38.

1936 a fair welle, i.e. the Well of Youth from which 'Mandeville' claims to have drunk *et vnques me semble qe ieo vaille mieltz* W 84/42. The source of this account is the *Epistola Presbiteri Iohannis*, which 'Mandeville' used in detail; see F. Zarncke, 'Der Priester Johannes', *Abhandlungen der philologisch-historischen Classe der königlich sächsischen Gesellschaft der Wissenschaften*, viii (1883), pp. 128–54, 180–4. The relevant passage is quoted in the Egerton Version, note to 84/18.

1948 The worship of the ox is reported of the inhabitants of *Polumbum* by Odoric (Yule, p. 137, Van Den Wyngaert, p. 440), who follows this account with a description of the practice of self-mutilation (1965–70 above) in the kingdom of *Mobar* on the south-eastern coast of India, i.e. ten days' journey to the south of *Polumbum*. 'Mandeville' keeps these two accounts separate (W 85/24 and 87/40), and their merging in the Metrical Version is probably due to the author. Both accounts of idolatry describe the sacrifice of children.

1965–6 This graphic detail is supplied by the author. 'Mandeville', following Odoric, says merely *ascuns ont les bracz et les iambes tot froissez et ascuns les coustes*. And the author suppresses the statement that the words of the sacrificer (1967–70 above) precede his suicide.

1973 Isaiah 2: 8: *et repleta est terra eius idolis, opus manuum suarum adorauerunt quod fecerunt digiti eorum.*

1974 This account of ritual murder of the sick is reported by Odoric (Yule, p. 175, Van Den Wyngaert, p. 456) of the land of *Dondin* and by Marco Polo (ii. 275) of the probably identical land of *Dagroian* in Sumatra. The author has removed the story from its context (W 99/27), presumably because of its similarity with the preceding account of unnatural practices. See note to 2767 below.

2001 Only one bifolium of the next quire in the manuscript is extant, probably the second and seventh leaves of a quire of eight. The continuous text resumes with the account of the Valley Perilous (2322 above). If the author preserved the sequence of *Mandeville's Travels* in these missing leaves, the matter lost after 2001 would correspond to W 89/25–94/23 (chiefly a description of the communal habits of the naked Sumatrans and the rotundity of the world, enlivened with characteristic anecdotes); after 2161 matter found in W 96/26–130/31 (mainly an account of the Great Khan); and after 2321 matter corresponding to W 136/35–138/29 (relating the overthrow of the Assassins). But the author's general practice of abridgement, rearrangement, and interpolation prevents an exact discovery of the contents of the missing leaves, and indeed he incorporates out of context matter which might otherwise have occurred on those pages; e.g. see note to 1974 above. None the less, it seems likely that the lost leaves did contain descriptions of the Sumatrans, the Great Khan, and the Assassins, all of whom would have appealed to his strong narrative instinct.

2002–4 These lines conclude an account of the cannibals of Sumatra which 'Mandeville' derived from Odoric (Yule, p. 148, Van Den Wyngaert, p. 446). He, however, does not restrict the cannibals' victims to children. Line 2002 refers to the practice of keeping the victim in **her lardere** until he is fat enough to eat; cf. W 89/39 *et sils sount crassez, ils les mangent tantost. Et sils sount megres, ils les fount encrasser.*

2006 Iane, i.e. Java. The rhyme indicates that the author inherited a corrupt variant (cf. the better *Iaua* W 94/23) or at least misread the word himself. 'Mandeville' follows the account given by Odoric (Yule, p. 151, Van Den Wyngaert, p. 447), but the author is highly selective, elaborating the description of the spicery beyond the brief reference in his source. Marco Polo (ii. 254) gives a slightly larger list of spices than Odoric. Neither **notmygges** nor **cloves** are grown in Java.

2009–16 These details of the **brasile** are interpolated by the author. Neither Odoric, Marco Polo, nor 'Mandeville' mentions the nut.

2017 canelle, i.e. the inferior type of cinnamon obtained from the bark of *cinnamomum cassia* and sometimes called cassia. See Miller, p. 42.

2025–30 Despite the disclaimer of 2026 the author has considerably expanded the list of spices, cf. W 94/26 *gerger, clous de girofle, kanele, zeodoal, noiz muscat, et maces.* Chaucer, *The Romaunt of the Rose*, ll. 1368–70, gives a similar list:

> As clowe gelofre and lycorice,
> Gyngevre and greyn de parys,
> Canell and setewale of prys.

galingale was originally a mild ginger (the derivation, through OF., Arabic, and Persian, is from the Chinese *Ko-liang-kiang* 'mild ginger from Ko'), but it was also applied to the aromatic root of *cyperus longus*, an English species of sedge, which is probably the meaning here.

gilofres are properly cloves and not a separate spice as the author states; see *O.E.D.* s.v. *clove-gillyflower.*

quibibus is the spice of the cubeb, much like a grain of pepper, which is native to Java.

bayes are described by Bartholomaeus, xvii. 48 (f. 222va) as *þe fruyt of laury tree*; in another context the Cotton Version (43/16 and textual note) mistakenly speaks of a *braunche of the bayes or of olyue*, cf. W 31/31.

graynes of paradis, a learned formation existing alongside the more popular *greyn de parys*, are cardomum capsules, *amomum meleguetta*; see *O.E.D.* s.v. *grain sb.* I. 4.

alkenade is the spice, or more commonly the dye, distilled from the leaves of the Egyptian privet; the form is derived through OF. and Spanish from the Arabic *al-henna*; see *O.E.D.* s.v. *alcanna*.

2032–6 These details are interpolated by the author. 'Mandeville' merely relates *touz biens y ad plentee forsqe de vin* W 94/29, but in the next paragraph (in the corrupt text used by the author, cf. note to 2081–2 below) he speaks of an antidote against poison prepared from leaves, which may have prompted the author's invention of that licoure. Cf. 2067–72, 2080–2 above.

2038 Pathan The island kingdom of *Panten* is described by Odoric (Yule, pp. 155–9, Van Den Wyngaert, pp. 447–50) and by Marco Polo (ii. 280), previously thought to correspond to the province of Banjarmasin on the southern coast of Borneo and now more plausibly identified with Singapore island. See note by H. Cordier on Odoric (Yule, p. 155 n. 5).

2045–6 The trees which bear **breede** are sago-palms, also reported by Marco Polo (ii. 282), and the trees which bear **venyme** are the upas trees, which were falsely supposed to be mortally poisonous. The trees bearing **wyne** and **hony**, reported by the factual Odoric, are possibly coconut palms, which produce a potent drink when fermented, cf. 2070. The manner of tapping these products is traditional, cf. the modern extraction of rubber in Malaya. See the Egerton Version, note to 94/14.

2078 medicyim The curious form is probably due to the scribe's practice of producing eye-rhymes by the most unlikely spellings, cf. note to 2167 below. But *-m/-n* were permissible rhymes in ME., cf. 2229–30 above.

2081–2 Odoric (Yule, p. 157, Van Den Wyngaert, p. 448) reports that the antidote against poison is prepared from human excrement, and this meaning is preserved by 'Mandeville' (*ses propres fiens* W 94/41). But in both manuscripts of Subgroup B (i) *fiens* 'dung' has been corrupted to *foilles* 'leaves', and the misunderstanding thus produced is reflected in the **iuys of þe same tree**. The error is also found in the Defective Version and its derivatives. See p. xii above.

2084 Calopide The form is not otherwise recorded and was probably invented by the author; similar examples of unique exotic place-names occur in 1520, 2353, 2368, 2416, 2438, 2925, all of them in rhyme, which possibly explains their creation. Elsewhere in ME. (e.g. Robert Mannyng)

place-names are often distorted for the sake of rhyme or metre. In his
account of *Panten* (see note to 2038 above) Odoric speaks of a *mare
mortuum* associated with reeds and miraculous stones and without a known
bottom, but the measurements of this **stondinge see** are interpolated by
the author, cf. W 95/29.

2096 The **reedis**, i.e. bamboo shoots, are reported by Vincent of Beau-
vais, *Speculum Naturale* xii. 67 (i. 920), whose measurements 'Mandeville'
adopts, and by Jacques de Vitry (p. 1100). The name **Thabies** is taken
from Brunetto Latini (p. 158): *les grandismes ions qui sont sor la mer que
li barbarin apelent Tabi*; but this is based on a misunderstanding of
Solinus l. 2 (ed. T. Mommsen, 1895, p. 182), where *Tabin* is the name
of the sea. The reeds themselves appear in later versions of the Alexander
legends, e.g. *the Prose Life of Alexander* (pp. 68, 104) and the *Epistola
Alexandri ad Aristotelem de situ Indiae* (p. 195).

2098 The form *femethes* is not recorded in *O.E.D.* or *M.E.D.* If its
meaning has not been distorted by scribe, translator, or author, it is
'paces, yards'; cf. W 95/30 *cez sont kannes, qils appellent Thaby, qi ont
xxx. toises ou pluis de long*. The word may be a by-form (and not a scribal
distortion) of ME. *fadom* (OE. *fǣðm*) 'the distance between a man's out-
stretched arms', i.e. six feet. A comparable and etymologically possible
sense of 'the distance between a man's outstretched legs', i.e. three feet,
could have developed from the basic OE. meaning of 'measurement', and
K. Sisam, *Studies in the History of Old English Literature* (1953), p. 65,
cites an example of the word used to translate 'cubit'. But cf. H 155/38
extanciones brachiorum, videlicet ffadoms.

2102 Precious stoones have been identified with the siliceous concre-
tions which form in the joints of bamboo. See the Egerton Version, note
to 95/4. 'Mandeville' curiously omits the vivid detail, related by Odoric,
that the amulet was inserted under the skin. The attribution of miraculous
properties to precious stones is commonplace; 'Mandeville', in a passage
omitted by the author (cf. W 79/45), lists the virtues of the diamond, cf.
note to 1855 above.

2111 This interpolated account of the three stones and their subsequent
erection at Stonehenge is due to the author's misunderstanding about the
size of the stones found at the roots of the bamboo; like Odoric, 'Mande-
ville' implies that these magic stones were no larger than ordinary gems.
The healing potion made in this fashion and the Stonehenge legend are
reported in almost all English chronicles, e.g. Matthew Paris, *Chronica
Maiora s.a.* 490 (i. 221), and Giraldus Cambrensis, *Topographia Hibernica*
ii. 18 (ed. J. F. Dimock, Rolls Series, 1867, v. 100–1); the ultimate written
source is Geoffrey of Monmouth, *Historia Regum Britanniae* viii. 11 (ed.
A. Griscom, 1929, p. 411). Cf. J. S. P. Tatlock, *The Legendary History
of Britain* (1950), pp. 40–2. The origin of this magic potion seems to have
been a genuine method of treating rheumatism by hot and steam baths;
see W. Bonser, *The Medical Background of Anglo-Saxon England* (1963),
p. 300; and this or a similar process is possibly commemorated in the

name of the so-called 'Heel Stone' (earlier *hele* 'health' stone) at Stone-
henge. Possibly associated with the myth reported by Geoffrey of Mon-
mouth is the legendary Irish pagan practice of commemorating a hero's
first killing by the erection of monoliths, an example of which is quoted
by R. Flower, *The Irish Tradition* (1947), pp. 2–3.

2123 The names of these giants, which do not occur in the list of famous
giants given by Vincent of Beauvais, *Speculum Historiale* ii. 92 (iv. 77),
nor in Geoffrey of Monmouth, loc. cit., have a distinctly biblical flavour;
cf. *Anakim* 'the sons of Anak' who supposedly dwelt at Hebron, and
Emims (Deuteronomy 2: 10–11).

2130 the mounte of Carloere, i.e. the site of the ring of stones, the
chorea gigantum, reported by Geoffrey of Monmouth (loc. cit.) in Kildare:
*quae est in Killarao, monte Hyberniae, ubi talis est lapidum structura qualem
nemo huius aetatis oculis prospexit.* Cf. Giraldus Cambrensis (loc. cit.): *in
Kildarensi planitie non procul a castro Nasensi.*

2132 In most versions of the legend Merlin alone is responsible for the
removal of the stones to Stonehenge, and Uther Pendragon is subse-
quently buried there; but in the ME. prose *Merlin* (ed. H. B. Wheatley,
E.E.T.S., o.s. 10, 1865, part 1, pp. 57–8) Uther Pendragon is associated
with Merlin in his plans to transport the stones from Ireland.

2140 Calomasse The form is very corrupt, cf. *Calonak* W 95/38 and
footnote 12, and it is possible that the author distorted the final syllable
to suit the rhyme, cf. note to 2084 above.

The country is called *Zampa* by Odoric (Yule, p. 163, Van Den Wyn-
gaert, p. 450) and *Chamba* by Marco Polo (ii. 267), i.e. Tchampa, formerly
a Buddhist kingdom in Indo-China. In conformity with his general
practice 'Mandeville' converts the kingdom into an **ile** in the Great Ocean
Sea. Both genuine travellers report the stories of the polygamous king and
the spawning fish; see the Egerton Version, notes to 95/14 and 95/24, and
the Bodley Version, note to 137/10.

2161 For a suggestion about the probable contents of the missing leaves
see note to 2001 above.

2162 The manuscript resumes just after the beginning of the account of
the medieval kingdom of *Cadeli,* probably Korea, derived from Odoric
(Yule, pp. 240–1, Van Den Wyngaert, p. 482). Like Odoric, 'Mandeville'
reports the legend of the vegetable lamb about the melon (a generic, not
specific, term in Latin, OF., and ME., from μῆλον 'apple' denoting several
kinds of gourds bearing sweet fruit) and then claims that the country
produces *longes pommes de bone odour et de bon sauour* (W 131/25, cf.
H 180/34), probably bananas or the **pomes of paradys** 1504. See the
Egerton Version, note to 130/1. H. Lee, *The Vegetable Lamb of
Tartary* (1887), p. 60, suggests that the myth originated in a distorted
account of the cotton-shrub. The author is responsible for the merging
of the separate accounts of the **litille lombe** and the **applis**.

2167 folle The form is due to the scribe's desire to give an exact eye-rhyme with **wolle.** Cf. 2252-3 and note to 2078 above.

2180 Caspery, i.e. the mountains of the Caucasus range adjoining the Caspian Sea, generally associated with the legend of Gog and Magog. The introduction of the legend at this point is, however, ultimately due to a misunderstanding by 'Mandeville' about the *montes Caspei* which Odoric reports in the kingdom of *Cadeli*, cf. note to 2162 above.

Legends of Gog and Magog and of the Ten Tribes of Israel are widely reported, but generally in isolation. 'Mandeville', in identifying **þe Iewes lynage** with **Goth and Magothes kynde,** is probably influenced by Jacques de Vitry (p. 1096) whose relation of Alexander's imprisoning of the Ten Tribes is immediately followed by the statement that he also confined the cannibal nations of Gog and Magog in the same place. See the Egerton Version, note to 131/5; *Kyng Alisaunder*, note to l. 5968; G. Cary, p. 296, and the authorities cited there.

2185 two and twenti kingis, traditionally the number of barbarian monarchs subdued by Alexander. The numerological significance of the number twenty-two survives at least until Spenser.

2187 Goth and **Magoth** are French forms of the names of the giants which are generally anglicized in translation. Cf. *Gogh et Magoh* H 181/18.

2208 the hie day of dome Legend associated the coming of Anti-christ and Doomsday with the escape of these imprisoned tribes. Cf. the *Pricke of Conscience* ll. 4467-72 (ed. R. Morris, 1863, p. 121):

> For þe Iewes has swylk a prophecy
> And says þus omang þam commonly,
> That þis folk ogayne þe worldes ende
> Sal com out and til Ierusalem wende
> With þair Crist, þat wonders sal wirke,
> And þan sal þai distroie Haly Kyrke.

The preceding passage (ll. 4456-66), introduced by *some says*, associates the imprisoned tribes with the queen of the Amazons exactly as in *Mandeville's Travels*. The prophecy was for a time held to have been fulfilled by the irruption of the Mongols into Europe; see Ricold of Montecroce (ed. J. C. M. Laurent, op. cit., p. 118) and cf. the Bodley Version, note to 47/29.

2212 The stronge walle of lyme and stone, sometimes known as Alexander's Gate, is part of the original legend and not identical, except in popular imagination, with the earth fortifications extending for one hundred miles eastwards from the Caspian Sea. See M. Letts, i. 184; A. R. Anderson, *Alexander's Gate, Gog and Magog, and the Inclosed Nations* (1932); R. Hennig, *Terrae Incognitae* (1950), ii. 169; the Egerton Version, note to 126/10.

2216 litil space, i.e. a pass across the Caucasus which 'Mandeville' calls *Clyroun* (W 131/46, cf. *Glyren* H 182/3), cf. *Direu* mentioned by Brunetto

Latini (p. 158). In all other versions the measurement **foure myle of brede** is applied to the pass, not the sea, and it seems possible that a scribe, not the author, is responsible for the altered sense here by reversing the couplet.

The pass may be the famous *Porta Caucasica* in the valley of the upper Tarek; or it may be the mythical 'Iron Gate' of Alexander, more prosaically the Pass of Derbend, which, in a passage omitted in the Metrical Version, 'Mandeville' mentions previously (W 126/31) from the account of Haiton (ed. L. de Backer, *L'Extrême Orient au Moyen Âge*, 1877), c. 1308. Derbend (Persian *dar band* 'a barrier, narrow pass') is ascribed to Alexander by Benjamin of Tudela (p. 99), cf. Marco Polo (ii. 52); but its originator appears to have been the Persian emperor Chosroes I who fortified the pass as part of his defensive wall against the 'White Huns'. See note to 2212 above, and cf. Pliny vi. 15 (ii. 366).

2227 The source of this **prophecie** about the pathfinder fox is not known, but there are classical and Arabic parallels; e.g. Sindbad's escape from being buried alive in the *Arabian Nights*. See the Egerton Version, note to 132/8. The author omits the important detail that the inclosed nations had never seen a fox previously and so chased it to its earth.

2241-9 These details are considerably enlarged by the author; 'Mandeville' merely claims that the Jews hope to subjugate and destroy, not convert, Christian men. The quotation from John 10: 16 is interpolated.

2251 þe londe of Bakkary is described in the apocryphal *Epistola Alexandri de situ Indiae* (ed. B. Kübler, *Iuli Valeri . . . res gestae Alexandri Macedonis*, 1888, pp. 202–3; and W. W. Boer, 1953, pp. 23–4), and it and its fabulous trees and beasts passed into the Alexander cycle. The author has once more enlarged the account of the wool-bearing trees in his source, where 'Mandeville' merely refers to the *arbres qi portent laine, auxi come barbis, dount homme fait des draps pur vestir* (W 132/39).

2262 ravenne The sense is not recorded in *O.E.D.* and its unfamiliarity is probably responsible for the scribal *there*, cf. the better **here**. Its meaning must be 'gall-nuts', the product of the *quercus infectoria*, which are rich in tannin and were widely used in the preparation of black ink; and its etymological root is OE. *hræfn*. See *O.E.D.* s.v. *raven* sb. 4. In OE. it was common to refer to ink by colour, e.g. *blæc*.

2270-1 The identity of the **pepleren,** and therefore the relevance of this couplet, is obscure. None of the indigenous poplar or willow trees have **beries**, although several bear catkins of a soft wool-like texture. **many** is possibly a scribally corrupt form of an earlier and better *grene*.

2278-9 This quotation is interpolated by the author.

2284 Preter Iohn All accounts of this fabulous emperor ultimately derive from the forged *Epistola Presbiteri Iohannis* (ed. F. Zarncke), and it seems certain that 'Mandeville' used a recension of this text; see note to 1936 above. But Odoric (Yule, p. 244, Van Den Wyngaert, p. 483)

identified the Khan of the Keraits, whom he found fifty days' journey
west of Cathay, as Prester John, and this distance is perhaps exag-
geratedly reflected in the estimate of the breadth of his empire in 2289,
foure monethis iourne þe ouergonge (cf. W 137/28 and H 184/44).
But the author has considerably abridged the detailed account given by
'Mandeville' of the emperor. See the Bodley Version, note to 99/6,
and the Egerton Version, note to 133/1.

2292–2307 'Mandeville' (W 135/38–136/45) reports that Prester John
holds sway over seventy-two tributary kings and is served in his court,
which numbers more than **thirti thousand** persons, by seven kings; but
he speaks of twenty, not **fourtie bisshoppes of lower degree**, and of
three hundred and sixty, not **foure hundrid erles**, and of seventy-two,
not **an hundrid dukes**. These numbers are expressed in roman numerals,
however, and variously corrupted in the extant manuscripts; for example,
manuscripts of Subgroup B (i) of the Insular Version and the affiliated
Defective Version give the number of **erles** as three hundred. It seems
likely that the author followed a text which was corrupt at this point,
although both **fourtie** and **foure** may be later errors introduced by
scribes and **hundrid** is probably a convenient round figure adopted by
the author for metrical reasons.

2308 Erropheroun At this point 'Mandeville' speaks of the land of
Milstorak before describing the castle of the Assassin chief, but there can
be no possible connection between *Milstorak* and **Erropheroun**. The
latter may be the invention of the author but, unlike similar examples (see
note to 2084 above), it does not occur in rhyme. 'Mandeville' describes no
city in terms exactly similar to those used by the author here; he says that
Latorin 'Peking' is larger than Paris and that *Iongo* 'Yenking' (i.e. an
alternate name for Peking) is larger than Rome, and he claims that the
principal city of Prester John is *Nise* (W 101/35, 113/35, 133/28); but none
of these cities can be identified with **Erropheroun**.
    The most plausible explanation of **Erropheroun** is that it is a gross
scribal distortion of *Caydoun*, the capital of the Great Khan near Peking
(Mongol *Daidu* 'Great Court'), built by Kublai Khan in 1267 and called
by Odoric (Yule, p. 217, Van Den Wyngaert, p. 471) *Taydo*, cf. Marco
Polo (i. 354). 'Mandeville' says that its walls extend for *xx. lieues*, cf. **foure
and fourty mile** 2314; that within the palace grounds is *vne mountai-
gnette*, cf. **a mounte** 2318; and that on this hill is built *vn autre palays*,
cf. **a castelle riche** 2320, which he describes in detail (W 105/28–107/30).

2310 Londene The reference is interpolated by the author. The best
accounts of fifteenth-century London are C. L. Kingsford, *Prejudice and
Promise in Fifteenth-Century England* (1925), pp. 107–45 and end-map,
and D. W. Robertson, *Chaucer's London* (1968). The fame of London is
celebrated in *London, thou art of townes A per se*, doubtfully attributed to
Dunbar, and its population is estimated in J. C. Russell, *British Medieval
Population* (1948), but cf. G. A. Williams, *Medieval London* (1963),
pp. 315–17.

2322 The relevance of this line is not certain. 'Mandeville' concludes his account of the Assassins with a description of the destruction of the Assassin stronghold of *Gathalonabez* (i.e. Shaikh ul-Jibal), the last of whom, Rukn ud-Din Khurshah, was hanged by Hulagu in 1256 (W 138/27); and if the missing leaf did contain the story of the Assassins (see note to 2001 above), it seems possible that this line is an imaginative addition to the original details of the destruction. Alternatively, it may be part of the account of the Valley Perilous which follows (2323–38). 'Mandeville' says that those who venture into the valley to plunder its riches *sount tantost estrangles de diable* (W 139/28). In neither case does 'Mandeville' mention the disposal of the **deede bodies**.

2323–38 This description of the Valley Perilous is based on the factual account of Odoric (Yule, pp. 262–5, Van Den Wyngaert, pp. 491–2) who reports his passage through a valley seven or eight miles long and strewn with corpses, possibly the pass of Reg-Rawan, some forty miles north of Kabul, leading to Tibet. See the Egerton Version, note to 138/1. The description of **that foule visage** is, however, the invention of 'Mandeville', possibly adopted from the legend discussed in the note to 758 above.

2329 clastrenne The word is not recorded in *O.E.D.*, and in *M.E.D.* s.v. *clastren* (derived from Late Latin *claustrare*) it is glossed 'to enclose (something), shut up'. Neither sense is applicable here, cf. W 139/31 *et ad les oilez si mouables et si scintillantz* and H 186/23 *et habet oculos mobiles et scintillantes*. If the author is correctly rendering his source, the sense must be 'sparkle, shine, glitter'. The development of these senses from Late Latin *claustrare* would be semantically difficult, and the form may be a corruption of *glistrenne* (OE. *glisnian*) or of *fast renne*.

2331 myddille erde (OE. **middelȝeard* and ON. *Miðgarðr*), i.e. the earth. The phrase belongs to the alliterative tradition, cf. **goold reede** 709.

2337–8 'Mandeville' makes no such claim; he says merely that Christians *qi sount en bone estate et astables en foy* (W 139/33) may pass the Valley Perilous without mortal danger but with great fear. And the interpolation makes nonsense of the final plea, in the complete versions, that the reader shall pray for 'Mandeville's' soul.

2340 twelff 'Mandeville' says *entrames xiiii* W 139/41 cf. H 187/3. The change may be due to a scribal corruption in the author's source or to the demands of rhyme. Similarly, 'Mandeville' claims that nine of the party survived, cf. **sevenne of his fellawis** 2347, and leaves the others' fate deliberately vague, cf. the definiteness of **for eueremoo** 2348.

2351–2 This quotation from Psalm 65: 12 is interpolated by the author.

2353 Ruspo The name does not occur elsewhere and is probably invented by the author, cf. note to 2084 above. 'Mandeville', however, reports the **ile** of cannibal giants, probably akin to the giants mentioned by Vincent of Beauvais, *Speculum Naturale* xxxi. 125 (i. 2392), and Isidore ix. 2. 132. See the Egerton Version, note to 140/11.

2368 Crasseran Like **Ruspo** 2353, the name does not occur elsewhere and is probably an invention by the author. The cotton shrub is reported by 'Mandeville' (W 142/38) and, ultimately, by Jacques de Vitry (p. 1099), but the vivid description in 2371–6 is interpolated by the author.

2374 cadasse, i.e. coarse wool. *O.E.D.* s.v. *caddis* records the word from about 1400.

2383 ǵerfans, cf. *gerfancz* W 142/42 and footnote 24, and *girfanz* H 188/5, i.e. the giraffe (Arabic *zurafa*). The animal is described in similar terms by Vincent of Beauvais, *Speculum Naturale* xix. 9 (i. 1387), who calls it *camelopardus*, following the account in Isidore xii. 2. 19. The giraffe, first brought to Rome in the time of Julius Caesar and always a rare animal in the classical arena, was chiefly known to medieval Europe by the written tradition. It was, however, independently reported by Marco Polo (ii. 422).

2387–8 This detail is interpolated by the author, probably on the analogy of the tortoise.

2389 chameliouns The plural form follows the conjunction **A** 'and'; see *O.E.D.* s.v. The chameleon is described by Vincent of Beauvais, *Speculum Naturale* xix. 6 (i. 1385); there are many similar accounts, e.g. Pliny viii. 51 (iii. 86), Solinus xl. 21 (p. 170), Isidore xii. 2. 18. 'Mandeville' describes the chameleon as *vne petite bestoille come vn cheueroun sauage* W 142/44– 143/19, cf. H 188/10.

2399–2414 These details are interpolated by the author from Bartholomaeus xviii. 21 (f. 276rb):

and it is yseyde þat þe camaleon lyueþ oonliche by ayre and þe wonte by eorþe and þe heryng by water and the criket by fyre, as þis vers meneþ.

Quatuor ex puris vitam ducunt elementis
camaleon, talpa, maris allec, et salamandra.
Terra cibat talpam, flamme pascunt salamandram,
vnda fit alleci, cibus aer camaleonti.

For the common medieval identification of the fabulous salamander with the **gamalioune** 'cricket' cf. Bartholomaeus, loc. cit., *þe criket hiȝt salamandra for þis beest quencheþ fyre and lyueþ in brennyng fyre*, and *Piers Plowman* B. xiv. 42.

2408 For the importance of **þe hirinǵe** in medieval England see A. R. Bridbury, *England and the Salt Trade in the later Middle Ages* (1955), pp. xvi–xviii.

2416 Barelide This name, not found elsewhere, is probably invented by the author, cf. note to 2084 above. 'Mandeville' reports both the

addris stronge 2421 and the **wilde swine** 2429, cf. W 143/21–4 and H 188/14–20, but he says nothing in these contexts of **huge forestis**. Elsewhere (W 84/32) he says that the Pepper Forest (see note to 1882 above) is infested with serpents, and the author's interpolation may have been inspired by this reference. Less plausibly, it may have been suggested by the later reference to *des grantz forestes toutz des chasteigns* W 152/34 in Cathay.

2429 The monstrous **wilde swine**, like the huge serpents and the **queinte beestis** 2443, are among the hazards encountered by Alexander in the *Epistola Alexandri de situ Indiae* (pp. 199–201) and retold by Vincent of Beauvais, *Speculum Historiale* iv. 54 (iv. 132).

2438 Orchepen This name is not found elsewhere, and the reference to the **cedrus** is interpolated. This combination exactly parallels that noted at 2416 above. Both appear to be the invention of the author. Cf. note to 2502 below.

2443 The **queinte beestis** are the fabulous monsters of Alexandrine legend; cf. *Kyng Alisaunder* (ll. 6504–615). But the author strangely omits the celebrated *odenthos* (W 143/27) and prefers only the *scyritae* among the many monsters described by 'Mandeville', who bases his account upon that of Vincent of Beauvais, *Speculum Historiale* iv. 58 (iv. 133), ultimately derived from the *Epistola Alexandri de situ Indiae* (p. 217). The reference to the **sixe leggis**, common to all versions of *Mandeville's Travels*, is based on a misunderstanding; cf. Vincent of Beauvais: *bestias habentes . . . latas ad sex prope pedum mensuram.* See the Egerton Version, note to 142/24.

2450 dusket The form is not recorded in *O.E.D.* or *M.E.D.* It may be a variant form of *dusked* pp. of *dusken*, cited in *M.E.D.*, but *dusketly* occurs in the *Book of St. Albans* in 1486, where it is suspiciously recorded by *O.E.D.* The form may have been influenced by *russet* 'of a reddish brown colour', recorded from *c.* 1400.

2452 Exedrath, apparently a corrupt reference to the 'Οξυδράκαι of Alexandrine legend (cf. *Oxidrate* W 145/42 and *Oxidrada* H 188/38). 'Mandeville' mentions these paragons (whose name he interprets as a place-name) in association with **Sinosople and also Dragmey** 2462. But he places the giant mice in the same unnamed island which the author styles **Orchepen** 2438 and refers to them very briefly: *et si ad des soriz auxi grantz come chiens, et chauue soriz auxi grantz come corbeaux* W 143/30. It is therefore possible (though less likely) that the author has invented the name **Exedrath**, as he has many others (see note to 2084 above), as the site of his inflated account of the mice.

2462 Sinosople is a corrupt form of the Γυμνοσοφισταί, 'the nakede wise' of the *Alliterative Alexander. Fragment C* (ed. W. W. Skeat, *The Wars of Alexander*, E.E.T.S., E.S. 47, 1886, pp. 223–45), who historically opposed Alexander's advance on the banks of the Hydaspes in the Punjab and passed into the Alexander cycle as paragons of virtue who shamed the emperor into peace. See the Egerton Version, note to 144/1, and G. Cary, p. 148. The scribal form of the name is identical with that of manuscripts of Subgroup B (i) of the Insular Version, cf. the better *Gysonophe* W 145/42 and footnote 15, and *Synosepulis* H 188/39. See pp. xiv, xv above.

Dragmey, i.e. the land of the Brahmans. Cf. *Bragmey* W 144/30. The ultimate source of all accounts of the Brahmans is the apocryphal Dindimus correspondence (ed. B. Kübler) which 'Mandeville' found in Jacques de Vitry (p. 1108) and Vincent of Beauvais, *Speculum Historiale* iv. 66–71 (iv. 135–7), cf. notes to 2251 and 2443 above. 'Mandeville' reports separately two very similar accounts of Alexander's confrontation by the Γυμνοσοφισταί and the Brahmans, and the author has blended them into one. Cf. Subgroup A of the Defective Version which omits the account of the former. See F. Pfister, 'Die Brahmanen in der Alexander-sage', *Berliner Philologische Wochenschrift* (1921), pp. 569–75.

2471–8 These pious details are interpolated by the author. 'Mandeville' says merely *en le temps iadis le roy Alisandre enuoya despier ceux de celle isle pur ceo qil voloit gaigner lour pais* W 145/29.

2491–3 This detail, with the quotation from James 2: 13, is interpolated by the author, who clearly shared the more favourable of the estimations of Alexander's character current in medieval Europe. Cf. G. Cary, pp. 226–57.

2494–2505 This account of **Anguilande** is interpolated by the author. Although 'Mandeville' in other contexts mentions both þe **Graueled See** and the **ryuer of Ronnemare** (see notes to 2548 and 2647 below) and variously reports of the presence of **ful goode cristen men** in lands of plenty throughout the empire of Prester John, he says nothing which is identifiable with this description, and it seems probable that the interpolation is the invention of the author.

Anguilande is clearly connected with **angle** 2497, but it is not clear which reference inspired the other. Such naïve attempts at etymology are characteristic of all medieval chroniclers, e.g. Capgrave. The reference to the language of these inhabitants (2504–5) is due to a false association of **Anguilande** with the continental homeland of the Angles (Bede, *Historia Ecclesiastica* i. 15). Cf. 2520–1, and Bartholomaeus xv. 14 (f. 173[rb]).

2502 This reference to olive trees is the third interpolation concerning trees, cf. the references to **cipres** 2418 and **cedrus** 2440. If the missing leaves contained an interpolation concerning *palme*, it would be certain that the author was consciously describing the four trees which went to the making of the True Cross. In a passage omitted by the author 'Mandeville' quotes a traditional belief, *in cruce sunt palma, cedrus, cypressus, oliua* (W 5/32 and H 150/28): see the Egerton Version, note to 5/10. Even without the fourth reference to *palme* in the extant manuscript, the supposition remains highly probable.

2507 Pikteine, cf. *Pitan* W 147/27 and *Pycan* H 189/8. The name ultimately derives from the *Trispithami* of Pliny vii. 2 (ii. 522), whose account of these people follows his description of the apple-bearing islanders. Vincent of Beauvais, *Speculum Naturale* xxxi. 128 (i. 2393), relates the fable without assigning the country a name, but elsewhere as part of the Alexander cycle (e.g. *the Prose Life of Alexander*, p. 89) it is a field *Actea*. The author has falsely identified **Pikteine** with the home-land of the Picts, thought in the Middle Ages to lie in the marches of Scythia and *Albany* (see note to 1647 above), and so interpolates the reference to **Englisshe** 2521. But this error was widespread (e.g. Matthew Paris i. 113) and stems from a confusion of Albany and the legendary Albion of antiquity (i.e. the Old Irish name for Pictavia), styled *Albanye þat now is called Scotland*. See J. S. P. Tatlock, pp. 8–9.

2524 The coming of **Engist** and **Horn** is related in the *Brut* (ed. F. W. D. Brie, E.E.T.S., o.s. 131, 1906, p. 50): *þere were ii. breþerne, prynces and maistres of þat straunge company. þat on me callede Engist, and þat oþere Horn.* The stages by which this early legend evolved into the earliest of the extant ME. romances, *King Horn* (ed. J. Hall, 1901), are not discoverable. See L. A. Hibbard, *Medieval Romance in England* (1924), pp. 83–96, and W. H. French, *Essays on King Horn* (1940).

2528 The quotation from Luke 4: 24 is interpolated by the author.

2529 Dendros is probably an invention of the author, cf. note to 2084 above. 'Mandeville' does not name the island where the inhabitants eat raw fish and flesh (W 147/32 and H 189/18). The references to the altitude of this land (2535–6) and to the solar cooking (2541–6) are interpolated by the author, but they occur elsewhere in *Mandeville's Travels*. The former is reported of Earthly Paradise (W 150/30 and H 190/14); and the latter occurs in the description of the Bedouin (W 33/34 and H 164/1). 'Mande-ville' does not claim that any land is so hot that its inhabitants have to shelter by day (2538), but in the account of þe **lande of Ermes** (1868 above and note) he states that the natives lie in water during midday (W 81/42).

2548 Rennomare This second reference to the Beas (the classical Hyphasis), the tributary of the Indus which marked the eastward extent of Alexander's penetration, occurs in its proper context. Cf. 2499 above; *Epistola Alexandri de situ Indiae*, p. 205; and see W. W. Tarn, *Alexander the Great* (1948), ii. 32 and end-map. The scribal form of the name, cf. the better *Buemar* W 147/33 and footnote 11, is similarly corrupted in manuscripts of Subgroup B of the Insular Version and its affiliates, the Defective and the Harley Versions. See pp. xiv, xv above.

2554–5 The extent of the **wildirnesse** and the name of **Eufronere** are both details interpolated by the author. The latter may be an invention, cf. note to 2084 above, but equally plausibly it may be a corrupt form of *Euphrates*, in the upper reaches of which the Dry Tree was traditionally sited. Cf. Odoric (Yule, p. 103, Van Den Wyngaert, p. 417).

2556-70 In this account of the miraculous trees are blended three originally distinct legends: viz. that of the Dry Tree which was destined to bloom before Doomsday (see *Kyng Alisaunder*, note to l. 6755 and the authorities cited there); that of the trees of Paradise which disappear at night (cf. *The Prose Life of Alexander*, p. 90); and that of the trees of the sun and moon; see G. Cary, p. 337, and the authorities cited there, especially Marco Polo i. 127-9.

All three legends are briefly and separately mentioned by 'Mandeville' (W 35/33, 135/30, 147/34), the third at this point in the text, and the author has conflated and expanded the references. 'Mandeville' has apparently misinterpreted the phantom fruit associated with exceptional longevity (2565-70), as a reference to the golden apples of the Hesperides, perhaps from a confused reminiscence of the story of Alexander's visit to the golden images of the gods before he reached the river **Rennomare** 2548.

2571-84 This confused account of Alexander's visit to the trees of the sun and moon is interpolated by the author. 'Mandeville' merely mentions the trees *qi parlerount au roy Alisaundre et li deuiseront sa mort*. But, as related in the *Pseudo-Callisthenes* (Budge, op. cit., ii. 164) and the *Epistola Alexandri de situ Indiae* (pp. 213-14), the prophecy specifies that Alexander shall never return into **Greke there he was kinge** but die by poison in Babylon. See the Egerton Version, note to 147/9.

2585-96 Inspired by these references to Alexander, the author interpolates the names of the Nine Worthies. 'Mandeville' mentions all except **Arthoure** and **Ectare** in various other and incidental historical contexts. Cf. the interpolation of the Seven Sages 549 and note above.

2598 Traprophan, i.e. Ceylon (Sanskrit *Tamraparni*), is described by Vincent of Beauvais, *Speculum Historiale* i. 79 (iv. 28), ultimately from Pliny vi. 24 (ii. 398-408). 'Mandeville' reports the presence of **noble cristen puple** in the island (W 148/37), undoubtedly a reference to the legendary faith of Prester John and to St. Thomas of India and not to the historical missions of the thirteenth and fourteenth centuries. The author with characteristic distortion converts the whole island (2608) and interpolates the reference to perpetual daylight (2605-6). The latter, in origin most probably describing northern Scandinavia, may have filtered into his knowledge through an anglicized version of an Old Norse saga or the lost *Inventio Fortunata* of Nicholas of Lynn; a fragment of which (in my possession) describes what is now Long Island.

2610 Orrille and **Argille** are the semi-mythical islands of *Chryse* and *Argere* in the Indian Ocean reported by Pliny vi. 23 (ii. 398), Isidore xiv. 3. 5, and Vincent of Beauvais, *Speculum Historiale* i. 79 (iv. 28 duplicate).

2616-18 'Mandeville' mentions neither **Engelath** nor any beryl-producing country. The name is probably invented by the author. Isidore xvi. 7. 5 and Vincent of Beauvais, *Speculum Naturale* viii. 48

(i. 518), place the source of beryl in India, and the interpolation here possibly stems from this tradition.

2620 Eufronone is apparently a gross scribal distortion of *Taprobane*, cf. W 149/29 *en celle isle de Taprobane y a grauntz mountains dor*, and H 189/40. The scribal confusion of *E-* and *T-* (paralleled in **Ephan** 1778 above) is not uncommon, and although this form presents an extreme example of corruption, the subsequent distortion is by no means inexplicable.

2625–30 These details do not occur in *Mandeville's Travels*. For other interpolations concerning trees see notes to 2416, 2438, 2502 above.

2631–6 'Mandeville' describes the griffon in these terms at the end of his account of Bactria (cf. 2251 above and W 132/43). There seems no good reason why the author should have inserted the reference here and not in its proper context. The description is derived from Vincent of Beauvais, *Speculum Naturale* xvi. 90 (i. 1210), cf. Isidore xii. 2. 17, and Marco Polo (ii. 404).

2632 Gripes (< Latin *gryphs* 'griffon') is first recorded as a loan-word in 1204. The word had a secondary sense of 'vulture' in Late Latin, and the author may have used that sense here, cf. **griffouns** 2635 which appear to be separate birds; although in other ME. contexts (e.g. *Sir Eglamour*, ll. 848–51) both words are used interchangeably. If the author adopted the form *gripes* from a Latin source (where it meant 'griffons'), described the bird exactly as 'Mandeville' describes the griffon, and then, not having recognized the meaning, interpolated a reference to the more common form *griffoun* (W 132/44 *griffoun*, H 182/34 *grifo*), his confusion would lend support to the argument for his use of a Latin version of *Mandeville's Travels*. See p. xiii above.

2637 The **hugie ampten** which guard the gold mines of the deserts east of India are described by Herodotus iii. 102 (ii. 128) and, finally, by Vincent of Beauvais, *Speculum Naturale* xx. 134 (i. 1536). But their association with the mines of **Orrille** and **Argille** and of **Eufronone** (see notes to 2610, 2620 above) is found only in *Mandeville's Travels*.

2647 the Graueled See, previously mentioned at 853 and 2498 above, is described as the first of the marvels of Prester John's empire after 'Mandeville' has concluded his account of the imperial court (see note to 2292–307 above, W 134/39 *la mer arenouse*, cf. **Mere Arenous** 2650). The primary source of this description is the *Epistola Presbiteri Iohannis* (ed. F. Zarncke, p. 914), and the **See** is probably identical with the *mare arenosum* reported—but not seen—by Odoric (Yule, p. 107, Van Den Wyngaert, p. 419) after he had visited *Cassan* (i.e. **Casseyne** 2753). The legend, which is probably based on some mythical account of the shifting sands of the desert, is embellished in all versions of *Mandeville's Travels* by the imaginative addition of the **goode fisshes** 2664.

2667 allaes, i.e. lignum aloes, a precious wood said to float down the

rivers of Paradise. See the Bodley Version, note to 37/23. 'Mandeville'
reports its presence in the Ganges (i.e. **Phison** 2705) in terms which have
caused the author to link it falsely with the Gravelly Sea: *en la quelle
riuere y ad molt des preciouses pierres et molt de lignum aloes et molt de
grauell dor* W 150/36, where the phrase *grauell dor* has been equated with
the **smale white sonde** 2652 of the Sea. See Miller, pp. 33–6.

2671–4 'Mandeville' sites Earthly Paradise and **the londe of derkenes**
beyond the desert confines of the empire of Prester John (W 149/43) and
not, as here, beyond the impassable Gravelly Sea.

2673 the londe of derkenes, probably based on distorted accounts of
an Arctic winter (cf. note to 2598 above), is described elsewhere in
Mandeville's Travels (W 128/35) as *Hauysoun,* probably the district of
Hamschen between the Black Sea and the Balkhar Dagh mountains, and
associated with the legendary imprisonment of the Persian persecutors of
Christians under the rule of the despot Shapur II. This story has possibly
inspired the author to interpolate the details of the **spritis** 2677–82. But
such references are not uncommon. Two manuscripts which contain
Mandeville's Travels (The Queen's College, Oxford, MS. 383 and Bodleian
Library MS. Additional C 285) also contain the prose *Gast of Guy*; and
Lincoln Cathedral MS. A. i. 17, ff. 250^v–7, tells the story of a woman who
attempted to alleviate the pains of purgatory by earthly assistance.

2685–700 This description of Earthly Paradise closely accords with that
of Vincent of Beauvais, *Speculum Historiale* i. 63 (iv. 24), cf. Isidore xiv.
3. 2. But 'Mandeville' has substituted the traditional wall of fire by a
moss-covered stone wall. See Letts, i. 214–15.

2701–8 All medieval accounts of Earthly Paradise mention the **faire
springenge welle** and the **foure streemes.** 'Mandeville' probably
followed the description given by Jacques de Vitry (p. 1098). Cf. Honorius
of Autun, loc. cit.; Gervase of Tilbury ii. 17 (p. 6); *Kyng Alisaunder,*
note to ll. 1499–1500; C. R. Beazley, *The Dawn of Modern Geography*
(1906), ii. 459.

2709–16 These details, interpolated by the author, belong to the tradi-
tional idea of Paradise, cf. the OE. *Phoenix,* ll. 74–80, and they are also
found, derivatively and independently, associated with the May garden.
Cf. Bartholomaeus xv. 11 (f. 186rb) and *The Franklin's Tale,* ll. 203–4:

> That nevere was ther gardyn of swich prys
> But if it were the verray paradys.

2714 without ioie The manuscript reading makes some sense as
punctuated, but an emended phrase *with alle ioie* would be a stylistic
improvement.

2717–44 'Mandeville' says nothing of **purgatorie** nor of the burning
gate of Paradise (see note to 2685–700 above). The interpolation, prompted
by the earlier reference to Earthly Paradise and in accord with current
ideas of geography which traditionally sited purgatory and hell in the

north, here supported by quotation from Jeremiah i. 14, is based on the teaching of Aquinas, *Commentarium in quatros libros sententiarum magistri Petri Lombardi* xxi. 1 (ed. M. F. Moos, 1947, iv. 1045–61).

2753 Casseyne, i.e. the Tartar province of Kenchan, visited by Odoric (Yule, p. 245, Van Den Wyngaert, p. 484), who called it *Cassan*. Cf. Marco Polo (ii. 18). The name is a corruption of *Changgan*, the Arabic style for the city of Si-nganfu, the capital of the rich and populous province of Shensi.

2760–4 These details are interpolated by the author. 'Mandeville' describes the rotundity of the world and claims that *les terres Prestre Iohan, emperour de Ynde, sont dessouz nous* W 91/34; but he says nothing of the different seasonal cycle of the southern hemisphere.

2767 Ribooth, i.e. Tibet, is described by Odoric (Yule, pp. 247–56, Van Den Wyngeart, pp. 484–6), whose account of the ritual disposal of the body is followed, with some minor additions, by 'Mandeville'. The practice is well attested. Cf. Herodotus iv. 26 (ii. 224); Vincent of Beauvais, *Speculum Historiale* i. 87 (iv. 32–3); Marco Polo (i. 292); William of Rubruck (Rockhill, p. 152, Van Den Wyngaert, p. 234); R. A. S. Macalister, *The Archaeology of Ireland* (1929), p. 166. Both Odoric and 'Mandeville' (W 153/29, H 191/7) confine their accounts to the ceremonial after the natural death of a parent. The author has conflated this description with an earlier account of the ritual murder of the sick in Sumatra, which he has already incorporated; see note to 1974 above. The use of this material a second time (i.e. at 2772–2801) suggests that the author was deliberately exploiting the more sensational parts of his source. Some of the details in this interpolated description are invented by the author, viz. 2772–85, and others are altered; in the original account of the Sumatran practice the idol pronounces the sick man's death, which is achieved by suffocation, cf. 2800–3. What follows after 2803 is based upon the account of the Tibetan rite.

2814 a charger faire, cf. *vn grant plateu dor ou dargent* W 153/31. The detail, not found in Odoric, is supplied by 'Mandeville'.

2825 The quotation is from the Roman burial service.

2842 The use of skulls as drinking vessels in Tibetan monasteries is attested by S. Hedin, *Trans-Himalaya* (1909), ii. 76, and cf. i. 375–9.

2847 anoþer ile 'Mandeville' does not name this land (W 153/44 and H 191/35) and the marginal rubric *Sepharage* is mysterious, unless it be a misplaced and mis-spelled reference to **Sapheran** 2925 (which, however, has its own marginal rubric). Odoric, however, describes the palace of the rich sybarite as being in Manzi, a rich and populous province of southern China (Yule, p. 254, Van Den Wyngaert, p. 487). Cf. Marco Polo (ii. 144–6).

2852 lorde of þat londe 'Mandeville' says that the land was ruled by *vn riche roy et puissant* and that this sybarite was merely *vn bien riche*, and Odoric adds that there were four such men in the kingdom.

2858 Cf. W 153/46 *ccc.*^{m·} *cheuaux chargez des bledz et de riz.* Odoric reports an annual revenue of three hundred thousand ass-loads of rice but says nothing of corn.

2876–9 These details are interpolated by the author.

2898–2923 The ultimate source of this remarkable interpolation may be Pliny vii. 2 (ii. 518), who relates that the *Hirpi* are able to walk over charred wood without injury, and the form **Tipiscenes** certainly appears to be Latin. But the description is largely a reworking of other similar marvels reported by 'Mandeville' and may therefore be the invention of the author. The evilly arrayed women 2910–13 may be related to the women of Chaldea, described in 1791–8 above; and the murder and eating of the sick (2914–23) recall very closely the practices already related by the author (see notes to 1974, 2767 above). The use of the dead man's skin as a ẟarnement to ẟone inne 2919 may be an imaginative extension of the genuine Tibetan practice of converting the skull into a drinking cup (2842–5 above); and the wool-bearing feet (2901–5) may be similarly based on the account of the wool-bearing trees (cf. W 132/40). Other men's marvels frequently find a resting-place in manuscripts of *Mandeville's Travels*; e.g. the interpolation of *þe ile of Hogge* in MS. Royal 17 B. xliii f. 70ᵛ and the monstrous-faced natives in the Bodley Version 141/14 fn.; and in view of the author's consistently uninhibited approach to his material the land of **Tipus** may have no literary source except, perhaps, the reference to the bound feet of the Chinese women which, in a passage omitted by the author, concludes the account of the rich Chinaman and his long nails. But see note to 2949 below.

2901 shoilinẟe The most likely meaning of this otherwise unrecorded form is 'sloping, flat-footed'; cf. *O.E.D.* s.v. *shoal* vb.² 3. Derivation from *shield* or *shell* (cf. MLG *schellen* 'to peal') is possible but, in the context, unlikely.

2925 Sapheran is not mentioned by 'Mandeville', who says nothing of saffron nor of its strange manner of collection (2936–49). The name, and possibly the whole description of the country, is possibly inspired by the term *saffron orientalis*, cf. Bartholomaeus xvii. 41 (f. 220ᵛᵇ): *tweye maner saffron, oon is ortensis and haþ þe name of gardynes for he groweþ þerinne . . . þe oþer hatte orientalis and haþ also þe name of þe place þat he groweþ inne.* A close parallel is afforded by the Essex place-name Saffron Walden, the centre of saffron cultivation in fifteenth-century England. The *crocus sativus* (Arabic *za'faran*) introduced into Spain by the Arabs, produces a yellow dye and a spice used in cookery, medicine, and as a perfume. Cf. the *Libelle of Englyshe Polycye*, l. 58.

2949 The abrupt ending of the Metrical Version in the middle of a page, which is not the ending of the manuscript, is probably due to the loss of

the final leaves of the scribe's exemplar. After the account of the rich
Chinaman 'Mandeville' concludes his account of the world with some
characteristically false personal details. The interpolations concerning
Tipus and **Sapheran** may represent an attempt to compensate for the
missing leaves by an earlier scribe and not, as suggested in notes to
2898–2923 above, be interpolated by the author.

GLOSSARY

Th is select glossary gives words and forms in the English text which may not be immediately intelligible. Generally the forms and the line references are those of the first occurrence. The past participle prefix *i-/y-* is disregarded in alphabetical arrangement. n denotes a lexical reference in the Commentary.

a, an *prep.* on, in, by 785, 768.
accounte *inf.* estimate, calculate 2319; **accountith** *pr. pl.* 864; **accountid** *pt. 3 pl.* 338; **accounted, accountid** *pp.* 531, 94.
addris *n.* snakes 2421.
adiamaundes *n.* diamonds 1855.
adoun *adv.* downwards 967.
afferde *pp.* afraid 2434.
affiaunce *n.* belief 176.
aȝen, *see* ayayne.
aire, eire *n.* heir 672, 2788.
aire *n.* air 2412.
alkenade *n.* spice 2030 n.
allaes *n.* aloes 2667.
alle and some *n. phr.* all and one 2774.
allemyȝht, allemyȝhty, almyȝhti, almyȝte, *adj.* almighty 1035, 817, 1, 2467.
amatistes *n.* amethysts 327.
amonge *adv.* here and there, in parts 322.
amorowe *adv.* on the morrow 850.
ampten *n.* ants 2637.
amyd, amyddes *adv., prep.* in the middle (of) 342, 229.
and *conj.* and 2; if 40.
angle *n.* promontory 2497.
angur *n.* vexation 2453.
anone right *adv. phr.* at once 1071.
apaid *pp.* satisfied 2489.
apertly *adv.* clearly 399.
apparail *n.* clothes 598.
appendith *pr. 3 s.* belongs 2501.
araied *pp.* adorned 324.
archeris *n.* embrasures 193 n.
areche *inf.* reach 544.
arered *pt. 3 s.* resurrected 1204.
asone *adv.* as soon 241.
assaie *pr. pl.* test 1431.

atte *prep.* at 5; *prep.+def. art.* at the 948.
atwynne *adv.* apart 1270.
auncestres *n.* forebears 20.
autere, autiere *n.* altar 962, 1475.
awhere *adv.* anywhere 2617.
axe *inf.* ask 1569; **axest** *pr. 2 s.* 1601.
axinge *n.* request 1570.
ayayne, ayein, ayen, ayenne, aȝen, aȝenne *adv.* again 2679, 684, 851, 862, 734, 1375.
ayens, ayenst *prep.* against 352, 1601.

ballokkis *n.* testicles 1870.
barbicans *n.* defence towers 190.
batailid *pt. pl.* armed, arrayed for battle 1807.
bawme *n.* balsam 1516.
bayes *n.* fruit of the laurel tree 2028 n.
beches *n.* precious stones 325 n.
bede *inf.* offer 1604.
bede, *see* byd.
beerdis *n.* beards 2906.
beere, bere *n.* bier 2810, 2802.
beeres, bere *n.* bear(s) 1324, 2444.
beldinge *n.* building 484.
bene *inf.* be 676; **beth** *pr. pl.* are 376.
bere *n.* outcry 2780.
bere, *see* beere *and* beeres.
bere, beren *pr. pl.* carry, bear 1500, 1491; **bore, ibore** *pp.* 1091.
berilles *n.* beryl stones 325.
bernes *n.* granaries 1519.
bete, beten *pt. pl.* beat 1018, 1009; **beten** *pp.* 964.
bicam *pt. 3 s.* went to 644.
bidene *adv.* together 2586.
bie *adv.* by 769.
biforn *prep.* before 20.
bigon *pp.* started 837.

bileue *n.* faith, belief 589.
bileueth, bilevith *pr. pl.* believe 2228, 571.
binethe *prep.* beneath 1870.
binynne *adj.* benign 7.
bistad *pp.* beset 1576.
blife, blive *adv.* gladly, quickly 2789, 2342.
blithe *adj.* happy 2477.
boldeli *adv.* without fear 679.
boon *n.* bone, body 712.
bore *n.* boar 2445.
botelle *n.* bottle 1712.
brede *n.* breadth 1248.
brenne *inf.* burn 1072; **bren** *pr. pl.* 1997; **brent** *pt. 3 s.* 786; **brennynge** *pr. ppl.* 783; **brent** *pp.* 1064.
brethe *n.* breath, blast of wind 855.
brid, bridde *n.* bird 1467, 1468.
brigges *n.* bridges 205.
brode *adj.* spacious, broad 747.
burgeis *n.* citizen, burgher 763.
buries *n.* berries 2264.
burthein *n.* burden 2381.
but . . . ne *adv. constr.* only 1844.
byd *inf.* bid 1569; **bade** *pt. 3 s.* 2574; **bad** *pt. pl.* 2488; **bede** *pp.* 782.

cadasse *n.* coarse wool 2374 n.
calcidoynes *n.* chalcedony stones 327.
Cane *n.* the Khan 1606.
canelle *n.* cinnamon 2017 n.
capitoly *n.* the Capitol 384.
carbuncles *n.* carbuncle stones 332.
careful *adj.* anxious 778.
cedrus *n.* cedars 2440.
cese *inf.* cease 920.
chameliouns *n.* chameleon 2389; *see also* **gamalioune.**
chapelette *n.* chapelet 1798.
chapmen *n.* merchants 2940.
charger *n.* large plate 2814.
chaundelers *n.* candlesticks 200.
cheine *n.* chain 928.
chere *n.* countenance 784.
chese *pr. pl.* choose 1833; **chese** *pt. s.* 921; **ches** *pt. pl.* 307.
cheuerele *n.* wild goat 2390.
clastrenne *pr. 3 pl.* sparkle 2229 n.
clepen *inf.* call 839; **clepeth** *pr. pl.* 666; **clepid** *pt. 3 s.* 156; **cleped** *pp.* 1293.
clergie *n.* knowledge of magic 1915.

clerk *n.* writer 74.
cleueth *pr. 3 s.* cuts, splits 1270; **cleuen** *pr. pl.* 2267.
cleueth *pr. 3 s.* adheres to 2410.
clois *n.* enclosure, wall 447.
closed, closid *pp.* enclosed, imprisoned 153, 2205.
cloustris *n.* clusters 2172.
clyme *adj.* still, clear, calm 1254 n.
cocadrilles *n.* crocodiles 1532.
cocatrices *n.* cockatrices, basilisks 1534.
comounlich *adv.* commonly 2423.
conduyt saf, save conduite *n.+adj.* safe-conduct 477, 1286.
conne *pr. pl.* know how to 64; **couth** *pt. 3 s.* could 2657.
coostis *n.* coasts, regions 538.
copere, copre *n.* copper 322.
coppe *n.* top 1754.
coppe *n.* cup 2843.
corious, curious *adj.* wonderful 484, 321.
cors, corse *n.* body, corpse 769, 771.
corseyntis *n.* saints 1124.
coruen *pp.* carved, hewn 391.
cosse *n.* kiss 682.
coteices *n.* precious stones 328 n.
councel *n.* consuls 307 n.
cours *n.* course, history of later development 69.
couth *adv.* clearly, widely 2695.
couth, *see* **conne.**
cracche *n.* stall 1089.
crafft *n.* skill 400.
crapotines *n.* toad-stones 328 n.
creaunce *n.* belief 1121.
crekettis *n.* crickets 2407.
crisolites *n.* chrysolites 327.
cristiante *n.* Christendom 738.
crofft *n.* hut 1086.
crois *n.* cross 448.
croniclis *n.* histories 80.
croun *n.* crown of the head 2912.
cuntre *n.* country 351.
curious, *see* **corious.**
curtasy *n.* noble conduct 1588.
curteisly *adv.* politely 1567.

debonernesse *n.* goodness 1949.
deedeli *adj.* mortal 8.
dele *n.* part 621; *see also* **somdele.**

delyueraunce *n.* disposal, granting 1760.

delyuere *inf.* dispose of, grant 1762.

demed *pp.* judged 1196.

dere *adj.* esteemed 11.

dere *inf.* injure 2105.

derst, durst *pt. 3 s.* dared 739, 745.

derworthli *adv.* lovingly, honourably 995.

devere *n.* appointed task, duty 1279.

dianes *n.* black gems 329 n.

di3te *pp.* placed, adorned 979.

displette *pp.* unkempt 1797.

distaunce *n.* strife, trouble 1022.

doloure *n.* grief 2782.

done *pr. pl.* do, cause to, put 686; **did** *pt. pl.* 435; **done, idoone** *pp.* 387, 1874; **doynge** *pres. ppl.* 2746; **do wai** *imp. 2 s.+adv.* stop 717.

dout *n.* awe, dread 1451.

drede *n.* doubt 1591.

drife, drive *inf.* chase, drive 2234, 2236; **droofe** *pt. 3 s.* 2190; **dryven** *pp.* 698.

dromedaries *n.* elephants 1660 n.

dusket *adj.* darkish 2450 n.

dwele *n.* delay 1583.

dyuers *adj.* different 25.

eche *adj.* each 1523.

echone *pron.* each one 147.

efft *adv.* again 559.

egge toole *comp. n.* sharp sword 2105.

eie, ei3en, ey3e *n.* eye(s) 784, 2329, 1682.

eighte, ey3te *num. adj.* eight 159.

eire, *see* aire.

eke *adv.* also 271.

emeraudes *n.* emeralds 330.

enchesoun *n.* reason 1080.

enioyneth *pr. 3 s.* adjoins 2674.

enpere *inf.* impair 562.

ensure *pr. 1 s.* assure 2623.

enterede *pp.* buried 522.

entringe *n.* entrance 2210.

environeth *pr. 3 s.* surrounds 1303.

erde *n.* earth 2331; *see also* myddille erde.

erst *adv.* previously 128.

ete, etenne *inf.* 2922, 2406 eat; **eeten, eetenne** *pr. pl.* 2004, 2511; **etenne** *pp.* 2832.

euenliche *adv.* even 394.

euerychone *pron.* everyone 2011.

eyren *n.* eggs 1500.

eyselle *n.* vinegar 508.

fairie, fayrie *n.* world of spirits 600, 1553.

fare *inf.* go, fare, behave 874; **ferde** *pt. 3 s.* 744.

fast *adj.* close 982.

fastned *pp.* fastened 931.

fayn *adv.* gladly 716.

feele, fele *adj.* many 2025, 22.

ferde, *see* fare.

fere *n.* fire 785.

fere, *see* yfere.

ferforth *adv.* far on 2742.

ferre ne nere *adv. phr.* no more nor less 84.

ferres *n.* firs 2629.

fers *adj.* bold 16.

ferst, frist *num. adj.* first 836, 73.

feterid *pp.* fettered 1051.

fett *inf.* fetch 2124; **fette** *pt. 3 s.* 363.

fine *n.* end 2799.

fleethe *pr. 3 s.* flies 1487; **fleen** *pr. pl.* 1375; **fli3e** *pt. 3 s.* 783; **fleende; fleenge** *pres. ppl.* 1472, 2826.

flete *inf.* float 1274.

flome *n.* river, water 1207.

floode *n.* river 1213.

flour *n.* flower, flour 2050; **bare the flour** *vb. phr.* excelled 2182.

floured *pp.* in blossom 2604.

folle *adj.* full 2167 n.; **atte folle** *adv. phr.* in every particular 2167.

fonde, founden *inf.* try 2236, 2232.

fonde, *see* fynde.

fonge *inf.* seize, grasp 2891; *pt. 3 s.* 143.

forcertainly, *adv.* surely 1755.

fordid *pt. 3 s.* destroyed 415.

fore *conj.* for 1576.

forgate *pt. 3 s.* forgot 780; **foryeten** *pp.* 776.

forgone *inf.* forgo 2518.

forleten *pp.* deserted 1549.

forlorn *pp.* lost 576.

forn *adv.* before 1100.

forshope *pt. 3 s.* transformed 673.

forsothe *adv.* indeed 23.

foryeten, *see* forgate.

foule *n.* bird 547.

foundid *ps. 3 s.* founded 419; *pp.* 837.

framwarde *prep.* away from 354.

free *adj.* generous, kind 1597.

freseth *pr. 3 s.* freezes 1545.

freten *inf.* eat, gnaw 2362.

frist, *see* **ferst.**

frith, fryth *n.* wood, wooded country 134, 2930.

froo *prep.* from 584.

fundacioun *n.* foundation 85.

fynde *pp.* refined 2070.

fynde *inf.* find 854; **fyndith** *pr. 3 s.* 2164; **fynde** *pr. pl.* 2188; **fonde, founde** *pt. pl.* 524, 640; **founde, ifounde** *pp.* 787, 2102.

fynde *inf.* provide for 1824.

gaderinge *n.* assembly 6.

gadren *inf.* gather 2775.

gaff, *see* **yeue.**

gamalioune *n.* chameleon 2408; *see also* **chameliouns.**

gan, *see* **gynne.**

garnement *n.* garment 2919.

gate *pt. 3 s.* acquired 425; **geten** *pp.* begotten 777.

geaunt *n.* giant 926.

gelte *n.* gilt 322.

gematry *n.* geometry 554.

gentil *adj.* noble 54.

gentilnes *n.* mark of nobility 2895.

geste *n.* tale 39.

gete, gote *n.* goat 1449, 1456.

gete *n.* jet 2325.

geth, *see* **gone.**

gilofres *n.* cloves 2028 n.

gliden *pr. pl.* roll, slide, slither 2329; **glidinge** *pres. ppl.* 742.

glistardes *n.* toads 1532 n.

gone, goo, goon *inf.* pass, go 1326, 1147, 2804; **goo** *pr. 1 s.* 194; **geth, goth** *pr. 3 s.* 915, 2447; **geth, gon, goo, goon** *pr. pl.* 936, 2923, 810, 1027; **igo, ygone** *pp.* 1565.

gote, *see* **gete.**

greces *n.* steps 967.

gripes *n.* vultures 2632 n.

grope *inf.* try to find 413.

grounde *n.* bottom 2093.

grym *adj.* fierce 529.

gynne *inf.* begin 2777; **gan** *pt. 3 s. auxil.* did 701.

ham, hem *pron.* them 147, 139.

handil *inf.* touch 1840; **handeleth** *pr. 3 s.* 2886.

hap *n.* fortune 788.

hastelich *adv.* hastily 731.

hastou *pr. 2 s.+pron.* hast thou 773.

hat, hight *pr. 3 s.* is called 1932, 543; **highte** *pt. 3 s.* 372.

haute *pp.* hatched 1498.

he, hee *pron.* they (*in rhyme only*) 130, 1793; *see p. xviii, fn. 1.*

heede *n.* monument, head-stone 1118 n.

hele *adj.* healthy 1411.

heled *pt. 3 s.* covered 771.

heles *pr. 3 s.* heals 1946.

hem, *see* **ham.**

hent *pt. 3 s.* grasped, seized 1034.

herborowid *pt. 3 s.* sheltered 1201.

here *inf.* hear 12; **herde** *pp.* 38.

hete, hiȝte *pt. 3 s.* promised 1612.

hevie *adj.* heavy 744.

hewe *n.* hue 2905.

hext, *see* **hie.**

heyght, hight *n.* height 1343, 1418.

hiduous *adj.* hideous 2780.

hie, hiȝe *adj.* high 321, 1614; **hier** *comp.* 542; **hext, hiest** *supl.* 2536, 2441; **in hie** *adj. phr.* on high 2563.

hight, highte, *see* **hat.**

hir *poss. adj.* their 163; **her** 562.

hir *pron.* her 673.

hiringe *n.* herring 2408.

holde, iholde *pp.* reputed, considered 501, 2561.

hole, hoole *adj.* whole 187, 363.

holiche *adv.* wholly 28.

honde *n.* hand 1183.

hope *n.* doubt 1303.

hope *pr. 1 s.* believe 1836.

huge, hugie *adj.* huge 1418, 1300.

hym *pron.* him, it 33; them 1170.

Ianivere *n.* January 310.

iaspes *n.* jasper stones 325.

iewise *n.* punishment 1924.

ihete, *see* **ete.**

ilome, *see* **lome.**

iles *n.* isles 612.

iourne *n.* journey, a day's travel 889.

ioynaunt *adj.* adjoining 2718.

irenne *n.* iron 1274.

issue *n.* entrance, outlet 853.

iugement *n.* trial 1139.
Iulli *n.* July 308.
iuys *n.* juice 1903.
iwis, iwys, ywysse *adv.* certainly 641, 102, 317.

kalendis *n.* Kalends 310.
kembid *pt. 3 s.* combed 710.
kene *adj.* fierce, eager 800.
kenne *pr. pl.* know 1187.
kepeth *pr. 3 s.* guards 1554.
kest *inf.* contrive, devise 1919.
kid *pt. pl.* made known 903; **kyd** *pp.* 2199.
kitte, kyt *inf.* cut 2542, 1965; **kyt** *pp.* 1826.
knave *n.* boy 1821.
konnynge *n.* skill 2787.
kyd, *see* **kid.**
kynde *n.* nature 860.
kynde *adj.* natural 2012.
kyne *n.* cattle 2430.
kynne *n.* family 22.
kyt, *see* **kitte.**

lain, layne *inf.* lay 1000; **laie** *imp. 2 s.* 859; **laidist** *pr. 2 s. sbj.* 862; **lay, leie** *pr. pl.* 1481, 2941; **laide, leide** *pt. 3 s.* 990, 638; **laid, laide** *pp.* 791, 1971; **leide** *pp.* lain 1000.
las, lasse *adj.* less 935, 339.
last *inf.* extend 1334.
lastage *n.* ballast 847.
leepres *n.* bay-trees 285 n.
lees, les, lys *n.* lie 1633, 308.
leest *supl. adj.* least 2169.
lefe, leve *adj.* loved 319, 11.
leide, *see* **lain.**
lenger *comp. adv.* longer 739.
lengest *supl. adj.* longest 2896.
lered *pp.* learned 609.
les, *see* **lees.**
leshes *n.* strips 2543.
lesinge *n.* lying 2854.
lesteneth *imp. pl.* listen 79.
lete *inf.* leave 2746.
lete *pt. pl.* caused 2341.
letheris *n.* leather 2936.
lette, lettinge *n.* delay, hindering 1725, 1831; **for lettinge** *vb. phr.* to prevent hindering 1831.
leued, leved, leveth, levid, *see* **liven.**
leuere *comp. adv.* rather 713.

leuk, leuke *n.* league 892, 896.
lewde *adj.* untaught, simple 609.
libardis *n.* leopards 801.
liche, lik *adj.* alike, like 801, 2122.
lifelood *n.* sustenance 2031.
lifft *adj.* left 1161.
liggen, liggeth, *see* **ly.**
light adoun *pt. 3 s.+adv.* dismounted 681.
ligoyns *n.* lynx-stones 335 n.
lisardes *n.* lizards 1907.
liven *inf.* live 548; **leueth** *pr. 3 s.* 2844; **leven, lif, liven, livith** *pr. pl.* 2424, 22, 2405; **leued, levid** *pt. 3 s.* 630, 1708.
lodehors *n.* pack-horses 2858.
lombe *n.* lamb 2165.
lome *n.* earth, loam 2237.
loos *n.* reputation 662.
lorn *pp.* lost 239.
lothe *adj.* reluctant 41.
loude or stille *adj. phr.* alive or dead 2487.
lust *pr. 3 s. impers.* it pleases 1817.
lyme *n.* lime, mortar 148.
lymme *n.* limb 2916.
ly, lie *inf.* lie, be buried 1560, 1067; **lieth** *pr. 3 s.* 520; **lien, lieth, liggen, liggeth, ly, lyne** *pr. pl.* 645, 1111, 2640, 1112, 1093, 1109; **laie, lay** *pt. 3 s.* 769, 1721; **leie, leye** *pp.* 713, 1982.
lys *n.* remission 2722.
lys, *see* **lees.**

macis *n.* nutmeg husks 2021.
maistry *n.* superior might 2190.
mamette, maumette *n.* idol 415, 341.
manyfoolde *adj.* numerous 2436.
marchaundise *n.* trading 1574.
mastikke *n.* gum of the mastic tree 616.
matere *n.* substance 42.
maumette, *see* **mamette.**
maunde *n.* maundy 1133.
medicine, mediciym *n.* antidote 1988, 2078 n.
meest *supl. adj.* greatest 2169.
mekelich *adv.* meekly 2467.
mele *n.* wheatmeal 2050.
meri *adj.* joyful 1152.
meruailis *n.* wonders 14.

messe *n.* food, dish 2872.
mete *n.* food 642.
mette *n.* make, kind, fashion 238.
meyne *n.* following, troop 135.
midwarde *n.* middle, centre 986.
Mighelmasse *n.* Michaelmas 51.
moch *adv.* much 2444.
moch, mochil, myche *adj.* much 389, 1729.
mochilness *n.* size 2390.
molles *n.* moles 2407.
moneth *n.* month 150.
monke, monek *n.* monk 1706, 1702.
moo *adj.* more 107.
moolde *n.* earth 2613.
moos, mos *n.* moss 2698, 2372.
more *comp. adj.* greater 178.
moselle *n.* piece 2840.
mot, mote *pr. 3 s.* must 885, 1286.
mountance *n.* space, duration 2783.
mowe *pr. pl.* may 819.
myche, *see* moche.
myddille erde *n. phr.* the terrestrial earth between heaven and hell 2331.
mydouernone *n.* middle of the afternoon 1543.
mynster *n.* church 939.
mys *n.* mistake, error 64.
myschapen *pp.* changed from (her) natural shape 722.
myse *n.* mice 2454.

naddres *n.* snakes 1430.
nam, *see* nym.
nawhere *adv.* nowhere 2272.
nedis *adv.* necessarily 1403.
nei3 *adj.* near 1815; ny3 and wide *adj. phr.* near and far 1369.
neme, *see* nym.
nempne *inf.* name 366; nempned *pt. 1 s.* 653.
nere *pt. 3 s.* were not 1910.
nere *comp. adj.* nearer 84.
nesshe *adj.* soft 1962.
net *adj.* bright, clear 2053.
neuen, neven *inf.* name 440, 213.
nome, *see* nym.
nones *n.*, used in the almost meaningless adv. phr. for the nones 323.
note *pr. 3 s.* does not know 1770.
nober *adv.* neither 640.
notmygges *n.* nutmegs 2019.
nouthe *adv.* now 233.

noy *n.* harm 2457.
nym, nyme *inf.* take 876, 1917; neme *pr. pl.* 838; nam, nome *pt. pl.* 2126, 2523; inome *pp.* 2159.
nys *pr. 3 s.* is not 1198.

ones, oones *adv.* once 1670, 597.
onicles *n.* onyx stones 333.
oo *num. adj.* one 2.
ordeined *pt. 3 s.* prepared, devised 732; ordeyned *pp.* 1915.
ordinance *n.* direction 1734.
ospringe *n.* descendants 1607.
othir *conj.* or 39.
oueragayn *adv.* adjacent to 2222.
ouergonge *n.* width 1732.
ouerheeled *pt. 3 s.* covered 2214.
ouerlonge *adj.* too long 40.
ouerright *adv.* overall 844.

paleis *n.* palace 146.
pare *inf.* pare, cut away 2820.
pas *inf.* pass 1151.
pay *n.* pleasure, satisfaction 2869.
pece *n.* piece 658.
peinted, peyntid *pp.* painted 392, 1396.
pepleren *n.* poplar trees 2270 n.
perfay *adv.* indeed 1707.
perisshid *pp.* pierced 2055; *see also* persshid.
peritotes *n.* green gems 331 n.
perre *n.* precious stones 409.
persshid *pp.* perished, drowned 1251; *see also* perisshid.
peynes, *see* pine.
philberdis *n.* hazel nuts 2024.
philosophie *n.* alchemy 1674.
pine, pyne *n.* pain, affliction 582, 1970; peynes *n.* torments 529.
pissemeris *n.* ants 2638.
plas *n.* place, palace 2299.
plenteuous *adj.* plentiful, abundant 659.
pocessioun *n.* wealth 1365.
prest *adj.* close at hand 367.
priuelie *adv.* stealthily 768.
processe *n.* passing of time 1397.
puple *n.* people 1037.
pyne, *see* pine.
pytte *inf.* put 2885.
pytte *n.* pit, ditch 842.

queinte *adj.* curious 2443; **queintist** *supl.* 2378.
quellid *pt. 3 s.* killed 1094; **quellid, quelleden** *pt. pl.* 1808, 380.
quibibus *n.* spice of the cubeb 2029 n.
quik *adj.* living 173.

raught, rauȝt *pt. 3 s.* reached, stretched 343, 408.
ravenne *n.* gall-nuts 2262 n.
rawe, rewe, rowe *n.* row, list 1256, 164, 1041.
realle *adj.* royal 752.
reame *n.* realm 1624.
rechace *inf.* relate 453.
rede *inf.* advise, inform 90.
reede *adj.* red 1073.
reflambines *n.* precious stones 331 n.
rehers *inf.* repeat, relate 75.
remewe *pr. pl.* go away 2146.
renneth *pr. 3 s.* flows, runs 1216; **ironne** *pp.* 69.
resoun *n.* sentence, words, text 526.
rewe, see rawe.
rialiche, rially *adv.* royally 323, 428.
richeli *adv.* richly 342.
rife *adj.* many 631.
right *adv.* directly 592.
rightis *n.* rites 2342.
ris *n.* rice 2848.
roche *n.* rock 1028.
roode *n.* cross 233.
rooff, rooffe, rove *n.* roof 344, 322, 945.
roosis *n.* roses 1073.
rooste, rostid *pp.* roasted 266.
rout *inf.* throw, fling 2822.
route *n.* assembly 2776.
rove, see rooff.
rynde *n.* bark 2018.

sain, sais, sayn, see sein.
salewe *inf.* greet 1567; **salewed** *pt. 3 s.* 1587.
sapheronne *n.* saffron 2926.
saphiris *n.* sapphires 330.
sarasens *n.* pagans 2587.
sardes *n.* precious stones like onyx 334.
sardoynes *n.* sardine stones 328.
saue, saufe, sauffe *adj.* safe 590, 821.
sauff *prep.* except 1348; *conj.* except that 2168.

saunz *prep.* except, without 1529.
sautere, sawtiere *n.* Psalter 58.
save *adv.* safely 1285.
sawe *n.* saying, custom 1831
scaped *pt. pl.* escaped 106.
scourgis *n.* whips, scourges 964.
sculle *n.* skull 2265.
se *n.* seat, capital city 1772.
se, see, sene *inf.* see 932, 1383, 30; **seest** *pr. 2 s.* 720; **sees, sene** *pr. pl.* 496, 2017; **sawe, seie** *pt. 3 s.* 31, 714; **syȝe** *pt. pl.* 1163; **sene** *pp.* 965.
secheth *pr. pl.* seek in pilgrimage 608.
seete, *n.* seat 1134.
sege *n.* siege 92.
sein, seine *inf.* say 38, 2926; **seith** *pr. 3 s.* 74; **saie, sain, sais, sayn, sayne** *pr. pl.* 2161, 1055, 617, 1412.
seinte *adj.* saint, holy 19, 195.
sekirly, sikerly, sikirlie, sikirly, sikirliche *adv.* surely 499, 757, 2228, 890, 2040.
selff *n.,* same 1026.
seme *n.* path, route 878.
semenge *pres. ppl.* seeming 1682.
sendalle *n.* rich silk material 993.
septemtrionalle *n.* north 1852.
sere *adj.* many 856.
seth, sith, sithens *adv.* since 37, 643, 1809.
isette *pp.* appointed 551.
setuale *n.* spice of the setwall 2028.
shafftis *n.* spears 2109.
shawe *inf.* show, reveal 1257; **shewe** *pr. pl.* 1781; **shewde** *pp.* 610.
shete *n.* sheet, burnous 2911.
shette, see shitteth.
shipperdis *n.* shepherds 1100.
shire *adj.* bright 1424.
shitteth *pr. pl.* shut 1481; **shette** *pt. 3 s.* 2211.
sho, shoo *pron.* she 744, 1612.
shoilinge *pres. ppl.* sloping 2901 n.
shope *pt. pl. refl.* decided 139.
shote *inf.* shoot 1003.
shuld *pt. 3 s.* should 1067.
sike *adj.* sick 1411.
siker *adj.* stable, fixed 1024.
sikerly, sikirly, sikirliche, *see* **sekirly.**
simulacre *n.* image 405.
sith, sithens, see seth.
sithe *n.* time 2478.

skille *n.* reason 1243.
sloo *inf.* slay 583; sloon *pr. pl.* 2109;
  slowe *pt. 3 s.* 250; slaine, slawe
  pp. 1805, 2916.
sloppes *n.* smocks, outer garments
  1793.
smale, smalle *adj.* small 2373, 346.
smaragdes *n.* emeralds 335.
smert *adj.* sharp 515.
smyt *pr. 3 s.* smites, billows, flares
  1424.
socoures *n.* strength 160.
soden, sodene *pp.* boiled 2532, 2817.
sogette *adj.* subject 1810.
solace *n.* consolation 1817.
solle *n.* sole 2903.
somat *adv.* somewhat 832.
somdele, somdelle *adv.* somewhat
  1249, 1001.
sonde *n.* sending 2345.
sonde *n.* sand 558.
sone *adv.* immediately 1435.
sope *n.* soap 1678.
sore *adv.* greatly 1545.
sothe *n.* truth 413.
sothely *adv.* truly 988.
sowdan *n.* sultan 1329.
sowdioure *n.* soldier 23.
spache, speche *n.* speech 1390, 2691.
spede *n.* protection 56.
spede *imp. 2 s.* preserve, bless 5.
spellid *pp.* killed 1910.
sperhauke *n.* sparrowhawk 1552.
stadies *n.* furlongs 1246 n.
stage *n.* place 433.
stampe *inf.* crush 2063.
standith, stant, stondith *pr. 3 s.*
  stands 1613, 718, 1541; stonding
  pr. ppl. 1240.
stap *inf.* step 1165.
staunce *n.* position 1925.
steven *n.* sound, voice 1152.
stied, sty3e *pt. 3 s.* ascended 1157,
  1162.
stonding, stondith, *see* standith.
stonen *adj.* made of stone 154.
stonge, *see* stynge.
stounde *n.* time 13.
stoute *adj.* brave, strong 678.
stracche *inf.* stretch, pass, take 1088.
straught, strau3t *adv.* straight,
  directly 1171, 407.
streme *n.* sea, river 819.

stronde *n.* shore 2346.
stynge *inf.* bite, pierce, stab 1435;
  stonge *pp.* 516.
swat *pt. 3 s.* sweated 1192.
swynke *pr. pl.* toil 2510.
swythe *adv.* quickly 2233.

table *n.* tablet, piece of wood 524.
take *inf.* overtake, catch 803; tane *pp.*
  taken 651.
talkinge *n.* recitation, tale 36.
tane, *see* take.
tene *n.* vexation 2453.
thare, thore *adv.* there 2547, 630.
thekke *pr. pl.* roof, thatch 2931.
thenkith *pr. 3 s. impers.* it seems 790.
thenne *adv.* thence 1186.
theremyd *adv.* therewith 2489.
þeretille *adv.* for so long 458.
þereto *adv.* about it 33.
thilk *adj.* that, the same 972.
tho, thoo *adj.* those 102, 105.
thoo *adv.* then 297.
thore, *see* thare.
thou3 *conj.* though 42.
throu3, throuh, throuhe *adv.*
  through 400, 2244, 470.
throwe *n.* moment 2256.
tide *n.* time 1368.
toflattered *pt. 3 s.* shattered 244.
tofore *adv.* before 445.
tonned *pr. pl.* put into casks 2070.
toolde *pp.* called, held 539.
toole, *see* egge toole.
topaces *n.* topaz stones 333.
tothe *n.* tooth 894.
trauailid *pt. 3 s.* travelled 29;
  trauailid *pp.* 24.
tre, tree *n.* wood, tree 587, 1664;
  treene, trene *pl.* 2018, 2418.
tretis *n.* composition 43.
treuli *adv.* honourably 1433.
trouble *adj.* turbid 1841.
trowe *pr. 1 s.* believe 530; trowen *pr.*
  pl. 590.
trowes *n.* troughs 2062.
truage *n.* tribute 375.
turmentid *pt. pl.* tortured 587.
turne *inf.* convert 2245.
twey, tweye *num. adj.* two 2258, 809.

vndirnome *pp.* understood 1473.

vndirtake *inf.* undertake, take down, take note of 1555; **vndirtoke** *pt. 3 s.* 31.

valoures *n.* value, worth 943.
veleny *n.* evil, shame 1604.
veniaunce *n.* vengeance 789.
venym, venyme *n.* poison 2077, 2046.
verament, verement *adv.* truly 393, 49.
veritee *n.* truth 1063.
vermidore *n.* rubies 330 n.
vetailis *n.* victuals 483.
virris *n.* glass vessels 857.
visage *n.* face 2327.
voide *adj.* empty 2316.
vois *n.* voice 772.
vouchsaue, vouchith saue *pr. 3 s.* requires 2550, 2144.

wake *inf.* watch without sleeping 1556.
walt *pr. 3 s.* beats down 1842.
wan, *see* **wyn.**
wardeynes *n.* keepers 1480.
wasshe *inf.* wash 1147; **wasshed, wosshe** *pt. 3 s.* 992, 1135.
weende, wende *inf.* go 556, 461; **wendith** *pr. 3 s.* 465; **wende** *pr. pl.* 1992.
welle *adv.* very 805.
wene *pr. 1 s.* think 296; **wente** *pt. pl.* 588.
wene *n.* doubt 29.
were *inf.* defend 1827.
were, where *n.* danger, doubt 1491, 1943.
werie *adj.* weary 41.
weten, wite, witen *inf.* know 79, 2149, 1432; **wete, wite** *pr. 2 s.* 21, 1137; **woste** *pr. 2 s.* 718; **wist** *pr. 3 s. and pl.* 643, 517.
where, *see* **were.**
wight, wyght *adj.* brave, bold 678, 16.
wight *n.* weight 2947.

wise *n.* manner 760.
wisse *inf.* teach, know 884.
withe *n.* willow branch 1923.
without *prep.* without 276.
witte *n.* skill, craft 1919.
witterly *adv.* certainly 1281.
wolden *pt. pl.* wished 825.
wolle *n.* wool 2902.
wombe *n.* stomach 2818.
wonde *pt. 3 s.* wound 993.
wonder, wondur *adv.* wonderfully, very 1690.
wondir *adj.* wonderful 2200.
wondris *n.* wonders 12.
wone *n.* plenty 2031.
wone *inf.* dwell 2230; **wone** *pr. pl.* 2694.
woned *pp.* wont 1749.
worch *inf.* work 1347.
worme *n.* dragon 690.
woste, *see* **weten.**
wrought, wrouȝt *pt. pl.* worked 1345, 1342.
wyght *n.* man 704.
wyght, *see* **wight.**
wyn *inf.* win, pass 2224; **wan** *pt. 3 s.* 109.

yaf, yaffe, *see* **yeue.**
yates *n.* gates 161.
yede, yoode *pr. 3 s.* went 771, 779; **ȝede** *pt. pl.* 55.
yeelde *inf.* surrender 2481; **iyolde** *pp.* 104.
yerde *n.* yard (in measurement) 2909.
yete, yette, yitte, ȝete, ȝit, ȝitte *conj.* yet 1611, 21, 1154, 94, 910.
yeue, yeve, yif *inf.* give 1723, 2801, 2797; **yeueth** *pr. 3 s.* 2015; **ȝaff, yaff** *pt. 3 s.* 401, 1120; **yafe, yaffe** 508, 421; **yeuen** *pp.* 2516.
yfere, in fere *adv.* together, in company 1272, 309.
ynowe *adj.* enough 249.
yssue *n.* outfall 2088.
yve *n.* ivy 1892.
ywysse, *see* **iwis.**

INDEX OF NAMES

THE scribal forms of the names of persons and places mentioned in the Metrical Version are listed with their line references and their modern forms. Biblical names are identified by the forms of the Authorized Version, and the names of Roman monuments (which are indexed collectively under **Rome**) are identified, where possible, by the forms preferred by S. B. Platner, *A Topographical Dictionary of Ancient Rome* (revised by T. Ashby, 1929). n indicates a reference in the Commentary.

Neyesburghe, Wieselburg, 469.
Nicholas, St. Nicholas, 606, 653.
Nile, the Nile, 1293, 1630.
Noe, Noah, 920, 929, 1699, 1710, 1739, 2689.
Nostre Dame de Marroe, a church at Cairo, 905 n.
Nostre Dame de Sardinache, a church near Damascus, 1391 n.

Olivete, Mt. Olivet, 1155.
Olympe, Mt. Olympus, 539.
Orchepen, land of cedar trees, 2438 n.
Orrille, an isle in the Indian Ocean, 2610 n.
oure lady, the Blessed Virgin Mary, 242.
Ozie, King Uzziah of Judah, 121, 126.

Palestine, Palestaner, Palestine, 872, 1314, 1632.
Panterane, Patera, in Lycia, 652.
paradys, earthly paradise, 1294, 1504.
Parys, Paris, 513.
Pathan, Singapore, 2038 n.
Pathmos, Patmos, 619.
Paule, St. Paul, 812, 816, 913.
Percie, Persia, 1628.
Peroun, the river Belus, near Acre, 897 n.
Peter, Petir, St. Peter, 1049, 1128.
Phison, the Ganges, 2705.
Pikteine, land of the Tripithami, 2507 n.
Pilrym, Pylrym, Château Pelerin, 877 n., 899.
Polimpe, Quilon, 1928 n., 1929.
Politrade, a plain in Egypt, 1520 n.
Polumpe, Mt. Quilon, 1931, 1932.
Porte David, the western gate of Jerusalem, 1052.
Porte Tire, Tyre, 807.
Portepye, perhaps Perschembé [now Porto di Plas], 1548 n.
Preter Iohn, Prester John, 2284.
Pyncerasse, land of the Petchenegs, 490 n.

Raphao, Rafineh, 1535.
Rebecca, Rebecca, wife of Jacob, 1115.
Reede See, the Red Sea, 1655, 2646.

Remus, Remus, 101.
Rennomare, Ronnemare, the river Beas, 2499 n., 2548 n.
Ribooth, Tibet, 2767.
Romaines, the Romans, 307, 319, 356, 369.
Rome, Rome, 62, 82, 89, 133, 156, 157, 352, 375, 379, 411, 462.
— the arches of:
— seinte Alexi, arcus Arcadii, Honarii, et Theodosii, 195 n.
— Antonyne, arcus Claudii, 203 n.
— Constantine, arcus Constantini, 197.
— Iulii Cesaris, arcus Severi, 201 n.
— Theodosii, arcus, 196 n.
— Vaspasian and Tity, arcus Titi, 199 n.
— the brigges of:
— seinte Aungelle, pons Aelius, 207 n.
— Fabian, pons Fabricius, 209 n.
— Gracian, pons Cestius, 210 n.
— Iewes brigge, pons Fabricius, 208 n.
— senatoures brigge, pons Aemilius, 213 n.
— Theodosii, pons Probi, 211.
— Valerianus, pons Aurelius, 212.
— the hilles of:
— Capitoile, Capitolinus mons, 221.
— Euentine, Aventinus mons, 217, 257.
— Ianicle, Ianiculum, 217.
— s. Mary the More, Esquilinus mons, 221.
— Stephano in Soleo, Caelius mons, 220 n.
— Tanelle, the pseudo-Aventine, 219 n.
— the churches of:
— s. Alext, s. Alessio, 219.
— s. Antony, see note to 271.
— the holie Crois, s. Croce in Gerusalemme, 448.
— s. Iohn the Lateranense, s. Giovanni Laterano, 445, 451.
— s. Kirias, s. Cyriac, 294, 314 n.
— s. Laurence in Lucine, s. Lorenzo in Lucina, 204.
— s. Laurencis withouten the walle, s. Lorenzo fuori le mura, 288, 447.

Rome (*cont.*):

— s. **Maries** church þe more, s. Maria in Ara Coeli, 382 n.

— s. **Marie** church the more, s. Maria Maggiore, 446.

— s. **Maries the Rotounde**, s. Maria ad Martyres 360, 427.

— s. **Martynnes**, s. Martino ai monte, 202.

— s. **Petris**, s. Petro in Vaticano, 252, 364, 443.

— s. **Poules** wiþout þe walle, s. Paolo fuori le mura, 444.

— s. **Sabine**, s. Sabina, 218.

— s. **spirite**, s. Spirito in Sassia, 251 n.

— the **churcheyerdis** of:

— s. **Agace**, Praetextatus, on the via Appia, 278 n.

— s. **Agnes**, St. Agnes, on the via Nomentana, 289.

— **Appolinare**, Appollonus the senator, 282.

— **Calipodie**, Calipodius, on the via Aurelia, 277.

— **Concorde**, Gordian, on the via Latina, 283 n.

— s. **Eracene**, *cimiterium Cucumeris*, 290 n.

— s. **Felice in the Pynce**, St. Felix, on the via Portuensis, 280.

— s. **Felici**, St. Felicitas, on the via Salaria Nova, 291.

— s. **Heline**, SS. Peter and Marcellinus, on the via Labicana, 285 n.

— s. **Heremite þe Domicelle**, St. Domitilla, on the via Ardeatina, 293 n.

— s. **Kalixt**, St. Callistus, on the via Appia, 292.

— s. **Kiriace**, St. Cyriacus, on the via Ostiensis, 294.

— s. **Pancras**, St. Pancratius, on the via Aurelia, 277.

— s. **Petris Wille**, St. Peter's Well, 289 n.

— s. **Ponci**, St. Pontianus, 292.

— s. **Prescille**, St. Priscilla, on the via Salaria Nova, 290.

— s. **Sabines and s. Vrsus**, *cimiterium ursi pilati*, 287 n.

— s. **Saturnine**, *cimiterium Trasonis*, 291 n.

— s. **Vrsus**, *cimiterium ursi ad portesam*, 279.

— the **paleicis** of:

— **Adriane**, Castel s. Angelo, 246.

— **Anthion**, thermae Antoninianae, 248.

— **Camille**, templum concordiae et pacis, 271 n.

— **Claudius**, thermae Domitianae, 247.

— **Constantine**, thermae Constantinianae, 258.

— **Domician**, Domitiana domus, 263 n.

— **Eufemine**, house of Eufermianus, 255.

— **Iulius Cesare**, aedes Divus Iulius, 253.

— **Neroes**, Laterana domus, 231 n.

— **Octovian**, arcus Octaviani, 267.

— **Olimpias**, thermae Olimpiadis, 265.

— **Romulus**, templum concordiae et pietatis, 230, 234 n.

— **Surrie**, palatium Susurrianum, 232.

— **Titi and Vaspasine**, thermae Titi, 256.

— **Troiane**, thermae Traiani, 245.

— **Veneris**, templum Veneris et Romae, 269 n.

— the **templis** of:

— **Adrian**, sepulcrum Hadriani, 297.

— **Anthonine**, templum Dives Augustis, 304.

— **Appoline**, a shrine of Apollo, 303 n.

— **Colise**, Coliseum, 385 n.

— **Enee**, the *concha Parionis*, 303 n.

— **Ercules**, aedes Hercules Victor, 378 n.

— **Floree**, templum Flora, 299.

— **Iany**, templum Ianus Quadrifrons, 383.

— **Iouis**, aedes Iuppiter Feretrius, 367, 377 n.

— **Marci**, campus Martius, 305 n.

— **Martis**, aedes Mars, 305.

— **Neron**, secretarium Neronis, 304 n.

— **Numie**, aedes Vesta, 311 n., 367.

— **Ofilis**, templum Hercules Olivarius, 378 n.

Rome (*cont.*):
— **Pantheon**, Pantheon, 247, 311, 318 n., 426.
— **Pheby**, templum Febris, 299 n.
— **Veste**, of þe west, aedes Vesta, 313, 368 n.
— **Virgily**, aedes Bellona, 300 n.
— **the yates of**:
— **porte Apie**, Apize, porta Appia, 168, 281.
— — **Aurea**, porta Aurelia, 182.
— — **Azinarie**, porta Asinaria, 177.
— — **Campanie**, porta Capena, 165.
— — **Castelle Sancte Angeli**, *see* porte Petri.
— — **Collecte**, porta Collina, 181 n.
— — **Latyn**, porta Latina, 171, 284.
— — **Lucane** þe more, porta Labicana, 178 n.
— — **Mecroine**, porta Metrovia, 177.
— — **Numentane**, porta Nomentana, 180.
— — **Pauli**, porta Ostiensis, 166.
— — **Petri**, porta Aurelia, 183 n., 184.
— — **Portuens**, porta Portuensis, 183.
— — **Pyncine**, porta Pinciana, 180.
— — **Septim**, porta Septimiana, 181.
— — **Taury**, porta Taurina, 179.
— — **Tiberine**, porta Tiburtina, 179.
— — **Viridaun**, porta Viridaria, 185 n.
Romulus, Romulus, 101, 147, 155, 237 n.
Roodes, Rhodes, 746.
Ruspo, land of cannibal giants, 2353 n.

Sabanense, the Sabines, 113 n.
Sabbatory, an intermittent spring, 1538 n., 1540.
Sadorneye, Saidenaya, 808.
Salaman, Solomon, 1007.
Salemount, a salt mountain, 1753 n.
Salisbury, Salisbury, 2135.
Sapheran, land of saffron, 2925 n.
Sarra, Sarah, wife of Abraham, 1114.
Satelly, Adalia, 756 n.
Scalane, Tuscany, 115 n.
Seboyn, Zeboiim, 1259.
Segore, Zoar, 1259, 1263.

Sely, Mt. Anchilos, near Ephesus, 648 n.
Sem, Shem, son of Noah, 918.
Seneglaunce, a city near Calcutta, 1927 n.
Sichie, Scythia, 1639, 1806.
Siloe, Siloam, 1141 n.
Siloo, Scio, 614.
Siluester, Pope Silvester I, 414 n.
Simon leprous, Simon the Leper (St. Julian), 1200.
Sinosople, land of the Gymnosophi, 2462.
Sodome, Sodom, 1258.
Sopheos, Cos, 661.
Sophy, St. Sophia's, Constantinople, 500.
Soudan, the Sultan of Cairo, 1287, 1290.
Spolitane, people of Spolitium, in Tuscany, 116 n.
Stephen, St. Stephen, 937.
Sterens, Hesternit [*now* Sofia], 492.
Surrye, Syria, 1631.
Symeon, Simeon, a holy Jew, 1034 n., 1036.
Symon, Simon, a shepherd, 1105 n.
Synay, Mt. Sinai, 1361, 1362.
Syone, Mt. Sion, 1127.

Thamare, the Don, 1644.
Thano, Mt. Ararat, 1696.
Thesaurizo, Tabriz, 1742 n.
Tholome, the sage Ptolemy, 565 n.
Tholopeus, Scolopitus, king of Scythia, 1803 n.
Thomas, St. Thomas of India, 141, 2298.
Tibery, the Tiber, 206.
Tigree, the Tigris, 1626, 1630, 2705.
Tipiscenes, men of **Tipus**, 2900 n.
Tipus, land of wool-bearing men, 2899 n.
Tire, the Ladder of Tyre, 893 n.
Titus, the emperor Titus, 1017.
Traprophan, Ceylon, 2598 n.
Troy, Troy, 92, 110, 129.
Turky, Turkey, 592.

Vter Pendragon, Uther Pendragon, 2132 n.

Vaspacian, the emperor Vespasian, 1017.

Venise, Venice, 826, 829, 885, 1573.

Virgille, Virgil, 224 n.

Westmynstere, Westminster, 1167 n.

Yberie, Hiberia, 1658 n., 1673.

Ynde, India, 1296, 1858, 2282, 2291, 2309, 2653, 2662, 2748.

Ypocras, the sage Hippocrates, 565 n., 669 n.

Zorobabele, Zerubbabel, 1011 n.

APPENDIX A

THE HARLEY VERSION

THE Harley Version of *Mandeville's Travels* is extant in B.M. MS. Harley 82, ff. 35–104. In this selection editorial omissions are indicated by spaced dots, and a folio number which immediately follows such an omission does not necessarily precede the first words of that folio. The manuscript is badly stained in parts, and words and letters legible only by the aid of ultra-violet light are printed within square brackets and without footnote. Single letters are printed in heavy type at the beginning of those scribal chapter divisions where the scribe, while indicating the letter, has left large blank spaces for later insertion of larger initials. Modern chapter numbers are inserted to facilitate reference to other modern editions of the work. Arabic numerals within square brackets refer to lines of the Metrical Version. Marginal rubrics are not printed. Before vowels final *-i, -um, -us* are printed in italic where the scribe appears to have elided those syllables; however, in gerund forms (as elsewhere) final *d* has a distinct terminal flourish which may indicate a final case ending, and cf. 154/22, 155/6. In all other respects the editorial procedure follows that adopted for the Metrical Version, except that roman numerals with suprascript final letters have been expanded to their verbal equivalents wherever they are not textually corrupt or significant or inordinately long.

The manuscript has been collated for sense with its Anglo-French source, the Insular Version, printed by G. F. Warner and represented by the *siglum* W. In two cases where the scribe has left a blank space to mark an omission (188/2 and 28) the lacunae are filled by reference to that French text. The manuscript was bound for Harley with other originally separate parchment items, viz. ff. 1–3 a fragment of a register for the years 1307–11 of Nicholas de Quaplod, abbot of Reading, and ff. 4–34 a thirteenth-century *Martyrologium*. ff. 1–40 are now separately mounted.

The original collation of *Mandeville's Travels* (ff. 35–104) is discernible from contemporary signatures and catch-words, viz. a⁸ (lacks 1, 8), b–d⁸, f⁸, i–l⁸, quires e, g, and m (probably eights) being lost. The pages of this third item are of uneven length, measuring approximately 250 × 165 mm. The frame measures 170 × 116 mm. and contains twenty-eight long lines of one *cursiva libraria* hand of the last quarter of the fourteenth century, the hand of ff. 4–34 being similar to the hand

of the Reading chartulary extant in B.M. MS. Egerton 3031. The
scribe's punctuation is distinctive and consistent. It seems very likely
that ff. 35–104 were written at Reading abbey.

The text of *Mandeville's Travels* is carefully written and generally
free from scribal error and possibly lies at no more than one remove
from the lost archetype of the Harley Version. This version was cer-
tainly translated from a lost manuscript of the Insular Version of the
type classified as Subgroup B (i) in *Scriptorium* xviii (1964), 34–48, and
now extant in B.M. MS. Sloane 1464 and Bodleian Library MS. Addi-
tional C 280. This lost Insular manuscript gave a text markedly superior
to that preserved in either of these manuscripts.

[f. 35] . . . memorie. Et specialiter propter eos qui habent voluntatem
visitandi sanctam ciuitatem Ierusalem et alia loca ibidem, demonstrabo
eis quam viam melius possint tenere. Nam sepe transiui et equitaui in
multa bona [societate], pro omnibus honorificetur et laudetur deus qui
est benedictus in secula. Amen.   5

CHAPTER I

Nunc in nomine gloriosi dei, si volueris mare transire versus orientem
potes per mare et per terram diuersas tenere vias secundum partes
diuersas a quibus moueris, vnde multe earum tendunt ad vnum finem.

Et sciend*um* est quod non intendo demonstrare tibi omnes ciuitates,
villas, et castella per viam, quia fastidium generaret audientibus, sed   10
solummodo aliquas terras et loca principalia vt possis viam rectam
secundum tuum propositum tenere.

In primis ergo, si de partibus occidentalibus venerit sicut de Anglia,
Hibernia, Wallia, Scocia, vel Norwergia, potes si volueris ire per
Almaniam, per regnum Hungarie quod extendit se ad terram Poialine   15
et ad terram Pannonie et Alesie. Et est rex Hungarie potens et magnus
dominus habens sub se multa regna, nam tenet Hungariam et Panoniam
et magnam partem Cammonie et Bulgariam et magnam partem regni
Russie, de qua fecit ducatum qui durat vsque ad terram de Nislan et
vsque ad terram Prussie.   20

Et transeundo per terram istius regis venies ad ciuitatem de Clipron
et per castellum de Neselburgh et per Malleuillam, que scituatur versus
finem Hungarie. Et ibi transibis flumen de Damuby. Iste fluuius de
Damuby est magnus fluuius et venit in Almaniam subtus montes versus
Lumbardiam et recipit in se xl. alia flumina et currit per Hungariam,   25
per Greciam, per Traciam, et intrat mare versus orientem. Et ita velo-
citer intrat mare quod aqua illius per xx. leucas infra mare suam retinet

1 *The first words of the manuscript are irrecoverable*

dulcedinem. Deinde venies ad Belgrauam et ingredieris Bulgariam.
[f. 35ᵛ] Et ibi transibis pontem lapideum qui scituatur super fluuium
de Marro, et venies in terram de Pynseras et tunc in Greciam ad
ciuitatem Sterrensem et postea ad Fympapam, deinde ad ciuitatem
5 Dandrenopolim, et postea ad Constantinopolim, que quondam dicebatur
Bizantiam. Ibi moratur comuniter imperator Grecie.

Ibi est ecclesia sancte Sophie, tocius mundi pulcherima. Et ante istam
ecclesiam est ymago Iustiniani imperatoris, cupria deaurata et super
equum coronata, que habebat in vna manu pomum rotundum, sed
10 cecidit iam de manu. Et hoc, vt ipsi asserunt, significat quod imperator
iam perdidit maximam partem terre et dominii sui. Nam solebat esse
imperator Rome et Romanie, Grecie, Asie minoris, terre Surie et Iudee,
in qua est Ierusalem, Egipti, Perside, et Arabie, sed omnia amisit preter
solam Greciam et aliquas terras circumiacentes. Quidam temptabant
15 sepius pomum in manum remittere, sed noluit tenere. Per istud pomum
intelligitur mundus et dominium quod habuit super mundum. Et
alteram manum habet contra orientem eleuatam malefactoribus quasi
minando. Et stat ista ymago super quemdam gradum marmoreum.

CHAPTER II

[499] Item, apud Constantinopolim est vera crux Cristi et tunica
20 inconsutilis, spungea et arundo de quibus dabant sibi in cruce bibere,
et vnus de clauis cum quibus erat crucifixus. Quidam affirmant medi-
etatam crucis Cristi esse in Cypro in vna abbathia que dicitur mons
sancte crucis, sed non est ita. Nam illa crux in Cypro est crux Dismas
boni latronis, sed hoc incognitum est multis quia propter oblaciones et
25 alia emolimenta faciunt eam honorari et dicunt quod est vera crux
Cristi.

Et sciatis quod crux Cristi ex quatuor generibus lignorum, prout
sequens versus demonstrat: *In cruce sunt palma, cedrus, cypressus, olyua.*
Nam illa pars a terra vsque ad caput erat de cypresso. Et pars transuersa
30 ad quam erant manus confixe erat de palma. Et basis infra [f. 36] rupe
in qua erat crux fixa erat de cedro. Et tabula supra capud e[ius] erat
longitudinis vnius pedis et dimidi (in qua erat titulus scriptus ebraice,
grece, et latine) erat de olyua.

Et fecerunt Iudei crucem ex istis quatuor generibus lignorum quia
35 credebant quod Cristus tam diu pependisset in cruce quam diu crux
potuit durasse. Et ideo fecerunt pedem de cedro nam cedrus nec in
terra nec in aqua potest corumpi. Et aliam partem fecerunt de cypresso
bene odorante, ne forte corrupcio corporis eius noceret transeuntibus.
Et partem transuersam fecerunt de palma nam in veteri testamento qui

10 quod] MS. qr, *i.e.* quia (*not* qd, *the normal abbreviation of* quod) *but cf.*
W 4/37 qe   21 clauis] MS. *last letter badly formed*

habebat victoriam de suo inimico coronabatur palma in signum victorie.
Sic Iudei credentes se vicisse Cristum fecerunt istam partem de palma.
Et tabulam tituli fecerunt de oliua que significat pacem, prout historia
Noe testatur qui emittens columbam reportauit ad archam ramum oliue
in signum quod esset pax facta inter deum et hominem. Sic Iudei 5
credentes per mortem Cristi eis perpetuam pacem fore fecerunt partem
istam de oliua quia dixerunt quod seminauit discordiam inter eos. Et
sciatis quod saluator noster affixus erat cruci iacendo, et postea cum
cruce in altum eleuatus, et sic sibi maior pena fuit.

Item, in Grecia et ali[b]i cristiani vltra mare dicunt quod arbor crucis 10
quam nos vocamus cipressum erat de pomo de cuius fructu Adam
gustauit; et sic habent in scriptis suis. Et dicunt quod quando Adam
infirmabatur, misit filium suum Seth ad paradisum vt rogaret angelum
qui custodiebat paradisum quatenus mitteret sibi oleum misericordie
quo possit linire membra sua causa sanitatis recuperande. Qui Seth 15
abiit sed ab angelo intrare non est permissus, et dixit quod de oleo
misericordie non potuit habere. Sed tradidit sibi tria grana eiusdem pomi
et precepit quod mitteret in os patris, et quando arbor illa fructum
portauerit pater eius ab omni infirmitate liberaretur. Qui reuersus ad
patrem [f. 36ᵛ] inuenit eum mortuum, et misit ista tria grana in os eius. 20
Que creuerunt in tres magnas arbores de quibus erat crux facta que
portauit bonum fructum, Ihesum Cristum per quem Adam et omnes
ab eo descendentes sunt a morte perpetua saluati nisi forte per peccata
sua perpediantur.

Ista sancta crux abscondita erat in terra subtus rupem montis Caluarie 25
plusquam cc. annis quousque per Elenam matrem Constantini impera-
toris erat inuenta. Et erat ista Elena filia Choeli regis Anglie, que tunc
dicebatur Britannia maior, quam Constancius imperator pater Con-
stantini dum erat in partibus illis, ob nimiam eius pulcritudinem
accepit in vxorem. 30

Item, crux ista habuit viii. cubitos in longitudine et iii. cubitos et
dimidum in latitudine. Item, medietas corone cum qua erat coronatus
in cruce et vnus de clauis et ferrum lancie et multe alie reliquie sunt
in Francia in capella domini regis. Et iacet corona in quodam vase
cristallino pulcre ornato. Istas sanctas reliquias emit rex quidam Francie 35
a Ianuensibus quasquidam imperator eis ob nimiam necessitatem
argenti quondam impignorauerat. Et licet dicitur quod est corona
spinea vel de spinis facta, nichilominus est de iunctis marinis albis que
pungunt sicut spine. Nam sepe vidi et diligenter respexi, et illam apud
Parisium et illam apud Constantinopolim. Et erant iste due vna corona 40
facta de iunctis marinis, sed iam diuisa est in duas partes; quarum vna
pars est apud Parisium et alia apud Constantinopolim. Et vna de istis

10 alibi] MS. alii, *but cf.* W 6/32 *and* n. 5, en Grece et li Cristiens

preciosis spinis data erat mihi in magnam amicitiam et similis est albe
spine nam sunt plures fracture eiusdem corone in vase sicut mouetur
[f. 37] et portatur de loco ad locum ostendendo magnis dominis.

Item, scire te volo quod nocte qua Cristus captus est ductus erat in
5 quemdam gardinum, et ibi primo examinatus et a ribaldis Iudeis derisus,
et de spinis albis ibidem crescentibus coronatus. Et ita dure capiti eius
impresserunt quod sanguis ex omni parte corporis decurrebat. Et ideo
habet alba spina plures virtutes, nam qui portauerit vnum ramum super
se non timebit de fulgure, tonitruo, vel tempestate, nec in loco in quo
10 est potest malus spiritus intrare.

In isto gardino Petrus ter negauit Cristum. Postea ductus erat in vnum
gardinum qui fuit Anne coram episcopis et magistratibus legis, et ibi
fuit iterum examinatus, iterum a Iudeis derisus, et iterum de spinis quas
nos *berbers* vocamus ibidem crescentibus coronatus. Et habet illa spina
15 multas virtutes et fit bonus viridis succus de foliis eius.

Deinde ductus erat in gardinum Cayphe vbi fuit iterum vepribus
coronatus. Postea ductus erat in cameram Pilati, et ibi iterum exa-
minatus et in multis acusatis. Et vestierunt eum Iudei clamide et in
cathedra sedere fecerunt et de iuncis marinis pungentibus eum
20 coronauerunt et flexis genibus ante eum deridendo dixerunt *Aue rex
Iudeorum*. Et cum ista corona crucifixus erat, vnde vna pars est apud
Parisium et altera apud Constantinopolim.

[513] Item, hastam lancie habet imperator Almannie sed ferrum est
apud Parisium. Et tamen imperator Constantinopolis dicit quod ipse
25 habet ferrum lancie. Quodquidem ferrum multociens vidi, et est magis
largum quam est illud Parisium.

CHAPTER III

Item, apud Constantinopolim iacet sancta Anna, mater matris Cristi,
quam sancta Elena de Ierusalem transtulit. Item, sanctus Iohannes
Crisostomus qui fuit archiepiscopus eiusdem vrbis. Item, sanctus Lucas
30 [f. 37ᵛ] euangelista cuius ossa erant de Bitania vsque ad eandem vrbem
translata. Item, habent ibidem vasa lapidea marmori similia que ex
propria natura semper aquam sudant et deguttant, et in tanto ex se
ipsis sine humana manu implentur quod aqua orificia vasorum ascendit
et exit. Et lapidem de quo ista vasa fiunt vocant *enidros* qui semper
35 stillat aquam.

Constantinopolis est nobilis ciuitas et pulcra et bene murata et est
triangula, habens ex vna parte brachium maris quod a quibusdam
vocatur Hellepontus; alii vocant os Constantinopolis, alii brachium
sancti Georgii. Et istud brachium circumcingit et claudit duas partes
40 ciuitatis. Et ad caput istius brachii maris versus mare magnum solebat

26 Parisium] MS. Parisiᵘˢ   33 orificia] MS. oreficia

esse ciuitas Troiana in quadam amena planicie iuxta eundem fluuium
cita. Sed quia tantum tempus iam ab eius subuersione transit, vix in
aliqua eius parte apparet.

[521] Item, circa Greciam sunt plures insule, sicut Calistria, Calcas,
Ortage, Tesbeia, Minoa, Flaxon, Melo, Carpacia, et Lempne. In ista 5
insula Lempne est mons Achos alcior nubibus. Sunt eciam diuerse
patrie et diuerse lingue sicut Turcopoli, Pyncenandi, et Comangi, et
omnes obediunt imperatori. Item, Tracia et Macedonia de qua erat
magnus Alexander rex. In ista terra erat Aristotiles natus in vna ciuitate
que vocatur Strageres. Et ibi iacet, et est super tumbam eius vnum 10
altare vbi conueniunt homines terre illius pro arduis negociis tractandis,
et videtur eius quod per inspiracionem diuinam habent ibi meliora
consilia. Et faciunt magnum festum de eo omni anno ac si esset sanctus.
[535] In ista terra sunt montes excelsi valde. Et versus finem Macedonie
est quidam mons qui vocatur Olympus transcendens nubes, et separat 15
Macedoniam a Tracia. Est eciam ibi mons Athos et est tante altitudinis
quod vmbra eius protenditur vsque Lempne [f. 38] qui distat per lxxvi.
miliaria a predicto monte. Et in summitate istius montis est aer purus,
nec est ibi ventus vel aer mixtus. Et propter hoc nec auis nec bestia
potest ibi viuere. Et dicunt homines ibidem quod philosofi dudum 20
ascenderunt istos montes et habebant spongeas aqua plenas semper
naribus eorum appositas ne deficerent siccitate aeris. Et in summitate
moncium scripserunt digitis suis in puluere et abierunt et in fine anni
reascenderunt et inuenerunt scripturas sanas et integras in nulla parte
earum vitiatas. Vnde apparet quod montes illi purum aerem attingunt. 25

Item, apud Constantinopolim est imperiale palacium nobiliter et
solempniter ordinatum. Et iuxta istud palacium est quidam pulcher
locus pro hastiludiis et aliis ludis deputatus, habens solaria et diuersos
gradus in circuitu ita quod vnusquisque potest videre sine impedimento
visus alterius. Et subtus istos gradus sunt stabula equorum imperatorum 30
bene testudinata, et omnes columpne adinfra sunt marmoree.

Item, infra ecclesiam sancte Sophie imperator quidam voluit quon-
dam sepelisse vnum de parentibus suis. Et fodientes sepulcrum in-
uenerunt vnum aliud corpus super quod erat lamen aureum ebraicis,
grecis, et latinis litteris scriptum. Scriptura autem hec erat: *Ihesus* 35
Cristus nascetur de virgine Maria et ego credo in eum. Et data istius
scripture erat ante incarnacionem Cristi per bis mille annos. Et adhuc
est lamen istud in thesauria ecclesie, et dicunt homines quod iste erat
Ermes sapiens.

Et licet Greci sunt cristiani, tamen multum variant et discordant a 40
vera fide catholica; nam dicunt quod spiritus sanctus non procedit a
patre et filio sed a patre tantum. Et non obediunt ecclesie romane vel

9 Aristotiles] MS. Aristoles *In margin* Aristotiles   16 Macedoniam]
MS. Mecedoniā

pape, et dicunt quod tantam potestatem habet eorum patriarcha inter eos sicut papa inter nos. Et ideo Iohannes papa xxii[us] misit eis litteras qualiter tota cristianitas vna deberet esse et vni pape obedire, qui est verus vicarius dei [f. 38[v]] et cui deus commisit potestatem ligandi et
5 soluendi et nulli alii. Ac illi remittentes sibi diuersa responsa inter cetera dixerunt: *Potenciam tuam summam circa tuos subiectos firmiter credimus. Superbiam tuam nimiam tollerare non possumus. Auariciam tuam saciare non intendimus. Dominus tecum, quia dominus nobiscum est.* Et alia responsa non potuit habere ab eis.
10 Item, conficiunt sacramentum altaris de pane fermentato et reprehendunt nos quod conficimus sine fermento, nam Cristus die cene fecit corpus suum de pane fermentato. Et in die cene faciunt panem fermentatum et siccant contra solem et custodiunt per totum annum et dant infirmis loco corporis domini.
15 Item, dicunt quod non est purgatorium nec anime citra diem iudicii penas sustinent nec gaudiis perfruuntur. Dicunt eciam quod fornicacio non est peccatum mortale, immo est res naturalis; et quod homines et mulieres non debent nisi semel matrimonium contrahere; et qui sepius contraxerint, filii erunt illegitimi et in peccatis nati. Et pro modica
20 occasione dissoluunt matrimonium contractum. Presbiteri eciam eorum ducunt vxores, et dicunt quod vsura non est peccatum mortale, et vendunt beneficia ecclesiastica, et sic faciunt alii alibi, quod dolendum est. Nam Symonia hodie in ecclesia dei coronatur; deus illud emendet.
Item, dicunt quod in quadragesima nullus debet celebrare missas nisi
25 die sabbati et die dominica. Et non ieiunant die sabbati aliquo tempore anni licet sit vigilia natalis domini vel pasche, nec permittunt latinos ad altaria eorum celebrare. Et in casu quo aliquis celebrauerit, statim lauant altare aqua benedicta et dicunt quod super vnum altare non debet nisi vna missa tantum in die celebrari. Dicunt eciam quod Cristus numquam
30 manducauit sed similauit se manducasse. Et dicunt quod nos peccamus mortaliter radendo barbas nostras quia hoc est signum opprobrii Ihesu Cristi; et qui sibi radunt barbas ad hoc faciunt vt plus placeant mundo et mulieribus. Dicunt eciam quod peccamus grauiter manducando de animalibus in veteri testamento prohibitis, sicut de [f. 39] porcis, lepori-
35 bus, et aliis animalibus non ruminantibus. Dicunt eciam quod nos peccamus manducando carnes septimana carnipreuii, et quia comedimus carnes die Mercurii et oua et caseum die Veneris; et excomunicant omnibus a carnibus abstinentibus die sabbati.
Item, imperator Constantinopolis facit patriarchas, archiepiscopos,
40 episcopos, et dat dignitates et confert clericis beneficia ecclesiastica, et eos si habeat causam priuat. Et sic est dominus temporalium et spiritualium in terra sua. Et si volueritis scire eorum a.b.c. quales litteras habent, potes hic videre cum nominibus earumdem: [*the alphabet follows in the MS.*].

CHAPTER IV

Et quamuis ista non pertinent ad iter nostrum, tangunt tamen ea que promisi, videlicet demonstrare et declarare mores et aliquas consuetudines et diuersitates terrarum. Et quia ista terra primo variat et discordat in fide et litteris a nobis, primo de illa tetigi ad differenciam fidei nostre a fide eorum, et quia homines in nouis et extraneis semper delectantur. 5

Nunc ergo redeo ad iter meum. Prosequendo de Constantinopoli si volueris ire per Turkeyam, venies primo versus ciuitatem Nik, et transibis portum de Cheuetot. Et videbis semper ante te montem de Cheuetot bene altum, per vnam leucam et dimidiam a predicta ciuitate distantem. Potes eciam, si volueris, a Constantinopoli venire per 10 brachium sancti Georgii et per mare. Et tunc primo venies ad insulam de Sylo. In ista insula crescit gumma, que *mastyk* vocatur, super parua arbusta, et exit sicut serisa vel pruna.

Postea venies ad insulam Pathmos vbi Iohannes [f. 39ᵛ] apostolus scripsit Apocalipsim. Et erat idem Iohannes in passione Cristi xx[x]. 15 annorum, et postea passionem Cristi vixit lxii. annis, et in centesimo etatis sue anno moriebatur.

De Pathmos venies ad Ephesum vnam pulchram ciuitatem iuxta mare sitam. Ibi moriebatur sanctus Iohannes, et sepultus erat in quodam sepulcro retro altare in vna pulchra ecclesia quondam a cristianis 20 possessa et inhabitata. Sed in tumba eius non habetur nisi manna quia corpus eius translatum erat in paradisum. Et modo tenent Turci ciuitatem et ecclesiam et totam Assiam minorem, et est tota Assia minor iam vocata Turkeya.

Et sciend*um* est quod sanctus Iohannes fecit sibi foueam in vita sua, 25 et totus viuens in illam descendit; vnde multi negant eum mortuum sed quod ibi requiescit vsque diem iudicii. Et pro certo est ibi vnum magnum mirabile, nam terra sepulcri eius sepe visibiliter mouetur quasi bulliendo et puluis decurrit ac si violencia cuiusdam corporis viuentis interius sic mouetur; vnde omnes videntes in admiracionem vertit. 30

[652] Deinde ab Epheso venies per diuersas insulas maris vsque ad ciuitatem Pateran vbi erat sanctus Nicholaus natus. Deinde ad Mirream ciuitatem vbi erat gracia diuina in episcopum electus. Et sunt ibi bona vina et forcia, et vocantur vina Mirree. Deinde venies ad insulam Cretam quam imperator quondam dedit Ianuensibus. Deinde transibis 35 per insulas Chohos et Langho, de quibus Ipocras erat dominus.

In ista insula de Langho est filia Ipocrasis in forma immanissimi draconis, centum extanciones brachiorum (videlicet *ffadoms*) in longitudine habentis; vt dicunt ibidem, nam ego non vidi. Et vocant eam incole dominam terre, et habitat subtus testudines cuiusdam antiqui 40 castelli, et monstru[it] se bis vel ter in anno. Nec alicui facit malum nisi forte no[c]ant ei. Et erat ita mutata de vna pulcra puella in talem draconem per quamdam deam nomine Dianam. Et dicunt quod reuen[iet] [f. 40] ad propriam formam cum venerit vnus miles ita audax quod voluerit eam osculari in ore; sed postquam conuersa fuerit non diu viuet.

Non multum iam tempus preteriit ex quo vnus miles Hospitalis de
5 Rodes probus et audax dixit quod voluit osculari eam. Ascendit dextrarium, venit ad castellum, intrauit cauernam. Draco videns eum venientem leuauit caput contra eum, equus vero viso tam horribili monstro furibundus in fugam vertitur, et inuito milite altam rupem ascendit et de rupe in mare saliit. Et sic seipsum cum sessore perdidit.

10 Item, iuuenis quidam qui nichil sciebat de isto dracone egressus de naui, venit per terram ad castellum istud, et intrauit cauernam. Et in tanto introiuit quod inuenit quamdam cameram, et in camera vnam pulcram puellam sedentem, et in speculo respicientem caput suum pectentem et cetera membra corporis disponentem; et habebat multos
15 thesauros iuxta eam. Et credens eam mulierem comunem, accessit propius ita quod puella vidit vmbram eius in speculo. Et conuersa interrogauit quid vellet. Et dixit quod vellet esse amicus eius. Ac illa quesiuit ab eo si esset miles, et dixit quod non. Tunc inquit:

Non potes esse meus amicus. Sed vade ad socios tuos et fac te militem.
20 Et cras egrediar de ista cauerna et veniam ante te; et veni et osculare me in ore, et ne formides in aliquo quia non faciam tibi malum. Et licet videar tibi terribilis et abhominabilis hoc est per incantacionem. Ne timeas ergo quia non sum aliud quam vides iam. Et si volueris me osculari, habebis omnes istos the[sa]uros et eris meus maritus et dominus
25 istius terre.

[729] Et super hoc recessit [et ven]it ad socios suos qui fecerunt eum militem. Et in crastino [egre]ssit vt oscularetur puellam. Et quando vidit eam de cauerna [sua] in terribili forma egredientem, statim immenso timore percussus [in] fugam vertitur. Ac illa [prose]quitur
30 eum, et cum videret eum [f. 40ᵛ] fugientem nec aliquando modo [reuer]tentem, cepit clamare et rugire quasi [demens] et reuersa est. Et statim moriebatur iste miles.

Et non potuit aliquis miles eam postmodum videre quin statim moriebatur. Sed cum venerit aliquis qui voluerit osculari eam non
35 morietur; immo conuertet eam in propriam formam et erit dominus terre.

Deinde venies ad insulam de Rodes quam Hospitilarii tenent et gubernant. Istam insulam quondam abstulerunt ab imperatore; et vocabatur Collos et Turci adhuc sic eam nominant. Et ad istos insulares scribit apostolus in epistolis suis *Ad Collocenses*, et continet octingentas
40 leucas in longitudine.

CHAPTER V

De Constantinopoli transeundo per mare et per istam insulam de Rodes, venies in Cyprum vbi sunt forcia vina. Et primo sunt rubri,

deinde deueniunt alba; et quanto sunt antiquiora, tanto sunt [melio]ra,
clariora, et magis odorancia. Et transeundo per istud iter venies iuxta
Golfam vel Caribdim Sathelie, vbi quondam erat vna magna terra
habens vnam pulcram ciuitatem nomine Satheliam. Que ciuitas et patria
perierunt propter peccatum cuiusdam iuuenis hoc modo. 5

Erat quidam iuuenis qui multum amabat iuuenculam quamdam
pulcram et formosam puellam que subito moriebatur sepultaque erat
in vno sarchophago marmoreo. Et propter nimium amorem quem ad
eam habuit, nocte venit ad tumbam eius, aperuit, introiuit, cognouit
eam, et recessit. Decursis vero nouem mensibus, venit vox ad eum 10
dicens: Surge, vade ad sepulcrum talis mulieris, aperi, et vide quid tu
ibi in eam generasti. Et caueas quod non omittas, quod si nolueris, mala
tibi venient infra breue. Qui abiit et aperuit tumbam, et statim extra-
uolauit ca[pud] teterrimi horribile et disfiguratum ad videndum. Et
circumuo[lauit] ciuitatem et patriam, et statim descendit ciuitas in 15
abyss[um].

Sunt aque ibidem periculose et quasi sine fundo ad transfretan[dum].
Item, a Rodes ad Cyprum sunt pl[us]quam quingente leuc[e] [f. 41]
in longitudine,[1] sed si applicaueris ad primum portum, videlicet Thyri
vel Sur, de quibus superius dixi, venies per terram ad Ierusalem si 20
volueris, et tunc de Thyro venies ad ciuitatem de Achon in vna die, que
quondam dicebatur Tholomayda, que erat pulcra ciuitas cristianorum
supra mare sita, sed iam vastatur quasi et destruitur.

[881] Item, a Venisia ad Achon per mare sunt bis mille et quater viginti
leuce lumbardie. Et a Calabria vel Cicilia ad Achon per mare sunt mille 25
ccc. leuce lumbardie. Et insula Creta est recte in medio vie.

[892] Et prope istam ciuitatem Achon versus mare, ad cxx. stadia in
dextra parte versus meridiem, est mons Carmeli vbi morebatur Heliseus
propheta. Et ibi secundum quosdam ordo fratrum Carmelitarum
sumpsit exordium. Iste mons non est magnus nec altus. Et ad pedem 30
istius montis solebat esse vna ciuitas cristianorum, que dicebatur
Cayphas eo quod Cayphas illam fundauit, sed in toto destructa est.
Et in sinistra parte montis Carmeli est quedam villa Saffra nomine super
alium montem sita. Ibi nati erant sancti Iacobus et Iohannes euangelista,
et loco natiuitatis eorum est vna pulcra ecclesia. 35

[841] Et a Tholomayda que nunc Achan dicitur vsque ad montem
magnum qui Scala Thiri vocatur sunt c. stadia. Et iuxta istam ciuitatem
de Achon currit riuulus paruus qui Beleoun dicitur. Et ibi prope est
fossa Menneoun. Hoc est vna fossa rotunda centum cubitos habens in
latitudine, et est plena arena lucenti de qua fit vitrum bonum et clarum. 40
Et veniunt homines pro ista arena per mare et per terram; et cum
euacuata fuerit fossa de ista arena, in crastino erit ita plena sicut

---

[1] *Harley here omits matter corresponding to* W 14/35–16/29

prefuit, quod mirum est. Et est ventus validus infra fossam qui mirifico
modo arenam mouet et turbat. Et si quis mittat aliquod metallum infra
fossam inter arenam, conuertetur in vitrum. Et si vitrum factum de ista
arena remittatur infra fossam, conuertetur [f. 41ᵛ] in arenam. Et dicunt
5 quidam quod est aspirallum vel vena maris arenosi.

   Item, ab Achon supradicta ad iii. dietas venies ad ciuitatem Palestine
que quondam fuit Philistinorum et vocabatur Gaza, quod interpretatur
ciuitas diuiciarum. Et est pulcra ciuitas et populosa iuxta mare posita.

   Istius ciuitatis portas Sampson fortis abstulit et montem ascendit.
10 Hic eciam multos Philistinorum interfecit qui fraude et consilio vxoris
sue oculos eius eruerant, crines totonderant; vnde in medio conuiuii
eorum ductus et ab omnibus derisus et ludificatus domum euertit et se
ipsum cum tribus milibus Philistinorum oppressit, sicut in libro Iudicum
legitur.

15 [875] De Gaza venies ad ciuitatem Cesarie, deinde ad castellum pere-
grinorum, postea ad Ascalonem, deinde ad Iaffam, et tunc ad Ierusalem
si volueris.

   Sed si volueris primo ire per terram ad Babilonem vbi soldanus
moratur, pro gracia ab eo impetranda vt possis secure per patriam
20 transire, et a Babilonia ad montem Synai et sic redire ad Ierusalem.
Tunc de Gaza venies ad castellum Daire et transibus Siriam et ingre-
dieris desertum vbi via est sabulosa. Et durat istud desertum per viii.
dietas, sed per viam et dietas habebis semper hostilarias vbi inuenies
omnia necessaria vite. Et vocatur istud desertum Achilek. Et cum
25 ingressus fueris istud desertum venies in Egiptum et vocatur Egiptus
Canopia et in alia lingua Mersin. Et primo venies ad vnam bonam villam
que vocatur Balbeta, que sita est ad finem regni Halappe. Et ab illa
venies ad Babiloniam et ad Cayram.

CHAPTER VI

   In Babilone est vna pulcra ecclesia sancte Marie vbi morebatur vii.
30 annis quando fugit de terra Iude a facie Herodis. Ibi iacet corpus sancte
Barbare virginis. Ibi morabatur Ioseph postquam fuit venditus a
fratribus suis.

   Ibi eciam misit Nabugodonosor rex tres pueros in caminum ignis,
qui ebraice dicebantur Ananias, Azarias, et Misael, prout psalmus de
35 Benedicite testatur. Sed [f. 42] Nabugodonosor eos vocauit Sidrak,
Misaak, et Abdenago; hoc est gloriosus deus, virtuosus deus, et deus
omnium regnorum. Et hoc erat quia vidit, vt dixit, filium dei deambu-
lantem cum eis in medio ignis.

   Ibi moratur comuniter soldanus in suo castello magno et forti super
40 rupem posito. Hoc est ad Cayram iuxta Babilonem. In isto castello sunt
semper ad custodiendum illud et ministrandum soldano cum fuerit ibi

plusquam sex milia hominum qui omnes habent necessaria sua de curia.
Ego bene noui nam steti cum eo stipendiarius in guerris suis contra
Bedones per magnum tempus. Et filiam cuiusdam magni principis
terreni cum magna hereditate et diuiciis multis mihi in vxorem dedisset
si creatorem meum negare voluissem. Sed hoc non potui pro aliquo 5
promisso terreno.

Et sciatis quod soldanus est soldanus v. regnorum que conquisiuit
sua virtute et fortitudine, scilicet regni Canopie (hoc est Egipti), regni
Ierosolomitane de quo Dauid et Salomon fuerunt reges, regni Halappe
in terra Damyeth, regni Arabie quod fuit vni illorum regum qui 10
venerant in Bethlem adorare dominum. Et multas alias terras habet in
manu sua, et cum hoc est Caliphes quod est magnum quid. Soldanus
lingua eorum idem est quasi rex.

Et fuerunt aliquando v. soldani et nunc non sunt nisi ille tantum de
Egipto. Et primus soldanus Egipti vocabatur Marachon, qui fuit pater 15
Sahaladini. Iste erat Medus, et cepit Caliphem Egipti et occidit eum,
et fuit soldanus vi et armis. Postea regnauit filius eius Sahaladinus,
cuius tempore rex Anglie Richardus venit in Siriam qui multa mala
soldano et Saracenis fecit . . . Mellechmador. Iste erat secrete occisus
per fratrem suum vt reg[f. 43]naret post eum. Et regnauit et fecit se 20
vocari Mellechmanda. Et iste erat soldanus in recessu meo a partibus
illis.

Item, soldanus potest ducere de Egipto plusquam xx. milia hominum
armorum, et de Suria et de Turkeya et de aliis terris quas tenet l. milia,
et omnes isti sunt stipendiarii eius. Et sunt semper secum, exceptis aliis 25
de terra sua qui sunt quasi innumeri. Et quilibet istorum percipit cxx.
florenos per annum, et super hoc oportet quod teneat iii. equos et vnum
camelum.

Et per villas et ciuitates sunt amaralli constituti ad gubernandum
istos stipendiarios. Et habet vnus quadringentos, alius quingentos, alius 30
plures, alius pauciores, et tantum percepit amarallus per se quantum
omnes sub se. Et ideo cum soldanus voluerit aliquem nobilem militem
promouere, facit eum amarallum. Et quando tempus fuerit carum,
milites isti vendunt equos suos et arma, et fiunt pauperes valde. . . .

Item, ante soldanum nullus extraneus venit nisi fuerit vestitus vestibus 35
aureis tartarinis vel de cammoka more saracenorum. Et quam cito primo
videtur ab aliquo, siue sit ad fenestram siue alibi, oportet [f. 43ᵛ] quod
genuflectet et osculetur terram, nam ista est reuerencia illorum qui
voluerint secum colloquium habere. . . .

[1316] Et sciendum est quod ista Babilon de qua prefatus sum iuxta 40
quam moratur soldanus non est illa magna Babilon vbi diuersitates
linguarum miraculo dei erant inuente, quando illa magna turris Babel

13 quasi] MS. qd., *i.e.* quod *but cf.* W 18/42 come

cepit edificari, cuius muri lxiiii. stadiorum erant altitudinis, que in
magnis desertis Arabie super viam qua itur versus regnum Caldee sita
est. Sed diu est ex quo nullus ausus erat approximare ad turrim, quia
est deserta et in circuitu eius sunt immensi dracones, magni serpentes
5 et alie bestie venenose ita quod nullus potest accedere ad locum.

Ista turris cum ciuitate habebat in circuitu murorum xxv. miliaria,
sicut homines terre illius testantur, et prout secundum humanam
estimacionem potest comprehendi. Et licet vocatur turris Babilonis,
erant tamen diuerse habitaciones et multe magne edificaciones, multam
10 terram in circuitu ocupantes. Nam turris per se decem miliaria habebat
in quadro. Et istam turrim fundauit rex Nembrot qui fuit rex terre
illius et primus rex mundi.

Iste Nembroth in similitudinem patris sui statuam erexit et subditos
suos illam adorare coegit [f. 44] cuius exemplo alii domini ducti hoc
15 idem fecerunt, et sic ydola et simulacra inceperunt. Alii tamen affirmant
ydola inicium sumpsisse a Nino filio Beli rege Assiriorum qui in honore
patris statuam erexit sicut Nembrot. . . . Sed Cirus rex Persarum
fluuium ab eis abstulit. Turrim et ciuitatem destruxit nam fluuium in
trecentos sexaginta riuilos diuisit, iurauit enim quod ita meabilem eum
20 faceret quod miles siccis genibus illum transiret. . . .

Et quare de ista famosa Babilone fit iam sermo noster, vnum verbum
inserere quod in *Maundeville* non vidi sed in cronicis repperi. Dicit
enim Beda, *De Ymagine Mundi*, quod Nembrot gigas x. cubitorum
Babilonem edificauit, c. portis ereis firmauit, et fluuius Eufrates per
25 medium eius transit, cuius muri tante spissitudinis et densitatis erant
quod vix a Ciro rege Persarum et Medorum qui eam cepit destrui
potuerunt. Cuius ars est turris Babel, quam dicunt tenere in altitudine
quatuor milia passuum (id est quatuor miliaria) et ab angulo in angulum
c. passus.

30 Item, Ieronimus, *Super Isayam*, Babilonem in agro Senaar per cir-
cuitum murorum dicit xvi. milia passuum ab angulo vsque ad angulum
et similiter per circuitum lxiiii. milia passuum (id est sexaginta quatuor
miliaria); cuius ars turris Babel est que edificata fuit post diluuium per
Nembrot gigantem, qui ignem pro deo tamquam contrarium aquarum
35 adorare faciebat, cuius turris altitudo quatuor milia passuum (id est
quatuor miliarium) esse scribitur. Et [f. 44ᵛ] sunt ibidem strate
marmoree templa aurea platee lapidibus et auro fulgentes venaciones
regie omnis generis bestiarum infra murorum ambitum constitute, que
destructa fuit per Cirum et Darium reges Persarum. Hec in cronicis.

40 Item, a Babiloun vbi soldanus moratur eundo directe inter orientem
et septemtrionem versus istam magnam Babilonem sunt bene xl. diete
transeundo per desertum. . . .

[1292] [f. 45] Babilon sita est super mare Gion quod alio nomine
dicitur Nilus, quod venit de paradiso terrestri. . . . [f. 45ᵛ] Istud flumen

venit de paradiso per deserta Indie. Deinde intrat terram et currit longo
tempore per multas patrias subtus terram. Deinde exit sub vno monte
qui vocatur Aloth qui est inter Indiam et Ethiopiam, habens ab introitu
Ethiopie v. mensium dietas. Postea circuit Ethiopiam et Moretanam et
venit in longitudine per terram Egipti vsque ad ciuitatem Alexan- 5
driam. . . .

CHAPTER VII

[1445] [f. 46] Item, in deserto Damiete obuiabat quidam sanctus
heremita cuidam monstro, quod ab vmbilico superius formam gerebat
humanam, in cuius frontis medio erant duo magna cornua acuta et
incidencia, et ab vmbilico inferius corpus habebat caprinum. Inter- 10
rogatus ab heremita quid esset, dixit se esse creaturam mortalem qualem
ipsum deus creauerat et in deserto illo habitabat victum suum per-
quirendo. Et rogabat heremitam vt dignaretur pro se illum deum orare
qui ad saluandum genus humanum descendebat de celo, natusque erat
de virgine, mortem et passionem sustulit secundum quod nos scimus, 15
per quem viuimus et sumus. Et adhuc est caput cum cornibus apud
Alexandriam pro mirabili.
[1461] Item, in Egipto est ciuitas Cleopolis, hoc est ciuitas solis. In ista
ciuitate est quoddam templum rotundum in modum templi Ierusalem.
Presbiteri istius templi habent in scriptis datam fenicis auis que vnica 20
est mundi, que in fine quingentorum annorum quia tam diu viuit venit
ad templum istud et super quoddam altare infra templum ardet se. Et
ministri templi erga eius aduentum preparant altare et superponunt
diuersas species, sulphur viuum et alia que leuiter volunt inflammari.
Et venit ista auis et ardet se in cineres, et [f. 46ᵛ] proxima die sequenti 25
inuenies vermem viuum inter cineres. Et secunda die erit auis perfecta,
tercia die surgit et euolat. Et sic sunt numquam plures istius nature,
et certe est magnum dei miraculum et bene potest illa auis deo com-
pari. . . .
[1513] Item, iuxta Cairam extra ciuitatem [f. 47] est campus vbi 30
balsamum crescit. . . . [f. 47ᵛ] Dicto iam de balsamo, dicam tibi de vno
alio quod est vltra Babiloun et fluuium Nili versus desertum inter
Affricam et Egiptum. Hoc est granaria Ioseph que fecit pro bladis vel
frugibus custodiendis tempore quo fames preualuit in Egipto. Et sunt
pulcra et lapidea de quibus duo supereminent altitudine et magni- 35
tudine magis admiranda, et habet quodlibet eorum vnam portam pro
ingressu cum paruo ascensu terre quia terra circa ea multum vastata
est ex quo facta fuerunt. Et sunt adinfra serpentibus plena. Et super
ista granaria a dextra sunt plures scripture diuersarum linguarum, et
dicunt aliqui quod sunt sepulcra magnorum dominorum. Sed hoc non 40

est verum, nam comunis opinio per totam patriam longe et late, procul
et prope, est quod sunt granaria Ioseph, et sic scribitur in cronicis
eorum. . . .

Item, Egipcii habent diuersas linguas, diuersas litteras ab aliis
5 differentes, vnde ostendam tibi quales sunt et quomodo eas vocant ad
diuersitatem aliarum linguarum: [*the alphabet follows in the MS.*].

CHAPTER VIII

[f. 48] Iam vero antequam vlterius procedam, volo redire ad demon-
strandum tibi alias vias per quas itur ad Babilonem vbi soldanus
comuniter est, que est in introitu Egipti, eo quod multi homines primo
10 veniunt ibi, postea ad montem Synay. Deinde redeunt per Ierusalem
(sicut alias dixi) quia primo complent longiorem peregrinacionem et
redeunt per propinquiorem, licet propinquior sit magis digna (hoc est
Ierusalem) quia nulla alia peregrinacio habet comparacionem ad illam,
sed ad maiorem securitatem cupiunt magis complere longiorem pere-
15 grinacionem quam breuiorem.

Vnde si volueris directe venire ad Babilonem per aliam viam et
magis breuiter de partibus occidentalibus supranominatis et de aliis
partibus circumiacentibus, venies per Franciam, per Burgoniam
vel Burgundiam, per Lumbardiam. Non oportet per istam viam
20 demonstrare ciuitates et villas quia via est comunis et quasi nota
omnibus. Plures sunt portus vbi homines mittunt se in mari. Quidam
accipiunt mare apud Ianuam, quidam apud Venesiam, et veniunt per
mare Atriaticum quod vocatur Gulfa vel Caribdis Venisie, que separat
Italiam et Greciam in illa parte. Aliqui veniunt ad Naphes, aliqui ad
25 Romam, et de Roma ad Raudis, et ibi mittunt se in mare et in multis
aliis locis vbi est portus. Et tunc venies per Tussiam, per Campaniam,
per Calabriam, per Appuliam, et per insulas Italli, et per Chous, per
Sardaniam, et per Ciciliam que est magna insula et bona. In ista Cicilia
est quidam gardinus multos diuersos fructus habens omni tempore anni
30 viridis et floridus, tam in yeme quam in estate.

[1428] Ista insula habet in circuitu trecentas quinquagintas leucas Fran-
corum et inter Ciciliam et Italiam non est nisi paruum brachium maris
quod vocatur Far de Mersin, et in Ciciliam intrat mare Atriaticum et
mare Lumbardie. Et in Cicilia sunt serpentes per quos homines probant
35 filios [f. 48ᵛ] suos si sint legitimi vel non. Nam si sint legimiti serpentes
repunt circa eos nichil ledentes, et si sint adulteri mordent et venenant.
Et sic plures probant filios suos si sint sui vel aliorum.

[1416] Item, in ista insula est mons Ethna qui eciam dicitur mons Gibel.
Et vulcana semper ardencia sunt, namque vii. loca ardencia diuersas
40 flammas diuersorum colorum emittencia et per variaciones istarum

flammarum sciunt homines terre quando tempus erit carum, frigidum
vel calidum, humidum vel siccum. Et qualitercumque tempus se habebit
sciunt per istas flammas. Et de Italia ad ista vulcana sunt xxv. miliaria.
Et dicunt homines quod sunt vie inferni.

Item, si volueris venire per Pisam secundum quod multi veniunt vbi 5
est brachium maris vel per aliquem portum ibidem in partibus illis, tunc
venies per insulam de Gref que est Ianuensium. Deinde applicabis in
Grecia ad portum de Miroth vel ad portum Valone vel ad ciuitatem de
Duras vel ad aliquem portum in partibus illis. Et tunc venies ad
Constantinopolim, postea transibis per aquam ad insulam Cretam et ad 10
Rodes et ad Cyprum. Et sic a Venesia ad Constantinopolim, tenendo
magis rectam viam per mare, sunt mille octingente octoginta leuce
Lumbardie.

Deinde a Cypro venies semper per mare dimittendo Ierusalem et
totam patriam a parte sinistra vsque ad Egiptum, et applicabis ad 15
ciuitatem Damiete que quondam erat fortis ciuitas in introitu Egipti
sita. Et de Damieta venies ad ciuitatem Alexandriam que similiter sita
est super mare. Et in ista ciuitate decollata erat sancta Katerina.
Sanctus eciam Marcus euangelista marterizatus et sepultus, sed im-
perator eius ossa ad Venisiam transtulit.   20

Et adhuc apud Alexandriam est vna pulcra ecclesia interius dealbata
sine pictura, et sic sunt omnes alie ecclesie ibidem que quondam fuerunt
cristianorum interius albe facte nam pagani et saraceni eas [f. 49] sic
dealbauerunt vt ymagines sanctorum in eis quondam depictas delerent
et abluerent.   25

Item, ista ciuitas Alexandria continet bene xxx. stadia in longitudine
et nisi decem in latitudine, et est pulcra ciuitas valde. Et in illa intrat
fluuius Nili in mare (sicut alias dixi) et in isto flumine Nili inueniuntur
lapides preciosi et lignum aloes quod venit de paradiso terrestri, et
ponitur in multis medicinis et est bene carum. Et ab ista Alexandria 30
venies ad Babilonem vbi soldanus moratur, que eciam sita est super
istud flumen Nili. Et ista via propinquior est eundo directe ad Babi-
lonem. . . .

Ab isto mare habebis quatuor dietas et tunc venies per desertum ad
vallem de [f. 49ᵛ] Helym et tunc ad montem Synay. . . .   35

Item, retro altare istius ecclesie est locus vbi Moyses vidit [f. 50]
dominum in rubo ardenti, et quando monachi intrant istum locum
discalceant se, eo quod dixit dominus Moysi: *Discalcia te quia locus in
quo stas sanctus est* . . . prout dicit Dauid in psalmo: [f. 50ᵛ] *Mirabilia
testimonia tua domine.* . . .   40

Deinde ascendens super montem sancte Katerine qui multo altior est
monte Moysi. Et in loco vbi erat [f. 51] sepulta non est ecclesia nec
capella nec aliquod habitaculum, sed est magnus aceruus lapidum circa
locum vbi positum erat corpus eius ab angelis. . . .

CHAPTER IX

[2541] Et comedunt et assant carnes suas et pisces super calidas petras contra solem. Et sunt fortes homines et bellicosi et est quasi infinita multitudo eorum. . . . Libenter contra eum bellarent si causam haberent [f. 51ᵛ] et sic sepe fecerunt eodem tempore quo steti cum eo. Et habent
5 vnum scutum et vnam lanceam tantum sine aliis armis. . . .

[1106] In Ebron regnauit xxxiii. annis et dimidio et ibi sunt sepulcra patriarcharum, scilicet Adam, Abrahe, Isaac, et Iacob, et eorum vxorum, videlicet Eue, Sarre, Rebecce, et Lie in declino montis. Et super eos est vna pulcra ecclesia cornuta vel angulata in modum castelli quam
10 Saraceni curiose custodiunt. Et habent locum in maximam veneracionem propter sanctos patres ibidem quiescentes, nec permittunt cristianum quemquam vel Iudeum intrare sine speciali gracia soldani. Nam reputant cristianos et Iudeos tanquam canes et quod non sunt digni tam sanctum locum intrare. Et locus vbi iacent dicitur duplex
15 spelunca vel duplex [f. 52] cauerna vel duplex fossa eo quod vnus super alium positus est. . . .

In ista valle est campus vbi homines extrahunt de terra quamdam rem quam *cambil* vocant. Et comedunt et vendunt eam homines loco specierum. Et licet faciant foueam tam profundam et largam sicut
20 possunt, in fine anni erit ita plena sicut prefuit; et hoc miraculose. Et ad ii. miliaria de Ebron est sepulcrum Loth filii fratris Abrahe, et prope Ebron est mons Mambre de quo vallis nomen accepit. Ibi est vna arbor quercina quam saraceni *Airpe* vocant. . . .

[f. 52ᵛ] De Ebron venies in dimidio die ad Bedleem si volueris, nam
25 non sunt nisi v. leuce et est pulcra via per siluas et planicies multum delectabiles. Bethleem est parua ciuitas longa et angusta, magnis et bonis fossatis in circuitu bene firmata. Bethleem quondam dicebatur Effrata, vnde in psalmo *Ecce audiuimus eum in Effrata*. Et versus finem ciuitatis ad orientem est pulcra ecclesia et graciosa, habens turres et pinnacula
30 subtiliter facta. Et infra ecclesiam sunt xliiii. columpne marmoree.

[1060] Et inter istam ecclesiam et ciuitatem est campus floridus, et dicitur floridus propter miraculum quoddam ibidem factum. Nam erat quedam puella propter fornicacionem sibi impositam iniuste et sine culpa morti adiudicata istoque in loco ardenda erat. Cumque fuissent
35 spine et strues accense, virgo stans orabat vt si esset innocens et immunis a peccato sibi imposito, dignaretur deus eam liberare et hoc omnibus demonstrare. Et sic fiduciam habens in domino ingressa est ignem. Et statim ignis extinctus est et locus factus est rosetum delectabile, et rami accensi rosas rubeas produxerunt et rami inaccensi rosas albas,
40 et iste fuerunt prime rose vise tunc temporis in mundo. Et sic fuit ista virgo gracia dei a morte liberata, et locus campi floridi nomen accepit quia plenus erat rosis florentibus.

[1084] Item, iuxta chorum istius ecclesie supradicte in parte dextra descendendo per xvi. gradus est locus vbi Cristus natus erat, nobiliter marmoree coopertus et [f. 53] graciose auro, azura diuersisque coloribus depictus. Et ibi iuxta ad iii. passus est presepe bouis et asine. Ibi eciam prope est puteus vbi stella cecidit que perduxit iii. reges orientales ad 5 istum locum. . . .

[1092] Item, subtus claustrum istius ecclesie per xviii. gradus a parte dextra est charnerum cum ossibus innocentium. Et ante locum vbi Cristus erat natus est sepulcrum sancti Ieronimi presbiteri cardinalis, qui bibleam et psalterium de ebreo transtulit in latinum. Et extra 10 monasterium est cathedra vbi sedebat quando illa transtulit. . . .

[1099] [f. 53ᵛ] De Bethleem ad Ierusalem sunt ii. miliaria et ad dimidiam leucam ab Bethleem in via versus Ierusalem est vna ecclesia vbi angelus denunciauit pastoribus natiuitatem Cristi. In ista via est sepulcrum Rachelis matris Ioseph patriarche que moriebatur statim postquam 15 peperit Beniamin, ibique sepulta erat iuxta Iacob virum suum. Et misit Iacob super eam xii. lapides grandes in signum quod habuit xii. filios.

In ista via ad dimidiam leucam a Ierusalem reapparuit stella tribus regibus que ad tempus abscondita erat propter Herodem. In ista eciam via sunt plures ecclesie cristianorum per quas semper transitum 20 facies. . . .

CHAPTER X

[996] [f. 54] Et ad ii. miliaria a Bethleem contra meridiem est ecclesia sancti Karicoti qui fuit abbas ibidem, de cuius morte monachi multum doluerunt et adhuc sunt depicti dolentes et lugentes sicut in morte eius lugebant, quod valde triste est ad videndum. . . . 25

[f. 54ᵛ] Item, infra istam ecclesiam in dextra parte iuxta chorum ecclesie est mons Caluarie vbi Cristus crucifixus erat, et est alba rupes in quibusdam sui partibus cum rubedine mixta. Ista rupes scissa vel cauata est, et ista scissura dicitur Golgatha. . . . Et ibi est vnum altare et ante istud altare iacent Godfridus de Boilloun, Baldewinus et alii qui 30 fuerunt cristiani reges in Ierusalem. . . . Et postea per multum tempus erant plures sancti monachi [f. 55ᵛ] et heremite in partibus illis prout in libro Vitas Patrum legitur. . . .

[986] Item, in medio chori istius ecclesie est quidam circulus in quo Ioseph ab Aramathia corpus domini posuit quando depositum erat de 35 cruce, et ibi lauit vulnera eius. Et istum circulum dicunt homines esse recte in medio mundi.

Item, in ecclesia sancti sepulcri versus aquilonem est locus vbi dominus noster erat incarceratus. Nam in pluribus locis incarceratus erat. Et ibi est pars cathene cum qua erat ligatus. Ibi eciam apparuit Marie 40

Magdalene post resurreccionem suam quando credidit eum esse orto-
lanum. . . .

Item, versus ecclesiam sancti sepulcri est ciuitas debilior quam alibi,
et hoc propter magnam planciem que est inter ecclesiam et ciuitatem.
5 Et extra muros ciuitatis ad orientem est vallis Iosaphat que tangit muros
in modum magne fouee et large. Et desuper istam vallem Iosaphat extra
ciuitatem est ecclesia sancti Stephani vbi erat lapidatus, et iuxta istum
[f. 56] locum est Porta Aurea que non potest aperiri. Per istam portam
ingressus est dominus die palmarum cui porte vltronie sunt aperte
10 sedens super asinam, et adhuc apparent pedes asine ibidem in tribus
locis super lapides durissimos.

Item, ante ecclesiam sancti sepulcri versus meridiem ad cc. passus est
magnum hospitale sancti Iohannis, a quo Hospitilarii inicium sump-
serunt. Et infra palacium infirmorum istius hospitalis sunt centum
15 viginti quatuor columpne lapidie; et in muro domus preter numerum
supradictum sunt quinquaginta et quatuor columpne lapidie que sus-
tenant domum.

[954] Et ab isto hospitali eundo versus orientem est vna pulcra ecclesia
que dicitur sancta Maria magna. Deinde est vna alia ecclesia satis prope
20 que dicitur sancta Maria Vatyns. Ibi Maria Cleophe et Maria Magda-
lene sparsis crinibus dominum in cruce lamentabantur.

CHAPTER XI

Et ab ecclesia sancti sepulcri ad clx. passus versus orientem est
templum domini, pulcra domus rotunda et bene alta plumboque
cooperta magnamque planiciem habens in circuitu sine edificio aliquo,
25 lapidibus marmoreis albis solidatam. In istud templum non permittunt
saraceni cristianum vel Iudeum intrare, nam reputant indignum quod
tam mala gens in tam sanctum locum ingrederetur. Sed ego intraui ibi
et alibi ad libitum vbi volebam. . . .

[f. 56ᵛ] In isto templo erat Carlemagnus rex quando angelus domini
30 detulit sibi prepucium circumcisionis Ihesu Cristi quod apud capellam
suam de Ayes portauit. Postea Charolus Caluus illud apud Pictauiam
detulit et postea ad Charters.

Item, sciendum est quod istud non est templum a Solomone factum,
nam illud non stetit nisi mille centum et duo annis vsque ad tempus
35 Titi filii Vaspasiani imperatoris, qui Ierusalem obsedit et Iudeos
destruxit eo quod Cristum sine licencia imperatoris occiderunt; vnde
ciuitate a Tito capta templum cum baptisterio succendit, Iudeos ad
undecim centum milia t[r]ucidauit, multos incarcerauit, alios in serui-
tutem vendidit, et sicut illi Cristum pro xxx. denariis vendiderunt, sic
40 Titus xxx. Iudeos pro vno denario dedit. . . .

[f. 57] Postea vero Bethel vbi archa domini cum reliquiis Iudeorum erat

posita. Istam archam cum reliquiis Titus post destructionem Ierusalem
Romam secum duxit. In ista archa erant tabule x. preceptorum, verga
Aaron, virga Moysi cum qua mare rubrum secuit et separauit et populum
per siccum transduxit; cum ista virga rupem percussit et fluxerunt aque,
et multa alia mirabilia cum ista fecit.   5

Item, vnum vas aureum manna plenum, vestimenta ornata [f. 57ᵛ] et
tabernaculum Aaron, vna tabula quadrata aurea cum xii. lapidibus
preciosis, vna pixidis de iaspide viridi cum xii. figuris nominis dei, vii.
candelabra aurea, xii. olle auree, quatuor thuribula aurea, vnum altare
aureum, iii. leones aurei super quos erat cherubin aureum, xii. palmas   10
habens in longitudine circulus signorum celi cum tabernaculo aureo,
tube argentee, vna tabula argentea, vii. panes ordeicii, et omnes alie
reliquie que erant ante Cristi incarnacionem. . . .

Ibi denunciauit angelus Zacharie natiuitatem filii sui Iohannis bap-
tiste. Ibi optulit Melchisedech domino panem et vinum in signum   15
sacramenti futuri. Item, super istam rupem cecidit Dauid postquam
vidit angelum percutientem populum, rogans dominum vt misereretur
sui et populi, et exaudita est oratio eius. Et propter hoc in loco isto
templum edificare voluit sed prohibitus est a domino, eo quod vir
sanguinum erat et quia occidit Vriam suum nobilem militem propter 20
vxorem suam. Et ideo omnia que erant ordinata et preparata ad templi
constructionem reliquit filio suo Salomoni [f. 58] qui edificauit templum
et rogauit dominum vt quicumque eum in isto loco Bethel puro corde
inuocassent, eos propicius exaudiret eisque consiliator et auxiliator in
omnibus iustis peticionibus existeret. Et concessum est ei a domino. 25
Et ideo vocauit illud Salomon *templum consilii et auxilii dei.*

Item, extra portam istius templi est quoddam altare vbi Iudei
columbas et turtures offerre consueuerant. Et modo Saraceni super illud
rotas cum vnco quodam fecerunt vt per solem horas diei videant et
discernant. Et inter istud altare et templum occisus erat Zacharias filius 30
Barachie. Et de pinnaculo istius templi Iudei sanctum Iacobum fratrem
domini primum episcopum Ierosolimorum precipitauerunt.

Et ad introitum istius templi versus occidentem est porta speciosa per
quam Petrus et Iohannes transierunt quando Petrus claudum quemdam
ibidem sanauit et erexit, dicens ei: *in nomine Ihesu Nazareni surge et* 35
ambula. Et iuxta istud templum in parte dextra est vna ecclesia plumbo
cooperta que vocatur Scola Salomonis. Et ab isto templo satis prope
versus meridiem est templum Salomonis in quadam magna placia et
bene plana pulcre situm. In isto templo fuerunt quondam milites templi
qui dicebantur templarii, et hic inicium et fundamentum ordinis eorum 40
habuerunt ita quod hic habitabant milites, et in templo domini canonici
regulares. . . .

Et subtus istam ecclesiam descendendo per xxii. gradus iacet [f. 58ᵛ]
Ioachim pater sancte Marie. . . . Item, scien*dum* est quod fuerunt

quondam tres Herodes famosi propter eorum crudelitatem. Iste de quo superius locutus sum Herodes erat Ascoloni[f. 59]ta; et qui Iohannem baptistam decapitauit erat Herodes Antipas; et qui sanctum Iacobum occidit et Petrum incarcerauit erat Agrippa. . . .

5   Et ab ista ecclesia ad cxx. passus est mons Syon vbi est pulcra ecclesia sancte Marie vbi morabatur et moriebatur. Ibi erant quondam canonici regulares cum suo abbate, et ab ista ecclesia delata erat ab apostolis in vallem Iosephat. Ibi est lapis quem angelus de monte Synay sancte Marie detulit, et est eiusdem coloris sicut rupes sancte Katerine. Et ibi 10   iuxta est porta per quam egressa est sancta Maria eundo versus Bethleem.

Item, in introitu montis Syon est vna capella in qua est lapis grandis et magnus cum quo Ioseph ab Aramathia Cristum in sepulcro clausit, et istum lapidem viderunt iii. Marie die resurreccionis a monumento reuolutum et angelos dicentes eis quia surrexit Cristus. Ibi eciam est 15   pars columpne ad quam Cristus erat flagellatus, et ibi iuxta erat domus Anne qui erat tunc temporis pontifex Iudeorum. . . .

Et ibi est altare super quod sancta Maria angelos missa canentes [f. 59ᵛ] audiuit. Ibi eciam apparuit dominus primo post resurreccionem discipulis suis ianuis clausis et dixit eis *Pax vobis*. . . .

20   Item, mons Syon est infra ciuitatem et est ciuitas altior et fortior ex illa parte quam ex aliqua alia, quia ad pedem montis est vnum pulcrum et forte castellum a soldano edificatum.

Item, in monte Syon sepulti erant Dauid et Salomon et plures alii Iudei reges de Ierusalem. Ibi est locus vbi Iudei corpus domini precipi- 25   tasse volebant. . . .

Item, sub monte Syon versus vallem Iosephat est fons quidam qui vocatur *Natatorium Syloe*. Ibi erat Cristus post baptismum lotus. Ibi aperuit oculos ceci nati. Ibi sepultus erat Ysaias propheta. Item, in introitu Natatorie Syloe est ymago quedam lapidea antiquo opere dudum 30   ab Absolon filio Dauid facta, que vsque hodie *manus Absolon* vocatur. Et ibi iuxta est arbor de Sehur super quam Iudas postquam [f. 60] tradidit Cristum desperans suspendit se. . . .

[1122] Item, ex alia parte ad cc. passus a Ierusalem est vna ecclesia vbi solebat esse caua leonum. Et subtus istam ecclesiam descendendo per 35   xxx. gradus sepulta erant xii. milia martirum tempore Cosdre regis, quorum corpora per leones in vna nocte diuina prouidencia erant coadunata.

Item, ab Ierusalem ad ii. miliaria est mons Gaudii pulcher locus et deliciosus. Ibi iacet sanctus Samuel propheta in vna pulcra tumba. Et 40   dicitur mons Gaudii eo quod peregrini venientes de partibus istis ibidem primo vident sanctam ciuitatem.

Item, inter Ierusalem et montem [f. 60ᵛ] Oliueti est vallis Iosephat sub muris ciuitatis (sicut alias dixi), et in medio istius vallis est riuulus quidam qui dicitur Torrens Cedron. . . .

[1175] Item, in medio istius vallis Iosephat est ecclesia sancte Marie in qua descendens per viginti quatuor gradus ad sepulcrum eius, et erat etate quando moriebatur sexaginta quatuor annorum. Et iuxta sepulcrum beate Marie est vnum altare vbi Cristus remisit Petro sua peccata. Et ibi iuxta versus occidentem sub vno altare est fons quidam de 5 paradiso veniens. . . . Et iuxta istam ecclesiam est vna capella iuxta rupem que vocatur Gethsemane. Ibi osculabatur Iudas Cristum. Ibi captus erat a Iudeis. Ibi dimissis discipulis suis abiit et orauit patrem dicens: *Pater si potest fieri transeat a me calix iste*. Et venit ad discipulos suos et inuenit illos dormientes. Et in rupe supra capellam apparent 10 digiti saluatoris sicut rupi adhesit quando Iudei eum capere volebant. Et vltra illum locum ad iactum vnius lapidis versus meridiem est vna alia capella vbi Cristus sanguinem sudauit. Et satis prope ibidem est sepulcrum regis Iosephat a quo vallis nomen sumpsit. . . .

Ab ista valle est mons Oliueti et dicitur Oliueti propter oliuas ibidem 15 crescentes. Iste mons altior est ciuitate Ierusalem [f. 61] et super istum montem omnes vici ciuitatis videntur. . . .

[1197] Et descendendo de monte Oliueti versus orientem est vnum castellum Bethania nomine. Ibi morabatur Simon leprosus, et ibi dominum in suo hospicio recepit postea ab apostolis baptizatus. . . . In 20 eodem loco Maria Magdalene lacrimis lauit pedes domini et capillis tersit, et ibi dimissa sunt ei peccata sua. Ibi eciam ministrabat Martha domino. Ibi suscitauit dominus Lazarum earum fratrem quatriduanum mortuum. Ibi habitabat Maria Cleophe. . . . Et in medio vie a monte Oliueti ad [f. 61ᵛ] montem Galilee est vna ecclesia vbi angelus sancte 25 Marie suam mortem intimauit. . . .

[1225] Et inter istum montem et istum gardinum currit riuulus aque. Ista aqua quondam erat amara et salsa sed per benedictionem Helisei prophete in dulcedinem versa est. Et ad pedem istius montis penes planiciem est fons quidam magnus qui in flumen Iordanis intrat. Ab 30 isto monte ad Iericho superius nominato est vnum miliare eundo versus flumen Iordanis. Item, iuxta viam de [f. 62] Iericho sedebat cecus et clamabat *Ihesu fili Dauid miserere mei* et statim visum recepit.

Item, ad ii. miliaria ab Iericho est flumen Iordanis, et magis prope per vnam leucam est vna pulcra ecclesia sancti Iohannis baptiste vbi 35 Cristum baptizauit. Et ibi iuxta erat domus Ieremie prophete. Et a Iericho ad iii. miliaria est mare mortuum, et inter Iericho et istud mare est terra Dengadde. Ibi quondam crescebat balsamum, sed homines arbores illius radicitus extrahentes apud Babiloniam plantauerunt et adhuc vocantur vites Dengadde. 40

CHAPTER XII

Item, ex vna parte istius maris descendendo ab Arabia est mons Moabitarum, vbi est quedam caua que *Karna* dicitur, et super istum

montem Balach filius Boor duxit Balaam vt malediceret et excomuni-
caret populum Israel. Istud mare mortuum separat Iudeam ab Arabia
et extendit de se Zoara vsque ad Arabiam. Aqua istius maris salsa est et
amara, et si terra fuerit ista aqua irrigata non fructificat. Et terra illius
5 sepe suum mutat colorem. Et proicit ista aqua ex se omni die et ex omni
parte quamdam rem quam homines *aspaltum* vocant, et sunt magna
frustra equinis corporibus grossiora.

[1238] Et de Ierusalem ad istud mare sunt cc. stadia. Istud mare dᶜ. et
lxxx. stadia continet in longitudine et cl. in latitudine. Et dicitur
10 mortuum eo quod non currit, nec homo nec bestia in eo potest mori,
et hoc sepe extitit probatum. Nam homines qui mortem meruerant in
eo sepe submersi fuerant et per tres dies vel quatuor ibidem morantes
mori non poterant; nam non recipit aliquid in se vitam habens nec
aliquis de eo potest bibere. Et si imponas ferrum supra natabit, si vero
15 plumam ad fundum descendit, et hoc est contra naturam. Et similiter
ciuitates ibidem constructe propter peccatum contra naturam perierunt.
Et ibi iuxta sunt arbores poma portantes visu pulcra matura et bene
colorata, sed si frangantur vel diuidantur per medium, cineribus sunt
plena in signum quod terra et ciuitates ille ira dei igne infernali in
20 cineres redacte erant. Aliqui istud mare vocant [f. 62ᵛ] lacum de
Alficide, alii flumen diaboli, alii flumen fetidum.

[1255] In istud mare dei vindicta descenderunt iste v. ciuitates, Sodoma,
Gomorra, Aldama, Seboyma, et Segor, propter peccatum sodomiticum
quod in eis regnabat. Sed Segor precibus Loth diu erat saluata, nam
25 sita erat in declino montis. Et adhuc apparet in parte sub aqua, nam
quando tempus fuerit clarum et tranquillum, eius muri infra aquam
videntur. . . .

Item, in istud mare intrat flumen Iordanis nec vltra currit, et hoc est
miliario vno ab ecclesia sancti Iohannis baptiste vbi cristiani se comuniter
30 lauant et balneant. Versus occidentem et miliario vno a flumine Iordanis
est mare Laboth quod Iacob pertransiuit veniens de Mesopotamnia.
Iste fluuius Iordanis non est [f. 63] multum magnus vel largus, bonis
tamen piscibus habundat, et venit de monte Libani de duobus fontibus
qui vocantur Ior et Dan. Et ab istis fontibus nomen et originem trahit.
35 Et transit per lacum qui Marron dicitur et per mare Tiberiadis et sub
montibus Gelboe, et est pulcra vallis nimis ex vtraque parte fluminis et
venit de montibus Libani totum in longitudine vsque desertum
Pharaonis. Isti montes diuidunt regnum Sirie et terram Phinicie. Super
istos montes crescunt arbores cedrine portantes longa poma et magna
40 ad quantitatem capitis humani. . . .

Item, in isto fluuio Iordanis Naaman Syrus lauit se et a leprosia
mundatus est. Et circa flumen Iordanis sunt multe ecclesie vbi plures
cristiani habitant. Et satis prope est ciuitas de Hay quam Iosue obsedit
et cepit. . . .

Item, a mari mortuo eundo versus orientem extra terminos promissionis [f. 63ᵛ] terre est quoddam castellum pulcrum et fortissimum in monte situm, quod lingua eorum Carac dicitur et sonat in latino *regaliter*. . . . Et satis prope est sepulcrum Ioseph filii Iacob, nam Iudei egredientes de Egipto ossa eius secum tulerunt [f. 64] et ibidem 5 sepelierunt. . . .

Nam Iulianus imperator ex sua crudelitate istam partem cum ceteris ossibus concremauit sicut apparet, et istud est per papas et imperatores approbatum. Et pars sub [f. 64ᵛ] mento et quedam porcio cinerum et discus in quo erat caput post decollationem missum sunt 10 apud Ianuam. . . .

Item, a Sebasta ciuitate ad Ierusalem xii. sunt miliaria. Et inter montes istius patrie est fons quidam qui quater in anno suum mutat colorem, nam aliquando est viridis, aliquando rubeus, aliquando clarus, aliquando turbidus, et vocatur fons Iob. . . . 15

In ista terra habitant plures Iudei sub tributo sicut et cristiani. Et si volueris scire litteras Iudeorum qui ibidem et alibi morantur, sunt tales cum nominibus subscriptis: *Aleph*ᵃ, *Beth*ᵇ, *Cunel*ᶜ, et cetera quere in originali.

CHAPTER XIII

De ista terra Samaritanorum de qua locutus sum venies ad planicies 20 Galilee dimittendo montes a latere, et est Galilea vna de prouinciis terre promissionis. In ista prouincia est ciuitas Naym et Capharnaum, Corosaym, Bethsay[da] [*end of* f. 64ᵛ, *the next quire is lost*].

CHAPTER XV

[f. 65] vnus deus quia Alkoranus eorum nil tangit de trinitate. Sed dicunt quod deus habet verbum quia aliter esset mutus, et quod habet 25 spiritum bene sciunt quia aliter non viueret. Item, quando aliquis eis loquitur de incarnacione quomodo per verbum angeli deus sapientiam misit in terram et in virgine Maria inumbrata erat et per verbum dei die iudicii mortui resuscitabuntur, dicunt quod hoc est verum. Et dicunt quod verbum dei magnam vim habet, et qui ignorant verbum 30 dei deum ignorant. Et dicunt quod Ihesus Cristus est verbum dei, et sic dicit eorum Alkoranus ibi vbi dicit quod angelus loquebatur Marie dicens, Maria deus tibi euangelizauit verbum ex ore suo et vocabitur nomen eius Ihesus Cristus. . . .

[f. 66] Alii Agareni ab Agar, et alii proprie Saraceni a Sarra [f. 66ᵛ] 35 sed sunt alii qui dicuntur Moabbite et Ammonite a duobus filiis Loth. . . .

Iam ostendam si placet quales litteras habent cum nominibus: *Ohnoy*, *Betach*, et cetera in originale. Et istas quatuor litteras habent plus propter diuersitatem quia locuntur in gutture, sicut nos de Anglia

habemus duas litteras plures in nostra lingua quam in eorum a.b.c.,
videlicet þ et ʒ, que dicuntur *þorn* et *ʒok*.

CHAPTER XVI

[f. 67] **P**ostquam superius de terra sancta et aliis terris circumiacen-
tibus et de diuersis viis ad eandem terram et ad montem Synai et ad
5 Babilonem minorem et ad alia loca superius nominata tendentibus
locutus sum; modo tempus deposcit vt de aliis terris et insulis diuersis
gentibus et bestiis vltra terminos illos loquar, quia vltra illas superius
nominatas sunt plures alie patrie, diuerse regiones, et insule per quatuor
flumina paradisi terrestri diuise.
10 [1623] Nam Mesopotania et regnum Caldee et Arabie sunt inter dua
flumina Tigris et Eufrates. Et regnum Medorum et Persarum sunt inter
dua flumina Nili et Tigris et regnum Sirie (de quo superius locutus
sum). Et Palestina et Finecia sunt inter Eufrates et mare Mediterraneum,
quod mare extendit se in longitudine a Marrok super mare Hispanie
15 vsque mare magnum, ita quod durat vltra Constantinopolim per iii.
milia et xl. leucas Lumbardorum.
[1639] Et versus mare occeanum in Indiam est regnum Sichie montibus
vndique clausum. Deinde sub Sichia et a mari Caspeo vsque ad flumen
de Thamar est Amazonia. Hec terra feminarum est vbi nulli sunt
20 homines sed omnes mulieres.
[1647] Deinde est Albania, magnum regnum et largum, et vocatur
Albania quia homines illius albiores sunt ceteris in partibus illis. Et
sunt ita magni canes et feroces ibidem quod insecuntur et occidunt
leones.
25 [1657] Postea vero est Hircania, Bactira, Hyberia, et multe alie regiones.
Et inter mare rubrum et mare occeanum versus meridiem est regnum
Ethiopie et Libie superioris, que terra Libie inferior incipit ad colump-
nas Herculis extendens se versus Egiptum et versus Ethiopiam.
[1613] In ista Libia mare altius est terra, et apparet itinerentibus quod
30 totam terram vellet transcurrere, et tamen metas suas non excedit. Et
in ista terra est mons quidam ad quem nullus approximare potest. In
ista terra Libie qui se vertit contra orientem vmbra corporis sui erit
a dextris, et in partibus nostris erit a sinistris.
[1619] Mare Libicum piscibus caret nam aqua illius propter nimium
35 solis calorem semper bulliens eos viuere non permittit. Et multe alie
terre sunt [f. 67ᵛ] quas omnes numerare longum esset, sed de aliquibus
earum plenius tibi inferius loquar.
Si ergo versus Tartariam, Persidam, Caldeam, vel Indiam transire
volueris, mare apud Ianuam vel Veniciam vel ad aliquem portum
40 superius nominatum accipies et venies per mare et applicabis ad

31 approximare] MS. approxiari

Trepezondam, que est bona ciuitas et vocabatur quondam Porta
Poncium. Ibi est rex Persarum et Medorum et aliarum terrarum
ibidem. . . .

[1545] De Trapezonda venies per paruam Armeniam si volueris. In ista
patria vltra ciuitatem de Layais est quoddam antiquum castellum super 5
rupem situm, quod Castellum Imperatoris dicitur, et iuxta ciuitatem
de Percipie, que est in dominio domini de Crok, qui est diues homo et
bonus cristianus. Nisum quemdam super vnam perticam inuenies
formosum nimis et elegantem quem custodit vna pulcra domina de faire.
Qui voluerit istum nisum vii. diebus et vii. noctibus (et quidam dicunt 10
tribus diebus et tribus noctibus) solus sine socio et sompno vigilare,
ista pulcra domina in finem vii. vel iii. dierum dabit sibi peticionem
quamcumque imprecari voluerit de rebus terrenis. Et hoc sepe extitit
probatum.

[1581] Et rex quidam Armenie magnus [f. 68] et valens princeps istum 15
nisum quondam vigilauit. Et ad finem vii. dierum venit ista domina
precipiens vt peteret quia debitum suum bene fecerat. Qui dixit quod
magnus et potens erat rex in terra diuiciis satis habundans, et nil vellet
petere nisi illam pulcram dominam et de ea suam voluntatem. Et domina
ad eum: Fatuus es et nescis quid petis, terrenum quidem petere deberes, 20
et ego spiritualis sum nec me habere potes. Et rex semper perseuerabat
nil aliud petens preter illam. Et domina ad eum: ex quo, inquit, non
possum te a tua voluptate retrahere, ego dabo tibi et omnibus ex te
descentibus donum sine aliqua peticione. Me, inquit, carebis. Guerram
continuam sine firma pace semper habebis, in subieccione inimicorum 25
tuorum vsque in nonam generacionem eris, bonis et diuiciis semper
egens. Et numquam postmodum erat rex Armenie in terra, immo
semper extiterunt in subieccione et sub tributo Saracenorum.

[1573] Item, filius cuiusdam pauperis hominis similiter vigilabat et
petiit quod posset esse fortunatus in mercando. Et domina concessit, 30
et erat postea nominatissimus et famosissimus mercator mundi per mare
et per terram, et deuenit ita diues quod nesciuit m¹. partem bonorum
suorum. Et sic iste pauper in peticione sua sapientior erat dicto rege.

Item, miles quidam Templi vigilauit similiter et petiit bursam auro
semper plenam. Et domina concessit sed adiecit in fine quod petiit de- 35
structionem ordinis sui, quia ob confidenciam illius burse futuri erant ita
superbi quod propter eorum superbiam destruerentur. Et sic fuit. Et
caueat bene quod semper vigilet quia si dormiat in parte vel in toto
non erit amplius visus super terram.

Ista non est via recta ad partes superius nominatas nisi forte aliquis 40
voluerit ista mirabilia videre, et ideo si viam rectam tenere volueris,
venies de Trepezonda ad magnam Armeniam ad vnam ciuitatem que

33 dicto] MS. dīte

vocatur Artiron. Ista erat quondam magna ciuitas et opulenta, sed a Turcis multum destructa et vastata est. Vino tamen et fructu caret.

In ista patria terra alta est et calida valde [f. 68ᵛ] et sunt ibi dulces aque et fontes perlucidi qui veniunt subtus terram de Eufrates, flumen
5 paradisi a predicta ciuitate per vnam dietam distante. Et venit istud flumen de partibus Indie subtus terram, et in terra Altasar exit et currit super terram et transit per istam Armeniam et intrat in mare Perside. [1688] Transiens inde de ciuitate Artiron venies ad vnum montem qui Sabissacol dicitur, et ibi iuxta est alius mons Ararath nomine, sed Iudei
10 ipsum Tano vocant. Super quem requieuit archa Noe, et adhuc ibi requiescita quando tempus clarum fuerit a longe videtur. Et continet mons bene vii. leucas altitudinis. Et dicunt quidam quod viderunt et tetigerunt archam et digitum suum in foramen per quod diabolus egrediebatur quando Noe *benedicite* dixit posuerunt. Sed qui talia verba
15 proferunt propriam voluntatem secuntur, quia super istum montem est tanta copia niuis, tam in estate quam in yeme, quod nulli homini patet ascensus; nec vnquam citra tempus Noe aliquis ascendit preter monachum vnum qui gracia dei ascendit et tabulam vnam de archa secum detulit, que in monasterio ad pedem montis hodie demonstratur.
20 [1701] Iste monachus montem istum ascendere multum desiderabat, vnde die quadam velle suum implere cupiens ascendit. Et cum iam terciam partem montis attingissit, vlterius pro lassitudine ire non potuit, vnde labore fessus obdormiuit. Qui post sompnum vigilans inuenit se ad pedem montis positum, qui dolens precibus continuis dominum
25 precabatur vt ipsum ascendere permitteret. Et venit ei angelus precepitque vt ascenderet, et sic fecit. Et numquam deinceps aliquis, quare talibus verbis non est fides adhibenda.

[1740] Et ibi iuxta est ciuitas Delasayne a Noe fundata, et satis prope est ciuitas de Any in qua quondam mˡ. ecclesie fuerunt. De isto monte
30 venies ad ciuitatem de Thauriso que quondam Faxis vocabatur, et est magna et pulcra ciuitas et per mercimoniis vna de nobilioribus mundi. Nam ibi confluunt mercatores pro omnibus mercimoniis habendis et est in terra imperatoris Perside, et dicunt homines quod imperator plus [f. 69] recipit de ista ciuitate causa mercimoniorum quam aliquis rex
35 mundi cristianus de toto regno suo.

[1750] Iuxta istam ciuitatem est mons salis, de quo vnusquisque pro rebus suis saliendis sine precio capit quantum sibi placuerit. Ibi eciam sunt multi cristiani sub tributo Saracenorum.

Ab ista ciuitate inde transiens venies versus Indiam per multas villas
40 et castella vsque ad ciuitatem Cadomam per x. dietas a predicta Thauriso distantem, que nobilis et regalis est ciuitas. Ibi estiuo tempore moratur imperator Perside quia patria frigida est et temperata. Et sunt ibi amene silue, flumina quoque nauigium portantia.

39 venies] MS. veĩens

Deinde viam versus Indiam semper tenens per multas dietas et multas
patrias venies ad ciuitatem Cassach nomine, que nobilis est ciuitas
tritici, vini, et omnium bonorum opilentissima. In ista ciuitate tres
magi reges gracia diuina sibi obuiauerunt et versus Bethleem vt Cristum
in carne natum adorarent cum muneribus similiter perrexerunt. Et ab 5
ista ciuitate ad Bethleem liii. sunt diete, et tamen infra ix. dies totum
miraculose peregerunt.

[1762] Deinde procedens venies ad vnam aliam ciuitatem Gethe nomine,
miliario vno a mari arenoso distantem. Ista nobilissima est ciuitas totius
terre imperatoris Perside. Ibi vocant homines carnes *Dabago* et vinum 10
Vapa. Et dicunt pagani quod cristiani in ista ciuitate diu viuere non
possunt, quin infra breue tempus morientur, et tam ab omnibus
ignoratur. Deinde venies per multas ciuitates et villas, quas numerare
longum esset, vsque ad ciuitatem Cornaam que quondam tam magna
erat quod muri eius xxv. miliaria in circuitu continebant, et muri adhuc 15
apparent sed ciuitas non est tota inhabitata. De Cornaa venies per
multas terras et plures villas vsque ad terram Iob, et ibi terminatur
terra imperatoris Perside. Et si litteras Persarum scire volueris, sunt
tales que hic scribuntur: *Aliu*ᵃ, *Bem*ᵇ, *Cem*ᶜ, et cetera in originale.

CHAPTER XVII

De ciuitate igitur Cornaa recedens venies in terram Iob, que pulcra 20
est patria et bonis omnibus [f. 69ᵛ] habundantissima et vocatur ab incolis
Sweze. In ista terra est ciuitas Temar. Iste Iob filius erat Cosre. . . .
[1776] In ista terra Iob nil humano corpori necessarium deest. Ibi
eciam sunt montes in quibus melius manna mundi inuenitur. Manna
dicitur panis angelorum et est res quedam alba melle et sucara dulcior 25
et deliciosior, et venit et generatur de rore celi super herbas terre illius
cadente, et coagulatur et fit dulcis et alba. Et ponitur pro diuitibus in
medicina nam ventrem laxat, malum sanguinem purificat, malencoliam
tollit. Ista terra Iob extendit se ad regnum Caldee, et est Caldea terra magna
valde et habet linguam propriam ceteris vltra mare grossiorem. Et 30
veniendo versus Caldeam transitum facies iuxta turrim Babilonie. Ista
est illa Babilon magna (de qua superius locutus sum) vbi lingue primo
mutate erant et inuente, a Caldea per quatuor dietas distans. . . .

Item, in Caldea est ciuitas Hur, vbi quondam morabatur pater Abrahe
ibique natus erat Abraham [f. 70] eodem tempore quo Ninus erat rex 35
Babilonie, Arabie, et Egipti. Iste Ninus ciuitatem Niniue a Noe primo
inceptam perfecit et conpleuit et ipsam a suo nomine Niniue appellauit.
Ibi iacet Tobias propheta, de quo loquitur sancta scriptura. De ista
ciuitate Hur dei precepto post mortem patris sui discessit Abraham vt
habitaret in terra Chanaan in loco qui Sichen dicitur, secum ducens 40
Sarram vxorem suam et Loth filium patris sui. Iste est Loth qui in

subuersione Sodome et Gomorre (sicut tibi alias dixi) saluatus erat. Item, Caldei suum proprium ideoma habent et sua proprias litteras prout hic apparent, [*four characters follow*] et cetera in originale.

[1800] Deinde iuxta Caldeam est Amazonia que terra feminarum dicitur,
5 vbi omnes sunt mulieres et nulli homines; non, vt quidam asserunt, quod homines ibidem viuere non possunt sed quia nolunt eos eis dominari. Nam in ista terra erat quondam rex et sicut in aliis terris homines coniungati. Vnde contigit regem istius terre Colopense nomine bellum contra Sichios suscepisse, qui rex cum toto nobili sanguine sui
10 regni in bello occubunt. Quod regina et alie domine terre, audientes se viduas factas et totum generosum sanguinem destructum, ad arma cucurrerunt et omnes alios homines in terra relictos gladiis occiderunt. Et sic ceteras mulieres secum viduas fecerunt. Et ab illo tempore et deinceps numquam aliquem hominem vltra septem dies inter eas esse
15 permiserunt. Nec infantem masculum nutriuerunt, sed quando societatem vel solacium hominum habere voluerint, ad partes vicinas se transferunt et ibi cum amasiis suis viii. vel x. diebus moram trahunt et tunc ad propriam redeunt. Et si forte inpregnate fuerint, si masculus fuerit, statim vt eundi vel edendi facultatem adeptus est, aut ad patrem
20 mittunt aut eum occidunt. Si vero femina, vnam mamillam cum calido ferro abscidunt; nam si sit nobilis et generosa sinistram mamillam amputant vt scutum melius regere et portare possit; si vero pedissequa, dextram ne forte impediretur archum trahendo.

In ista terra est vna regina que totam patriam [f. 70ᵛ] regit et gubernat,
25 et omnes eius preceptis parent et obediunt. Et faciunt semper reginam per electionem de valentioribus in armis, et sunt bone sapientes et valentes bellatores et sunt stipendiarii in auxilium aliorum regum sepe conducti, et digne et laudabiliter et victoriose in armis se gerunt et defendunt.

30 Ista terra Amazonia *immo* est insula aqua vndique cincta et circumdata exceptis duobus locis vbi sunt duo introitus. Et vltra istam aquam habitant earum amasii, quos quotiens eis placuerit vadunt et visitant.

Item, iuxta Amazoniam est terra Turmagitta bona quondam patria et deliciosa, cuius bonitate Alexander rex delectatus primam suam
35 Alexandriam ibi fundauit. Nam xii. ciuitates construxit quas a suo nomine Alexandrias vocauit. Sed ciuitas hec modo Celsita appellatur.

Item, ex alia parte Caldee versus meridiem est Ethiopia, magna patria ad fines Egipti se extendens, que in duas partes principales diuisa est, orientalem videlicet et meridionalem, que pars meridionalis Morecan
40 appellatur. Ibi sunt homines nigriores quam alibi.

[1834] Et in ista parte est fons quidam; aqua de die tam frigida est vt non bibatur, et in nocte tam calida vt non tangatur. Et vltra istam

14 eas] MS. eos   30 immo] MS. in vna

partem meridionalem transeundo per mare occeanum est magna terra
et magna patria propter nimium calorem inhabitabi*lis*, et omnes aque
Ethiope propter continuum solis calorem turbide sunt et salse. Homi-
nesque istius terre de facili inebriantur et parum appetunt comedere,
fluxumque ventris comuniter paciuntur, nec diu viuunt. Item, Ethiopia 5
Cusis appellata est et sunt in ea plures diuerse gentes. Quidam sunt vno
tantum pede incedentes mire et incredibilis velocitatis homines, et est
pes tam magnus et largus quod resupini contra solem vmbra illius totum
corpus tegunt.

In Ethiopia pueri primo sunt glauci, deinde crescente etate fiunt nigri. 10
In Ethiopia est ciuitas Saba in terra de qua vnus trium magorum qui
venerant Cristum in Bethleem adorare erat rex et dominus.

De Ethiopia per multas diuersas terras et patrias venies in Indiam in
tres principales partes diuisa[m], est enim India [f. 71] maior que alta
terra est et calida; India minor que temperata est ad terram Medorum 15
se extendens; et tercia pars versus septemtrionem frigidissima est, ita
quod propter nimium frigus et continuum gelu aqua fit cristallum, et
super istas rupes cristallinas crescunt optimi diamantes. Et apparent
turbidi coloris in modum glauci cristalli, in parte ad colorem olei se
trahentis, et sunt ita duri quod non possunt polliri. Et vocant homines 20
in ista patria diamantes *hamese*. Alii diamantes inueniuntur in Arabia
qui non sunt ita boni sed sunt molliores et magis bruni. Alii in Cipro
insula inueniuntur qui molliores sunt et bene possunt polliri. Alii
inueniuntur in Macedonia sed meliores et preciosiores sunt in India.
Inueniuntur eciam sepe duri diamantes in massa illa que egreditur de 25
aurifodina vbi homines aurum fodiunt quando massa illa in paruas
partes vel pecias diuisa fuerit. Contingit aliquando vnum reperiri ad
quantitatem pise, alium minoris quantitatis. . . . Et crescunt plures simul
parui et magni, et sunt quidam bene ad quantitatem nucis coruli, et
omnes naturaliter sunt quadrati et punctati subtus et supra sine aliquo 30
humano opere. Et crescunt simul masculus et femina, et de rore celi
nutriuntur et coeunt et generant et paruos filios iuxta eos producunt
qui omni anno multiplicantur et crescunt. Ego sepe probaui quod si
seruantur cum modica rupis porcione et non tollantur de radice et quod
sepe de rore maii rigantur, crescunt visibiliter et parui fient bene magni, 35
quia sicut vera margarita de rore celi coadunatur et ingressatur, eodem
modo facit verus diamas. Et sicut margarita ex sua natura rotunditatem
accipit, pari modo diamas virtute diuina quadraturam recipit. Et debet
diamas portari semper a parte sinistra vbi maioris est virtutis quam in
parte dextra, quia vis sue originis et essencie versus septemtrionem est 40
que est sinistra pars mundi et similiter [f. 71ᵛ] sinistra pars hominis
quando faciem suam contra orientem vertit. Et licet virtutes diamantis

2 inhabitabilis] MS. inhītabilē   14 diuisam] MS. dīsa

178 APPENDIX A

lapidarium tibi liquide demonstrat, ego tamen propter aliquos igno-
rantes virtutes eius hic tibi ostendam, prout ipsi in partibus illis trans-
marinis affirmant a quibus omnes sapientie et prophecia descenderunt . .

CHAPTER XVIII

[1856] [f. 72] Item, plures alie terre diuerseque patrie sunt ibidem, et
5 dicitur India ab Indo flumine per terram currente. In isto flumine sunt
anguille triginta pedum longitudinis. Et homines iuxta istum fluuium
degentes virides sunt et glauci pessimeque colorati.

In India et in circuitu Indie sunt plusquam v. milia insularum
habitabilium bonarum et magnarum exceptis aliis inhabitabilibus et
10 aliis paruis. Et in qualibet insula est magna copia ciuitatum, villarum,
et gentium sine numero. Nam Indi talis sunt nature quod terras suas
libenter non exeunt quia sunt directe sub Saturno, qui planeta duodecim
signa firmamenti triginta annis peragrat, et quia tam tardi motus est
homines sunt eo degentes et in natura cum eo participantes non sunt
15 multum mobiles. . . .

[1867] Item, venies per Indiam per multas diuersas patrias vsque ad
magnum mare occeanum. [f. 72�v] Deinde inuenies vnam insulam Ermes
nomine vbi mercatores Venicie et Ianue pro diuersis mercimoniis
emendis sepe conueniunt. Sed tanta est caliditas in ista terra quod,
20 propter nimium et intensum calorem magnamque corporis dissolu-
cionem, testiculi hominum corpus exeunt ad mediam vsque tibiam
dependentes, quod malum incole terre precauentes districte eos ligant
vnguentesque restrictiuis ad restringendum corpus se inungunt, vel
aliter non viuerent nec sustinerent . . . [*the next quire is lost*].

CHAPTER XXI

25 [f. 73] carnes eorum comedunt loco carnium ferinarum. Deinde venies
per multas insulas maris vsque ad vnam insulam Melka nomine vbi
eciam sunt homines pessime nature, nam in nulla re mundi tantum
delectantur sicut in morte et in occasione hominum. Libenter enim
humanum sanguinem bibunt, quem sanguinem *deum* appellant, et qui
30 plures possit occidere plus inter eos honoratur. . . .

Preteriens inde venies per mare occeanum per multas insulas vsque
ad vnam insulam pulcram et bonam nomine Nacumeran, continens in
giro plusquam mille miliaria. Cuius incole omnes vtriusque sexus capita
habent canina, qui Cenosaphali vocantur, et sunt rationabiles valde et
35 intelligibiles et bouem pro deo adorant. Et vnusquisque bouem aureum
vel argenteum in fronte portat in signum amoris sui dei. Et vadunt
semper nudi preter pannum paruulum de quo genua et membra
cooperiunt, et sunt magni homines et bellicosi et portant vnum scutum
magnum et largum cum quo corpus totum tegunt et vnam lanceam.

Et si aliquem in bello capiunt ipsum comedunt. Item, rex istius insule [f. 73ᵛ] multum diues est et potens et secundum suam legem deuotus valde. . . .

De ista insula recedens venies ad vnam aliam Silha nomine, que octingenta bene miliaria in circuitu continet. Istius insule magna pars 5 vasta est et deserta vbi tanta est copia serpentum, draconum, et cocodrillorum quod nullus ibidem morari potest. . . . [1898] Et istam aquam ex lacrimis eorum esse nam tam diu ibidem plorauerunt quousque [f. 74] lacum istum sic lacrimis impleuerunt. Et ad fundum istius lacus inueniuntur preciosi lapides et grosse margarite, 10 et in lacu crescunt magne arundines. Et sunt in eo multi cocodrilli, serpentes, et magni sanguisugi. Et rex terre omni anno semel licenciam dat pauperibus de isto lacu lapides preciosos colligendi, et hoc propter elemosinam et pro amore dei Ade. Et licet sic colligantur, sufficienter tamen inueniuntur. Et propter venenosas vermes infra aquam inungunt 15 sibi brachia et tibia de succo limonis, qui est quoddam genus fructus cuius odorem ferre non possunt, et sic non timent cocodrillos vel aliquod venenosum animal. . . .

Item, in ista insula et in aliis insulis ibidem mare est ita altum quod apparet quod tangit nubes et quod totam terram transcurrere et operire 20 vellet, et hoc est magnum mirabile quomodo potest sic teneri preter voluntatem die quod aer illud ita sustentat. Et ideo dicit Dauid in psalmo, *Mirabiles elaciones maris*, et cetera.

CHAPTER XXII

De ista insula transeundo per mare versus meridiem est vna alia insula magna et lata que Dodyn vocatur. In qua sunt gentes diuerse 25 nature ita quod pater comedit filium et filius patrem, maritus vxorem et vxor maritum. Nam si contingat patrem vel matrem vel amicum alicuius infirmari, statim filius venit ad presbiterum legis, rogans eum vt querat ab ydolo eorum vtrum pater eius ex illa infirmitate morietur vel non. Tunc presbiter et filius simul ante idolum veniunt et deuotis- 30 sime genua flectunt et cum magna deuocione questionem suam [f. 74ᵛ] ab eo querunt. Et diabolus infra ydolum respondet et dicit quod non morietur ista vice, et docet eos quomodo eum curabunt. Et tunc filius domum reuertitur et sicut doctus est ab ydolo patrem suum ab infirmi- tate curat et releuat. Et sic faciunt vxores pro viris suis, viri pro vxoribus, 35 amicus pro amico, et quilibet pro alio. Sed si ydolum dicat quod morietur, tunc presbiter cum filio et cum vxore infirmi ad eum accedit, et pannum super os eius ponit et sic flatu extincto eum suffocat et occidit.

Deinde totum corpus in frustra diuidit et incidit, et omnes cognatos 40

16 limonis] MS. linionis

et amicos inuitat vt de isto mortuo comedant, omnesque ministrallos
patrie quos inuenire possunt conuocant et eum cum maxima solemnitate
comedunt. Et postquam carnem comederint, ossa eius sepeliunt can-
tantes maximamque melodiam facientes. Et omnes cognati et amici qui
5 isti festo non interfuerunt sunt reprobati et verecundati, magnumque
dolorem faciunt quia numquam amplius pro amicis reputabuntur. Et
dicunt amici quod sic eius carnem comedunt vt eum de penis eripiant,
nam si vermes eum in terra comederent anima eius iuxta eos penam
maximam pateretur. Et quando carnem macilentam inueniunt, dicunt
10 amici quod grauiter peccauerunt quod eum tam diu languescere
fecerunt et tam magnam penam sine ratione pati permiserunt. Et quando
carnem crassam et pinguem inueniunt, hoc multum laudant et dicunt
quod statim sine pena in paradisum mittitur. . . .

CHAPTER XXVII

[f. 89] Terra hec de Chatay est in Assia profunda. Deinde citra est
15 Assia maior. Regnum de Chatay versus occidentem extendit se ad
regnum Tharsis, cuius regni vnus ex regibus qui venera[n]t in Bethleem
adorare Christum erat dominus. . . . [f. 89ᵛ] Et versus caput istius regni
est mons Choas altissimus mundi. Et inter mare Maure et Caspium ibi
est angusta via strictusque transitus eundi versus Indiam. . . .

CHAPTER XXVIII

20 [f. 90] Et a meridie deserta Indie ista est bona patria et opulenta et
bene populosa multasque bonas ciuitates in se continet. Sed due
principaliores sunt Bactira et Seomergant, quam quidam Sozmagant
appellant. . . . [f. 90ᵛ] In isto regno de Abchaz est vnum magnum
mirabile. Nam vna prouincia patrie bene tres dietas in circuitu habens
25 quam homines Hamysoun vocant, tota tenebris est cooperta sine aliqua
luce. . . .
[f. 91] Nunc vero superius versus Indiam est regnum Caldeorum
extendens se versus orientem a montibus Caldeorum vsque ad ciuitatem
Niniue super flumen Tigris sitam. . . . Deinde est Mesopotamnia que
30 incipit versus orientem ad fluuium Tigris ad vnam ciuitatem que Mosel
vocatur et protenditur in [f. 91ᵛ] occidentem vsque ad fluuium Eufrates
ad vnam ciuitatem que dicitur Roharz. . . .

CHAPTER XXIX

[2162] Venies per vnam regionem Cadilhe nomine et est bona patria et
magna. Ibi crescit quoddam genus fructus in modum cucumerum, et

16 venerant] MS. ven'at

cum fuerit maturus scindunt et diuidunt illum homines per medium et
infra inueniunt vnam bestiolam in carne, ossibus, et sanguine in modum
agnelli sine lana, quam homines cum fructu comedunt. Et est magnum
mirabile de isto fructu magnumque opus nature. Ego tamen, vt dixi,
eis non multum mirabar de hoc quia eodem modo erant arbores in   5
patria nostra fructus portantes qui fiunt aues volantes et sunt bone
[f. 92] ad manducandum. Et que cadunt in aquam viuunt, et que in
terram statim moriuntur. Et de hoc multum mirabantur ipsi.

Item, in ista patria sunt poma longa sapida et odorifera et pendent
c. simul in vno botro et c. in alio. Et habent folia longa et larga ad   10
longitudinem ii. pedum et amplius.

Item, in ista patria et in aliis terris ibidem sunt arbores portantes
gariofiles, nuces muscatas, grossas nuces Indie, cinomomum, multasque
alias diuersas species. Sunt eciam vites ibidem tam magnas vues
portantes quod vnus fortis homo vix botrum vnum cum vuis a terra   15
leuaret.

[2178] Item, in ista eadem regione sunt montes Caspie quos Vber incole
appellant, et inter istos montes Iudei x. tribuum quos homines Gogh et
Magoh vocant inclusi sunt. Ibi namque xxii. reges cum eorum populis
inclusi erant qui antea vltra montes Sichie morabantur. Et inter istos   20
montes Alexander rex eos fugauit et putabat quod virtute et labore
hominum suorum eos includeret. Et quando non potuit, deum nature
rogauit vt opus ab eo inceptum implere dignaretur. Et licet indignus erat
dei auribus, deus tamen ex sua gracia montes simul clausit. Et sic ex
omni parte excelsis montibus reclusi persistunt excepto vno latere, et per   25
illud latus currit mare Caspium.

Hic potest queri ex quo mare ex vno latere currit quare per illud mare
non exeunt vbi voluerint. Ad hoc respondeo: mare istud Caspeum
egreditur de terra subtus montes et currit per desertum a latere istius
terre vsque ad fines Perside; et licet vocatur mare, non tamen est mare   30
nec tangit aliquod mare, immo est lacus quidam vnus de maioribus
mundi. Et licet in istud mare se mitterent, nescirent vbi applicarent,
nullam namque linguam preter suam propriam intelligunt. Et ideo exire
non possunt.

[2215] Et sciendum est quod Iudei nullam propriam terram per totum   35
mundum habent nisi tantum istam infra istos montes. Et tamen sunt
tributarii regine Amazonie que diligenter et curiose eos [f. 92ᵛ] custodit
ne forte ex aliqua parte sue terre exeant, quia terra istius regine
coniungitur istis montibus. Contingit tamen aliquando quod quidam
illorum montes ascendunt, sed multitudo ascendere non potest. Montes   40
namque sunt ita excelsi et rostrati quod velint nolint ibi erunt quia
nullum egressum habent preter vnam paruam semitam virtute hominum
factam et durat bene per quatuor magnas leucas vbi terra est vasta et
deserta arida et sine aqua, quare homines habitare ibidem non possunt.

Et cum hoc sunt ibidem tanti dracones, serpentes, et alia venenosa animalia quod nullus transire potest nisi per maximum et durissimum hyemem. Et istum angustum transitum vocant ibidem homines *Glyren*. Et iste est transitus que regina Amozonie facit sic custodiri.

5 Et licet egredirentur nullam linguam preter hebream intelligunt et sic hominibus loqui nescirent. Et tamen dicitur quod tempore Anticristi exibunt et magnum dampnum et occisionem cristianis inferrent. Et ideo Iudei per alias mundi partes morantes filios suos semper hebreum docent sub ista spe vt quando illi de Caspeo exeunt eis loqui sciunt et
10 in cristianitatem ad cristianorum destructionem perducere valeant, quia bene sciunt per eorum prophetias vt dicunt quod illi de Caspeo exibunt et per totum mundum dilatabuntur, et quod christiani erunt in eorum subiectione plusquam illi vmquam fuerunt in cristianorum subiectione. [2226] Et si volueris scire qualiter egressum inuenient, ego sicut intellexi
15 tibi dicam. Tempore Anticristi vulpes quedam in locis illis vbi Alexander rex portas fecit foueam suam faciet, et in tantum fodiet et terram penetrabit vsque infra ad istas gentes perueniat. Et quando vulpem vident mirabuntur, eo quod numquam huius modi animal antea viderant. Omnia namque alia animalia secum inclusa habent preter vulpes.
20 Vnde statim ipsam fugabunt et persequentur quousque in suam foueam reingrediatur. At illi insequentes terram penetrabunt semper foueam sequendo vsque ad portas ab Alexandro factas et magnis lapidibus bituminatas peruenerint et istas portas frangent, et sic egressum inuenient.
25 [2250] De ista terra recedens venies [f. 93] ad Bakariam vbi sunt crudeles homines et maliuoli. In ista terra sunt arbores lanam sicut oues portantes de qua fiunt panni et vestes. Hic eciam sunt multi ypotami qui aliquando super terram, aliquando in aqua conuersantur, et sunt semiuiri equi semiequique viri, sicut alias dixi. Et nil preter homines
30 comedunt si eos capere possunt. Aque eciam istius terre et flumina sunt aquis maris amariora. Hic eciam griffones plus habundant quam in aliis partibus, et dicunt quidam quod habent partem anteriorem aquilinam et partem posteriorem leoninam, et verum dicunt quia talem effigiem habent. Vnus tamen grifo maior est octo leonibus et c. aquilis virtute
35 et fortitudine quia vnum magnum equum cum eius sessore, si eos inuenire poterit, volando ad nidum suum portabit, et eciam duos boues sicut ad aratrum simul ligantur. Habent namque vngulas anteriorum pedum ita magnas et largas sicut cornua bouis vel vacce de quibus faciunt ciphos ad bibendum, sicut nos de cornibus bubalinis facimus.
40 Et de costis et pennis alarum fiunt magni archus et fortes ad sagittandum.

De Baccaria igitur transiens venies per multas dietas per terram Presbiteri Iohannis magni imperatoris Indie, et vocatur regnum eius insula Pentexoria.

CHAPTER XXX

Iste imperator Presbiter Iohannes tenet magnam terram, et multe bone ciuitates et ville sunt in suo regno multeque diuerse insule magne et large quia hec terra India diuisa est per insulas propter quatuor flumina paradisi que totam terram in plures partes diuidunt. Et similiter in mari sunt multe insule. Melior ciuitas istius insule Pentoxorie Nisa 5 vocatur et est ciuitas regalis nobilis et diues valde.

Presbiter Iohannes multos sub se habet reges multasque diuersas gentes et est terra sua bona et diues valde. Non tamen ita diues sicut illa magni Chan quia mercatores non ita comuniter frequentant sicut illam magni Chan propter magnam loci distanciam; et ex alia parte, 10 inuenient in insula de Chatay quicquid necessarium fuerit [f. 93ᵛ] sericum, species, pannos aureos, et omnia alia mercimonia quecumque. Et licet in terra Presbiteri Iohannis melius forum haberent, timent tamen longam viam magnaque pericula maris in partibus illis. Nam in multis locis in mari ibidem sunt rupes adamantine que naturaliter ad se ferrum 15 trahunt. Et si naues alique cum clauis et vectibus ferreis inde transierint, statim rupes eas inseparabiliter ad se trahunt. . . .

Item, imperator iste Presbiter Iohannes semper filiam magni Chan accipit in vxorem, et econtra magnus Chan filiam Presbiteri Iohannis. Et sunt in terra sua multe diuerse res, multi preciosi lapides magni et 20 largi de quibus faciunt homines scutellas, discos, et ciphos magnos. Multaque alia diuersa mirabilia sunt ibidem, que omnia scribere stilus non sufficeret.

[2284] De principalioribus tamen sui regni et de suo statu et lege aliqua tibi in parte dicam et ostendam. Imperator iste Presbiter Iohannes 25 cristianus est et [f. 94] magna pars sue patrie similiter. Non tamen habent omnes articulos fidei prout nos habemus. Credunt tamen patrem et filium et spiritum sanctum, et sunt multum deuoti et inter se fideles valde et non curant de cautelis et fraudibus. Et habet sub se lxxii. prouincias et in qualibet prouincia est vnus rex, et isti alios reges sub 30 se habent, et omnes sunt ei tributarii.

[2647] In sua eciam terra multa sunt mirabilia. Nam in patria sua est Mare Arenosum totum de arena sine gutta aque, et venit et recedit cum magnis fretis sicut aliud mare facit. Et numquam fit stabile nec aliquo tempore quiescit. Et istud mare nemo potest transfretare nauigio 35 vel alio ingenio. Et ideo que vel qualis terra vltra istud mare fuerit penitus ignoratur. Et licet omnino careat aqua, inueniuntur tamen ibidem boni pisces genere quasi et similitudine a piscibus alterius maris differentes. Et sunt gustu sapidi et ad esum deliciosi.

Et tribus dietis in longitudine ab isto mari sunt magni montes a 40 quibus egreditur fluuius quidam a paradiso procedens totus ex lapidibus

35 transfretare] MS. transffetare *blotted*

preciosis sine aqua. Et currit deorsum per deserta cum magnis fretis
sicut Mare Arenosum et intrat istud mare et ibi perit. Istud flumen
quatuor diebus septimane sic currit et ducit secum magnos de rupibus
lapides, et statim vt ingressi fuerint istud mare, amplius non comparent
5 sed omnes perduntur. Et istis quatuor diebus quibus istud flumen sic
currit, nullus audet intrare; ceteris vero diebus bene possunt.

Item, vltra istud flumen magis versus deserta est vna magna planicies
arenosa inter montes sita. Et in ista planicie omni die sole oriente
incipiunt parua arbusta crescere, et crescunt vsque ad medium diem et
10 fructum portant. Nullus tamen audet fructum tangere quia est quasi res
fantastica vel de faire. Et post meridiem decrescunt et terram reintrant
ita quod sole occidente amplius non apparent. Et sic faciunt omni die
et istud est magnum mirabile.

Sunt eciam in isto deserto multi siluestres homines cornuti et horri-
15 biles et non locuntur sed vt porci grunniunt. Canes [f. 94ᵛ] eciam
indomiti in magna copia ibi habundant. Sunt eciam hic psitaci aues
quas lingua eorum *pistak* vocant, que naturaliter locuntur et homines
transeuntes per deserta salutant. . . .

Iste imperator comuniter moratur apud Susam ciuitatem et ibi est
20 suum principale palacium ita nobile et ita solempne sicut aliquid potest
estimari vel ymaginari. Et desuper principalem turrim istius palacii sunt
duo rotunda poma aurea et in quolibet pomo sunt duo carbunculi magni
et largi omni nocte clare fulgentes. Et principales porte istius palacii
sunt ex vno precioso lapide nomine sardonice circumligatura sine
25 bordura, et vectes portarum sunt eburnei. Fenestre eciam aularum et
camerarum sunt de cristallo. Tabule siue mense in quibus comedunt
quedam sunt de amaritibus, alie de amatistis [f. 95], alie ex auro cum
lapidibus preciosis. Columpne mensas supportantes sunt de eisdem
lapidibus. Gradus vero ascendendo versus thronum vbi sedet, vnus est
30 de onichino, alius de cristallo, alius de iaspide viridi, alius de amatisto,
alius de sardonice, alius de cornelino; septimus vero super quem pedes
suos ponit est de crisolito. Et omnes isti gradus circumligati sunt auro
cum lapidibus preciosis et grossis margaritis orientalibus. . . .

[2284] Item, per totam suam patriam et per omnes terras et patrias
35 ibidem in partibus illis homines comedunt semel tantum in die. Et
comedunt omni die in sua curia plusquam xxx. milia personarum,
exceptis venientibus et recedentibus. Sed xxx. milia sue patrie vel terre
magni Chan non tantum de bonis vno die expendunt sicut xii. milia in
partibus istis. Habet eciam vii. reges iugiter sibi seruientes, et post
40 mensem recedunt isti et alii loco eorum succedunt. Et cum istis regibus
assistunt sibi iugiter ministrando lxxii. duces et trecenti comites. Et in
sua curia comedunt omni die xii. archiepiscopi, xx. episcopi, et patri-
archa sancti Thome qui est quasi papa. Et archiepiscopi et abbates
[f. 95ᵛ] omnes sunt reges in patria ista. . . .

Item, iuxta insulam Pentoxoriam que est Presbiteri Iohannis est vna
magna insula longa et lata, Milstorak nomine, et est in dominio Pres-
biteri Iohannis. Hec insula cunctis bonis plena est. Ibi erat quondam
vir quidam prediues Calconabes nomine, qui in monte quodam
pulcherimum castellum habuit ita forte et ita nobile sicut aliquis posset 5
ordinare vel ymaginari. Et totum montem speciosis muris murauit, et
infra muros formosum gardinum fecit in quo erant arbores omnia
genera fructuum que inueniri possent portantes. Omnes eciam herbas
odoriferas et florigeras in eo plantauit. Erant eciam in gardino multi
fontes pulcri et perlucidi iuxta quos aulas et cameras mire pulcritudinis 10
construxit que omnes auro et azorio depicte erant et ornate. Et fecit in
eis multa diuersa mirabilia sicut gesta historiarum testantur diuersasque
bestias aues cantantes que per machinas ac si viue essent voluebantur.
Posuit eciam in gardino omnia genera auium et omnes bestias in quibus
homo delectari posset vel solacium habere. Misit eciam ibidem pul- 15
criores iuuenculas et domicellas quas inuenire poterat sub etate xv.
annorum et decores iuuenes cum eis eiusdem etatis, et erant omnes
vestiti vestibus aureis et dixit quod erant angeli. Fecit eciam iii. fontes
nobiles et deliciosos quos cum iaspide et cristallo auro lapidibus
preciosis et margaritis circumclausit et vallauit. Et sub terra conductum 20
habuit ita quod quando voluit isti tres fontes vnus curreret [f. 96] lacte,
alius vino, alius melle. Et istum locum paradisum vocauit.

Et quando aliqui probi milites vel bacularii audaces et fortes eum
videre venerant, in suum paradisum illos ducebat et omnes istas delicias
eis ostendebat diuersosque cantus auium et illas formosas puellas 25
necnon fontes lacte vino et melle manantes. Et fecit in vna alta et
sublimi turri diuersa instrumenta musicalia sonare sine visu, et dixit
quod erant angeli dei et quod iste erat paradisus ille quem deus amicis
suis promisit dicens *Dabo vobis terram fluentem lac et mel.* Deinde
pocionem quamdem eis dedit de qua statim inebriati erant, et tunc dixit 30
eis quod si amore ipsius mori vellent, eos post mortem in paradisum
istum poneret, et eiusdem etatis cum istis puellis essent et cum eis
semper viuerent et luderent semperque virgines perseuerarent. Et
postea dixit quod mitteret eos in vnum alium paradisum pulcriorem vbi
visibiliter deum nature in sua maiestate et gloria viderent, et tunc 35
optulerunt se suum velle in omnibus facere et implere. Tunc precepit
quod occiderent talem dominum et tales qui erant eius aduersarii, et
quod non timerent mortem quia mitteret eos in vnum paradisum cencies
iam pulcriorem. Et sic isti milites et bacularii multos nobiles magnates
in patria occiderunt, et plures sub spe istius paradisi seipsos inter- 40
fecerunt. Et sic homo iste per suas magnas seductiones de inimicis suis
se vindicabat.

18 MS. *has corrector's mark in margin*   37 tales] MS. talē

186   APPENDIX A

Cognita tandem causa et malicia istius Cacolonabes, nobiles et diuites
patrie conuenerunt et castellum illud obsederunt et ad solum prostra-
uerunt et ipsum occiderunt et omnes delicias et nobilitates istius
paradisi destruxerunt. Locus fontium et alia mirabilia adhuc ibidem
apparent sed diuicie recesserunt et non multum tempus iam preteriit 5
ex quo locus destructus et deletus erat.

CHAPTER XXXI

Item, iuxta istam insulam de Milstorak a parte sinistra versus flumen de
Phison [f. 96ᵛ] est vnum magnum mirabile. Hoc est vallis quedam inter
montes per quatuor miliaria bene durans. Quidam vallem incantatam
illam vocant, alii vallem diaboli, alii vallem periculosam. In hac valle 10
omni die et nocte audiuntur tempestates, murmuraciones, strepitusque
magni. Auditur eciam ibidem ingens sonitus timpanorum, acchararum,
et tubarum ac si esset magnum festum. Hec vallis est et semper extitit
demonibus plena. Et iuxta quosdam est quidam introitus inferni. In hac
valle est magna habundancia auri et argenti, vnde multi pagani et 15
cristiani similiter pro thesauro habendo sepe intrant, sed redeundo a
demonibus strangulantur et suffocantur et precipue pagani et cristiani
similiter qui causa cupiditatis intrauerunt.
[2327] Et in medio istius vallis sub vna rupe est caput diaboli cum facie
multum terribile ad videndum et horribile, et non plus apparet nisi 20
caput vsque ad humeros. Sed non est homo in mundo tam fortis et
animosus, cristianus vel alius, quin in aspectu eius tabescet et pauebit,
ita terribile est et ita acute quamlibet personam respicit. Et habet oculos
mobiles et scintillantes et tociens et tot vicibus modum sui vultus mutat
et mouet quod nullus versus eum audet approximare. Et de ore eius 25
egreditur ignis et fumus et tantus fetor quod vix potest aliquis sustinere.
Sed cristiani bone vite et stabiles in fide sine periculo bene intrant,
nam de peccatis suis confessi sunt et signo sancti crucis se muniunt ita
quod diaboli eis nocere non possunt. Sed licet sint sine periculo, non
sunt tamen sine magno timore et tremore quando visibiliter demones 30
circa eos vident, qui diuersos insultus in eos faciunt, diuersimodeque
in aere et in terra eis minantur tonitruo et diuersis tempestatibus
incessanter flagellantur, ita quod homo semper timet ne deus de
peccatis suis et malefactis vindictam sumat.
[2339] Et sciendum est quod quando socii mei et ego fuimus ad istam 35
vallem, eramus in magna perplexitate vtrum auderemus corpora [f. 97]
nostra fortune tradere et sub protectione dei intrare vel non. Et quidam
sociorum nostrorum consenserunt, quidam vero contradixerunt. Et
erant tunc nobiscum duo fratres minores de Lumbardia, boni et
perfecti viri, qui dixerunt quod si aliqui intrare vellent, ipsi eorum 40

comites libenter fierent. Quo audito, sub confidencia et protectione dei et illorum missas fecimus celebrari, confessi et comunicati fuimus, et sic xiiii.ᶜⁱᵐ intrauimus. Sed in regressu nostro eramus nisi nouem, et vtrum socii nostri reuertebantur an in valle perierunt ignotum erat
5 nobis; numquam tamen vidimus eos amplius, et duo erant Greci et iii. Hispanni. Alii vero socii nostri qui per vallem transire nolebant a latere per aliam viam perrexerunt vt nos precederent, et sic fecerunt. Et sic dictam vallem transiebamus.

Et vidimus in multis locis aurum, argentum, lapides preciosos, et alia
10 iocalia hic et illuc in magna habundancia vt apparuit; sed vtrum erat vt apparuit nescio quia non tetigi. Demones namque sunt valde subtiles et aliquando ad decipiendum homines faciunt aliquid apparere quod non est. Et ideo non tetigi, et similiter quia nolui a mea deuocione turbari, numquam enim ante vel post tam deuotus extiti, quid propter
15 timorem demonum quos in diuersis figuris circa me vidi, quid propter corpora mortua per totam vallem iacentia; quia si duo potentissimi reges hostiliter inter se bellum habuissent et maior pars exercitus cecidisset, vix tantos mortuos reddidisset sicut ibidem iacuerunt, quod valde horribile erat ad videndum.

20 Et ego multum mirabar quomodo tanta corpora et tam integra fuerunt quia pro maiore parte, vt apparuit, non putruerunt. Sed credo quod demones sic eos apparere fecerunt quia non potuit esse, vt michi videbatur, quod tot homines tam nouiter ingressi fuissent, nec ex alia parte quod diu et per longum tempus sine corrupcione esse poterant. Et
25 multi erant in habitu cristiano, sed credo quod erant decepti et capti cupiditate thesauri vel [f. 97ᵛ] quod habebant nimis trepida corda et non poterant sustinere pauorem. Et ideo magis deuoti fuimus.

Eramus eciam per ventum, tonitruum, et tempestates sepe ad terram prostrati, sed semper adiuuit nos deus. Et sic dictam vallem sine
30 periculo transiuimus, gracias deo in omnibus agentes.
[2353] Deinde vltra istam vallem est vna magna insula vbi sunt homines magne stature sicut gigantes xxviii. vel xxx. pedum longitudinis. Isti vestibus non vtuntur sed pelles bestiarum super eos pendent, et panem non comedunt sed carnes crudas edunt et lac bibunt. Domos eciam non
35 habent et libencius carnem humanam comedunt quam aliquid aliud. Istam insulam nullus voluntarie intrat nec ei approximat, quia si videant nauem cum hominibus statim mare intrant vt eos rapiant. . . .
[2367] [f. 98ᵛ] In ista patria et in multis aliis partibus ibidem et eciam magis citra seminant homines semen bombicis et crescunt inde parua
40 arbusta que bombicem portant, et sic faciunt omni anno et sic est bombex ibidem in magna copia. Item, in ista insula et in multis aliis ibidem est quoddam genus bosci tam durum et forte quod carbones

35 aliquid] MS. aⁱd (*not* aliqⁱd *as at* 189/5)

eius cineribus operti per totum annum et amplius ignem seruant et
portant. Iste arbores parua folia habent sicut [iuniperus].

[2377] Et [f. 99] sunt alie arbores que nullo modo possunt ardere vel
putrescere. Sunt eciam arbores auellane que nuces gerunt humano
5 capite grossiores. Ibi eciam sunt multe ozafles quas *girfanz* vocant. Hec
est vna bestia maculata altitudinis equi dextrarii, sed habet collum xx.
cubitorum longitudinis et caudam sicut ceruus, et vnam altam domum
bene potest transuidere.

[2389] Sunt eciam in ista patria multi chamaliontes. Hec est quedam
10 bestiola sicut siluestris capra, et vadit semper gula aperta eo quod de
aere viuit et numquam comedit vel bibit, et sepe mutat suum colorem
quia aliquando videtur vnius coloris, aliquando alterius, et potest se
mutare in omnes colores preter album et rubrum.

[2421] Sunt eciam ibidem serpentes magni et immensi cxx. pedum
15 longitudinis diuersisque coloribus colorati sicut rubri, virides, glauci,
indici, et nigri, et omnes sunt diuersis maculis aspersi. Sunt alii serpentes
cristati qui cristas super capita portant et directe super pedes gradiuntur,
et sunt octo passuum grossitudinis et amplius, et habitant in rupibus et
montibus, et habent semper guttur patens et apertum vnde venenum
20 semper deguttant et emittunt.

Sunt eciam ibi porci siluestres diuersorum colorum ita magni sicut
boues nobiscum, et sunt maculati in modum iuuenum hinnilorum. Sunt
eciam ibidem hericii ita magni sicut sunt hic siluestres porci; nos eos
porcos spinatos vocamus. Ibi sunt albi leones magni et potentes. Et sunt
25 alie bestie magnis dextrariis maiores quas homines *lonherantes* vocant,
et alii *dontes* eas appellant. Et habent caput nigrum, et in media fronte
tria longa cornua acuta vt gladius et incidencia, et habent corpus
[flauum]. Et sunt crudeles bestie ita quod elephantes fugunt et occidunt.

[2437] Sunt adhuc alie bestie crudeles et feroces, non multum vrso
30 maiores, et habent caput sicut aper et sex pedes, et in quolibet pede
duas vngulas largas [f. 99ᵛ] et acutas, et habent corpus simile vrso et
caudam sicut cauda leonis.

[2451] Sunt ibi eciam mures ita magni sicut canes, et sunt alii mures
sicut cornices. Et sunt ibidem auce rubie nostris aucis multum maiores,
35 et habent caput, collum, et pectus nigrum. Multa alia genera bestiarum,
et auium sunt in ista patria et in aliis terris circumiacentibus, de quib[us]
omnibus loqui nimis longum esset et fastidiosum. . . .

CHAPTER XXXII

[2461] [f. 100] Item, est vna alia insula Oxidrada nomine et alia que
Synosepulis vocatur, vbi sunt boni homines et fideles magneque fidei,

---

2 iuniperus] MS. *om. leaving blank Cf.* W 142/41 geneoure   28 flauum]
MS. *om. leaving blank. Cf.* W 143/28 fauues   36 quibus] MS. quib *with*
elision before vowel

et in consuetudinibus et bonis moribus pro maiore parte concordant
cum Bragmanis, et vadunt omnes nudi. In istas insulas intrauit Alex-
ander, et quando vidit eorum bonam fidem magnamque fidelitatem
dixit quod non offenderet eos sed peterent ab eo quicquid vellent
diuicias [f. 100ᵛ] vel aliquid aliud et libenter eis daret. Ac illi dixerunt 5
ei quod ille satis diues est qui habet viccum necessarium suo corpori,
et quod diuicie huius seculi transitorie vane sunt minimique valoris. ...
[2505] [f. 101] Item, vltra istam insulam est vna alia Pycan nomine.
Homines istius insule terram non excolunt nec laborant quia non
comedunt. Et sunt bene colorati et pulcre forme secundum eorum 10
magnitudinem quia sunt parui sicut nani. Non tamen ita parui sicut
pigmei. Isti viuunt ex odore pomorum siluestrium; et quando ad partes
longinquas se transferunt ista poma secum deferunt, quia si carerent
odore statim morerentur. Et non sunt multum rationales sed sunt
simplices et bestiales. 15
[2528] Postea est vna alia insula vbi homines sunt omnes pilosi et hispidi
preter faciem et palmas. Isti currunt super mare sicut super siccam
terram, et comedunt carnes et pisces crudos. In ista insula est vnum
magnum flumen ii. miliaria et dimidium habens in latitudine Remmar
nomine, et ab isto flumine sunt xv. diete eundo per deserta. 20
[2551] Ex alia parte fluminis, si quis transire posset, nam ego non fui ibi,
sed dictum erat nobis ab hominibus patrie quod infra illa deserta erant
arbores solis et lune qui Alexandro regi loquebantur et ei mortem suam
nunciauerunt. Et dicunt homines quod custodes arborum qui comedunt
fructum earum et balsamum quod crescit ibidem [f. 101ᵛ] viuunt 25
quatuor c. vel sescentis annis virtute fructus et balsami. ...

CHAPTER XXXIII

[2597] [f. 102] Item, versus partes orientales terre Presbiteri Iohannis
est vna insula bona et magna Taprobana nomine, nobilis et fructuosa,
cuius rex diues est valde, et tamen subiectus est Presbitero Iohanni, et
semper fit rex per electionem. In ista insula sunt due estates, ii. yemes; 30
fruges eciam bis in anno metuntur; gardini eciam omni tempore anni
sunt flogeri. Ibi habitant boni homines et rationabiles, et multi cristiani
inter eos qui diuiciarum suarum finem nesciunt. ...
[2609] Item, iuxta istam insulam versus orientem sunt due alie insule,
quarum vna dicitur Orilla, alia Argita, vnde tota terra est ex aurifodio, 35
et sunt iste insule recte vbi mare rubrum se separat a mari occeano.
In istis insulis nulle videntur que clare apparent preter vnam claram
stellam quam *Canapes* vocant. Luna eciam per totam lunacionem non
videtur nisi in secunda quadra.
[2637] In insula eciam Taprobana sunt montes aurei quos formice 40

34–5 MS. *has corrector's mark in margin*

curiose custodiunt et aurum purgant et purum separant a non puro.
Et sunt magne formice sicut canes ita quod nullus ad montes audet
appropinquare, quia iste formice statim in eos irruerent, et sic de isto
auro habere non possunt nisi magno et subtili ingenio. Et ideo quando
5 est magna et incensa caliditas formice abscondunt se in terra a tercia
hora diei vsque nonam; et tunc veniunt homines cum camelis, drome-
dariis, iumentis et aliis bestiis et eos clam et secrete [f. 102ᵛ] onerant
clamque discedunt antequam formice terram exeant. . . .
   Item, vltra terram, insulas, et deserta dominii Presbiteri Iohannis
10 eundo directe versus orientem nil inuenitur nisi montes et magne rupes
et regio tenebrosa vbi diebus vel noctibus lux nulla lucet, sicut illi de
patria testantur. Et durant ista deserta et tenebre vsque ad paradisum
terrestrem vbi Adam et Eua, primi parentes nostri, positi erant. . . .
   Paradisus terrestris, vt dicunt homines, est altior terra mundi, cuius
15 altitudo circulum lune (circa quem scilicet luna suum [f. 103] tran-
situm facit) tangit. Et ideo fluuius Noe attingere non potuit qui totum
mundum sub et supra destruxit preter paradisum solum. Et est para-
disus muro circumclusus, sed quali muro ignoratur. Et sunt muri, vt
apparet, musco cooperti, et non apparet lapis vel aliqua res probans de
20 quo murus factus est. Et extendunt se muri a meredie in boriam, et est
tantum vnus introitus ardenti flamma vndique clausus ita quod nulli
mortali patet ingressus.
   Et in eminenciori et altiori loco paradisi quasi in medio est fons,
quatuor fluuios ex se proiciens qui diuersas mundi terras circuunt.
25 Quorum primus dicitur Physon vel Ganges quod idem est; currit per
Indiam, in quo inueniuntur multi lapides preciosi, lignum aloes, et arena
aurea. Alius vero dicitur Nilus vel Gyon; iste transit per Ethiopiam et
Egiptum. Tercius dicitur Tigris, qui vadit per Assiriam et Armeniam
magnam. Quarti nomen est Eufrates; iste currit per Medos, per
30 Armeniam, et Persidam. Et dicunt homines quod omnes aque dulces
mundi sub et supra earum naturam et originem ab istis fontibus
paradisi accipiunt et ab eis exeunt. . . .

CHAPTER XXXIV

[f. 103ᵛ] Et sic reuertendo venies ad vnam insulam nomine Casson.
Hec patria lx. dietas habet in longitudine et plusquam l. in latitudine.
35 Hec est melior insula maiusque regnum in partibus illis excepto regno
de Chatay. . . . Et sunt in ea magne foreste castaniarum. Rex istius insule
diues est et potens princepsque magnificus, et tamen tenet terram suam
de magno Chan et ei obedit, quia hec est vna de prouinciis quas magnus
Chan habet sub se, excepta sua propria terra et exceptis multis aliis
40 minoribus [f. 104] insulis.
   [2765] De isto regno descendens venies in redeundo ad vnum aliud

regnum Ryboht nomine, et est similiter sub magno Chan. Hec patria
bona est et populosa, frugibus vino cunctisque aliis rebus opilentissima.
Incole istius patrie domos non habunt sed iacent in tentoriis de filtro
nigro factis. Et ciuitas regalis et principalis murata est lapidibus albis
et nigris, et omnes vici ciuitatis de eisdem lapidibus sunt bene paui- 5
mentati. . . .

In hac insula quasi per totam patriam est ista consuetudo quando
pater alicuius mortuus fuerit et filius honorem patri facere voluerit,
conuocat amicos, parentes, presbiteros, et ministrallos cum magna copia.
Et corpus defuncti super vnum montem deferunt in magno gaudio et 10
maxima solempnitate. Et tunc maior prelatus caput eius amputat et in
scutella aurea vel argentea magna et larga si diues sit ponit; et filio
tradit et alii cantant et dicunt orationes suas. Postea presbiteri et
religiosi totum corpus in frustra diuidunt et incidunt orationes suas
semper dicendo. Et aues patrie, que longa et antiqua consuetudine ad 15
hoc sunt assueti, veniunt et volant desuper sicut vultures, aquile, et
cetere aues que carnes comedunt, et presbiteri eis frustra ista proiciunt.
Ac ille leuantes paululum discedunt et comedunt et, sicut sacerdotes
nobiscum pro animabus defunctorum cantant *Subuenite sancti dei*, sic
presbiteri isti in eorum lingua tunc alta voce clamant et cantant, *Respi-* 20
cite et videte quam bonus erat homo iste quomodo angeli dei veniunt vt eum
in paradisum deferant. [f. 104ᵛ] Et tunc apparet filio quod est multum
honoratus quando aues patrem suum sic comederint, et qui maiorem
numerum auium habere poterit magis inter eos honoratur. Postea filius
cum parentibus et amicis domum reuertitur et eis magnum festum facit. 25
Et omnes amici toto tempore conuiuii de istis auibus locuntur, qualiter
ibi venerunt quinque, ibi viginti, et de hoc multum se glorificant et
delectantur loqui. Et cum fuerint sic domi, filius caput patris sui coquit
et vnicuique speciali amico dat parte carnis loco interferculi. Et de testa
ciphum facit in quo ipse et omnes amici cum maxima deuocione bibunt 30
in memoriam illius sancti hominis quem aues comederunt, et istum
ciphum seruat sibi filius tempore vite sue et de ipso bibit in memoriam
patris.

[2846] De ista insula redeundo per x. dietas per terram magni Chan est
vna bona insula, magnumque regnum nobilem et diuitem regem habens. 35
Et inter ceteros diuites sue patrie est vnus prediues qui non est princeps
vel dux, amarallus nec comes, et tamen multi sunt qui terras suas de
ipso tenent, quia diues est valde et habet omni anno de redditu ccc.
milia equorum frugibus et riso oneratorum. Et iuxta consuetudinem
terre illius nobilem vitam ducit, habet namque l. domicellas puellasque 40
ei iugiter ad mensam et ad lectum seruiunt et ministrant suumque velle
in omnibus implere parantur. Et quando sedet ad mensam iste domicelle
cibum ante eum deferunt v. semper fercula simul et veniendo vnam
cantilenam dulcissime cantant. Postea cibum parant et incidunt et in

os eius mittunt, quia ipse nil facit sed tantum manus super mensam tenet, habet namque tam magnas vngues quod nil potest tenere vel accipere. Et nobilitas hominum istius terre est habere magnas vngues et eas nutrire. Et plures sunt qui eas in tantum nutriunt quod totam
5 manum cum eis circuunt et est magna nobilitas. Inter eos nobilitas vero mulierum ibidem est habere paruos pedes, et ideo quando sunt nate, ita stricte [*the last two words are catchwords of the missing final quire*].

APPENDIX B

THE SCRIBAL TRADITION OF *MANDE-VILLE'S TRAVELS* IN ENGLAND

THE INSULAR VERSION is a French recension, made in England before 1390, of the author's original French text. It is studied by Guy De Poerck, 'La tradition manuscrite des *Voyages* de Jean de Mandeville', *Romanica Gandensia* iv (1956), and by M. C. Seymour, 'The Scribal Tradition of *Mandeville's Travels*: the Insular Version', *Scriptorium* xviii (1964). The version is printed by G. F. Warner, *The Buke of John Maundeuill*, Roxburghe Club (1889). The manuscripts are divisible into three subgroups; subgroups A and B are independently derived from the lost archetype, and subgroup C derives from a lost manuscript of subgroup B (i) which was carried into France before 1402 and there developed alongside the Continental Version with which it was sometimes conflated; see L. C. Schepens, 'Quelques observations sur la tradition manuscrite du *Voyage* de Mandeville', *Scriptorium* xviii (1964).

Subgroup A

1. British Museum MS. Harley 204.
2. British Museum MS. Harley 212.
3. British Museum MS. Harley 1739.
4. British Museum MS. Harley 4383 (printed by Warner).
5. British Museum MS. Royal 20 A.i.
6. British Museum MS. Royal 20 B.x (printed in part by Warner).
7. Bodleian Library MS. Bodley 841.
8. Bodleian Library MS. Ashmole 1804.
9. Durham Cathedral Library MS. B.iii.3.
   A manuscript sold at Sotheby's, 12 December 1966.

Subgroup B (i)

10. Bodleian Library MS. Additional C 280.
11. British Museum MS. Sloane 1464 (collated by Warner).

Subgroup B (ii)

12. British Museum MS. Sloane 560.
13. Leiden University Library MS. Vossius Lat. F 75.

Subgroup C

14. British Museum MS. Additional 33757 (collated by Warner).
15. Fitzwilliam Museum, Cambridge MS. CFM 23.
16. Durham University Library MS. Cosin V.i.10.
17. Bürgerbibliothek, Bern MS. 58.
18. Palais des Arts, Lyon MS. 28.
19. Bibliothèque Nationale MS. Fonds fr. 5633.
20. Bibliothèque Nationale MS. Fonds fr. 5635.
21. Bibliothèque Nationale MS. Ancien Fonds fr. 2810.

THE ROYAL VERSION is a Latin translation of a lost manuscript of subgroup A of the Insular Version, most closely related to MS. Royal 20 A.i. The scribal tradition of the version is examined, and the text printed in part, by M. C. Seymour, *The Bodley Version of Mandeville's Travels*, E.E.T.S., o.s. 253 (1963).

22. British Museum MS. Royal 13 E.ix (printed in part by Seymour).
23. British Museum MS. Harley 175.
24. British Museum MS. Cotton Appendix iv.
25. British Museum MS. Cotton Otho D.i (an epitome).
26. Hunterian Museum, Glasgow MS. T.4.1.
27. Jesus College, Cambridge MS. Q.B.18.
28. Durham University Library MS. Cosin V.iii.7.

THE LEIDEN VERSION is a Latin translation of a lost manuscript of subgroup B (ii) of the Insular Version, most closely related to MS. Sloane 560, and was made before 1390.

29. Leiden University MS. Vulcan 96.
30. Corpus Christi, Cambridge MS. 275.
31. British Museum MS. Egerton 672.
    Cardiff Public Library MS. 3. 236 (two leaves only).

THE HARLEY VERSION, a Latin translation of a lost manuscript of subgroup B (i) of the Insular Version which gave a better text than either of the extant manuscripts, is printed in part above.

32. British Museum MS. Harley 82.

THE ASHMOLE VERSION is an independent Latin translation of a lost manuscript of subgroup B (i) of the Insular Version.

33. Bodleian Library MS. Ashmole 769.

THE DEFECTIVE VERSION is an English translation of a lost manuscript of the Insular Version, most closely related to subgroup B (i). The earliest printed editions of this version by Pynson, De Worde, and

East are examined by M. C. Seymour, 'The early English printed editions of *Mandeville's Travels*', *The Library* xix (1964), and various later editions (all based on East's text) are listed by Mrs. Bennett, *The Rediscovery of Sir John Mandeville* (1954). The latest of these reprints was issued in Everyman's Library (no. 812) in 1928. With one exception, the manuscripts of this version are divisible into five subgroups; subgroups A and B derive independently from the lost archetype, and subgroups C, D, and E represent successive dependent stages in the transmission of the text of subgroup B. Two separate pages (from Chs. vi and ix of an inferior subgroup) of an otherwise lost manuscript of this version are printed by A. C. Cawley, 'A Ripon fragment of *Mandeville's Travels*', *English Studies* xxviii (1957). See also J. Vogels, 'Handschriftliche Untersuchungen über die englische Version Mandeville's', *Jahresbericht über das Realgymnasium zu Crefeld* (1891), and M. C. Seymour, 'The English Manuscripts of *Mandeville's Travels*', *Transactions of the Edinburgh Bibliographical Society* iv (1966).

Subgroup A (i)

34. Corning Museum of Glass, New York MS. 6.
35. Magdalene College, Cambridge MS. Pepys 1955 (ff. 1^v–6^r printed with MS. 75 below).

Subgroup A (ii)

36. Cambridge University Library MS. Dd.i.17.
37. Balliol College, Oxford MS. 239.
38. The Queen's College, Oxford MS. 383.
39. Bodleian Library MS. Rawlinson D 101.
40. Bodleian Library MS. Douce 33.
41. Bodleian Library MS. Ashmole 751 (extracts, printed by M. C. Seymour, 'Secundum Iohannem Maundvyle', *English Studies in Africa* iv, 1961).

Subgroup A (iii)

42. Cambridge University Library MS. Ff.v.35.
43. Bodleian Library MS. e Musæo 124.

Subgroup B

44. British Museum MS. Arundel 140.
45. British Museum MS. Royal 17 B. xliii.
46. British Museum MS. Harley 2386.
47. British Museum MS. Harley 3954.
48. Huntington Library, California MS. HM 114.
49. British Museum MS. Royal 17 C.xxxviii (independently derived).

Subgroup C

50. Rugby School MS. Bloxam 1008.
51. British Museum Additional MS. 33758.
52. Trinity College, Cambridge MS. R.4.20.
53. Bodleian Library MS. Douce 109.
54. Bodleian Library MS. Rawlinson B 216.
55. Bodleian Library MS. Rawlinson D 100.
56. MS. owned by the late H. L. Bradfer-Lawrence, of Ripon, Yorks. Bodleian Library MS. Lat. misc. e 85 (Chs. xiii–xv only).

Subgroup D

57. Chetham Library, Manchester MS. 6711.
58. Cambridge University Library MS. Gg.i.34, part 3 (Chs. i–ii derive from subgroup A).
59. Bodleian Library MS. Additional C 285.
60. Bodleian Library MS. Tanner 405.
61. MS. owned by Mr. B. Penrose, of Barbados Hill, Devon, Pennsylvania (part of Ch. xxxii interpolated from subgroup E).

Subgroup E

62. National Library of Scotland MS. Advocates 19.1.11.
63. Trinity College, Dublin MS. E.5.6.
64. Bodleian Library MS. Laud Misc. 699.
65. British Museum MS. Sloane 2319.
66. British Museum MS. Additional 37049 (an epitome, printed by M. C. Seymour, 'The English Epitome of *Mandeville's Travels*', *Anglia* 84, 1966).

THE COTTON VERSION is a conflation in English based on a lost manuscript of subgroup A of the Defective Version. The conflator expanded and altered his base text by detailed reference to a manuscript of subgroup A of the Insular Version. First printed in 1725 and subsequently reprinted many times, the version was edited in a modernized text by A. W. Pollard in 1900, in a diplomatic text by P. Hamelius, E.E.T.S., O.S. 153 and 154 (1919 and 1923), and by M. C. Seymour (Clarendon Press, 1967, and O.U.P., World Classics, 1968). Some aspects of its grammar are examined by H. J. van der Meer, *Main facts concerning the syntax of 'Mandeville's Travels'* (1929), and the manuscript is described by C. E. Wright, *English Vernacular Hands* (1960), p. 17, with a facsimile of f. 60^v.

67. British Museum MS. Cotton Titus C.xvi.

THE EGERTON VERSION is a conflation in English based on a lost manuscript of subgroup A of the Defective Version and a lost

English translation of the Royal Version. It is printed by G. F. Warner, op. cit., and in a modernized text by M. Letts, *Mandeville's Travels: Texts and Translations* ii, Hakluyt Society, 2nd series, cii (1953). Its textual composition is examined by M. C. Seymour, 'The origin of the Egerton Version of *Mandeville's Travels*', *Medium Ævum* xxx (1961).

68. British Museum MS. Egerton 1982.

THE BODLEY VERSION is an abridgement of the lost English translation of the Royal Version used by the conflator of the Egerton Version. It is printed by M. Letts, op. cit., and M. C. Seymour, op. cit. on p. 194.

69. Bodleian Library MS. Rawlinson D 99 (printed by Letts).
70. Bodleian Library MS. e Musæo 116 (printed by Seymour). See also his note, 'A fifteenth-century East Anglian scribe', *Medium Ævum* xxxviii (1969).

THE METRICAL VERSION, an English rendering in couplets, of a lost manuscript of subgroup B (i) of the Insular Version, is printed in the present volume.

71. Coventry City Record Office MS.

THE STANZAIC FRAGMENT is an English verse rendering, possibly based on the Cotton Version and on Pipino's text of Marco Polo. It is printed by M. C. Seymour, 'Mandeville and Marco Polo: a stanzaic fragment', *AUMLA* xxi (1964).

72. Bodleian Library MS. e Musæo 160.

THE IRISH VERSION was translated in 1475 by Fínghin Ó Mathghamhna from a lost manuscript of subgroup A of the Defective Version. It is printed, with translation, by W. Stokes, *Zeitschrift für celtische Philologie* ii (1898), and its origin is examined by M. C. Seymour, 'The Irish Version of *Mandeville's Travels*', *Notes and Queries* ccviii (1963).

73. British Museum MS. Egerton 1781 (ed. Gearóid Mac Niocaill and M. C. Seymour, Dublin Institute of Advanced Studies, *at press*).
74. Bibliothèque Municipale, Rennes MS. 598 (printed by Stokes).
75. British Museum MS. Additional 33993 (extracts, printed by Mary Doyle and M. C. Seymour, 'The Irish Epitome of *Mandeville's Travels*, *Éigse* xii, 1967).

EARLY ENGLISH TEXT
SOCIETY

LIST OF PUBLICATIONS
1864–1972

JUNE 1972

EARLY ENGLISH TEXT SOCIETY

The Early English Text Society was founded in 1864 by Frederick James Furnivall, with the help of Richard Morris, Walter Skeat and others, to bring the mass of unprinted Early English literature within the reach of students and to provide sound texts from which the New English Dictionary could quote. In 1867 an Extra Series was started of texts already printed but not in satisfactory or readily obtainable editions. In 1921 the Extra Series was discontinued and all publications were subsequently listed and numbered as part of the Original Series. In 1970 the first of a new Supplementary Series was published; unlike the Extra Series, volumes in this series will be issued only occasionally, as funds allow and as suitable texts become available.

In the first part of this list are shown the books published by the Society since 1938, Original Series 210 onwards and the Supplementary Series. A large number of the earlier books were reprinted by the Society in the period 1950 to 1970. In order to make the rest available, the Society has come to an agreement with the Kraus Reprint Co. who will reprint as necessary the volumes in the Original Series 1–209 and in the Extra Series. In this way all the volumes published by the Society should once again be in print by May 1973. The reprints at present ready are shown in the second part of the following list.

The subscription to the Society, which constitutes full membership for private members and libraries, is £3·15 (U.S. members $9.00, Canadian members Can. $9.50 a year for the annual publications in the Original Series, due in advance on 1 January, and should be paid by cheque, postal order or money order made out to 'The Early English Text Society', and sent to Dr. Anne Hudson, Executive Secretary, Early English Text Society, Lady Margaret Hall. Oxford. The payment of the annual subscription is the only prerequisite of membership. The books in the Supplementary Series do not form part of the issue sent to members in return for the payment of their annual subscription, though they are available to members at a reduced price; a notice about each volume is sent to members in advance of publication.

Private members of the Society (but not libraries) may select in place of the annual issue past volumes from the Society's list chosen from the Original Series 210 to date or from the Supplementary Series. The value of such texts allowed against one annual subscription is £5·00, and all these transactions must be made through the Executive Secretary. Members of the Society may purchase copies of books O.S. 210 to date for their own use at a discount of 30% of the listed prices; private members (but not libraries) may purchase earlier publications at a similar discount. All such orders must be sent to the Executive Secretary.

For particulars about commercial orders, see the note at the end of this list.

Details of books, the cost of membership and its privileges, are revised from time to time. This list is brought up to date annually, and the current edition should be consulted.

June 1972

LIST 1

ORIGINAL SERIES 1938-1972

O.S. 210 **Sir Gawain and the Green Knight,** re-ed. I. Gollancz, with introductory essays by Mabel Day and M. S. Serjeantson. 1940 (*for* 1938), *reprinted* 1966. £1·25

211 **The Dicts and Sayings of the Philosophers:** translations made by Stephen Scrope, William Worcester and anonymous translator, ed. C. F. Bühler. 1941 (*for* 1939), *reprinted* 1961. £3·75

212 **The Book of Margery Kempe,** Vol. I, Text (*all published*), ed. S. B. Meech, with notes and appendices by S. B. Meech and H. E. Allen. 1940 (*for* 1939), *reprinted* 1961. £3·50

213 **Ælfric's De Temporibus Anni,** ed. H. Henel. 1942 (*for* 1940), *reprinted* 1970. £2·10

214 **Forty-Six Lives translated from Boccaccio's De Claris Mulieribus by Henry Parker, Lord Morley,** ed. H. G. Wright. 1943 (*for* 1940), *reprinted* 1970. £2·75

215, 220 **Charles of Orleans: The English Poems,** Vol. I, ed. R. Steele (1941), Vol. II, ed. R. Steele and Mabel Day (1946 *for* 1944); *reprinted as one volume with bibliographical supplement* 1970. £3·15

216 **The Latin Text of the Ancrene Riwle,** from Merton College MS. 44 and British Museum MS. Cotton Vitellius E. vii, ed. C. D'Evelyn. 1944 (*for* 1941), *reprinted* 1957. £2·25

217 **The Book of Vices and Virtues:** A Fourteenth-Century English Translation of the *Somme le Roi* of Lorens d'Orléans, ed. W. Nelson Francis. 1942, *reprinted* 1968. £3·75

218 **The Cloud of Unknowing and The Book of Privy Counselling;** ed. Phyllis Hodgson. 1944 (*for* 1943), *reprinting.*

219 **The French Text of the Ancrene Riwle,** British Museum MS. Cotton Vitellius F. vii, ed. J. A. Herbert. 1944 (*for* 1943), *reprinted* 1967. £2·75

220 **Charles of Orleans: The English Poems,** Vol. II; *see above* O.S. 215.

221 **The Romance of Sir Degrevant,** ed. L. F. Casson. 1949 (*for* 1944), *reprinted* 1970. £2·50

222 **The Lyfe of Syr Thomas More, by Ro. Ba.,** ed. E. V. Hitchcock and P. E. Hallett, with notes and appendices by A. W. Reed. 1950 (*for* 1945), *reprinted* 1957. £3·15

223 **The Tretyse of Loue,** ed. J. H. Fisher. 1951 (*for* 1945), *reprinted* 1970. £2·10

224 **Athelston: a Middle English Romance,** ed. A. McI. Trounce. 1951 (*for* 1946), *reprinted* 1957. £2·10

225 **The English Text of the Ancrene Riwle,** British Museum MS. Cotton Nero A. xiv, ed. Mabel Day. 1952 (*for* 1946), *reprinted* 1957. £2·50

226 **Respublica:** an interlude for Christmas 1553 attributed to Nicholas Udall, re-ed. W. W. Greg. 1952 (*for* 1946), *reprinted* 1969. £1·50

O.S. 227 **Kyng Alisaunder,** Vol. I, Text, ed. G. V. Smithers. 1952 (*for* £3·75
1947), *reprinted* 1961.

228 **The Metrical Life of St. Robert of Knaresborough,** together £2·10
with the other Middle English pieces in British Museum MS.
Egerton 3143, ed. Joyce Bazire. 1953 (*for* 1947), *reprinted*
1968.

229 **The English Text of the Ancrene Riwle,** Gonville and Caius £1·75
College MS. 234/120, ed. R. M. Wilson with an introduction
by N. R. Ker. 1954 (*for* 1948), *reprinted* 1957.

230 **The Life of St. George by Alexander Barclay,** ed. W. Nelson. £2·00
1955 (*for* 1948), *reprinted* 1960.

231 **Deonise Hid Diuinite** and other treatises related to *The Cloud* £2·50
of Unknowing, ed. Phyllis Hodgson. 1955 (*for* 1949), *reprinted*
with corrections 1958.

232 **The English Text of the Ancrene Riwle,** British Museum MS. £1·50
Royal 8 C. i, ed. A. C. Baugh. 1956 (*for* 1949), *reprinted*
1959.

233 **The Bibliotheca Historica of Diodorus Siculus translated by** £4·00
John Skelton, Vol. I, Text, ed. F. M. Salter and H. L. R.
Edwards. 1956 (*for* 1950), *reprinted* 1968.

234 **Paris and Vienne translated from the French and printed by** £2·10
William Caxton, ed. MacEdward Leach. 1957 (*for* 1951),
reprinted 1970.

235 **The South English Legendary,** Corpus Christi College £3·15
Cambridge MS. 145 and British Museum MS. Harley 2277,
with variants from Bodley MS. Ashmole 43 and British
Museum MS. Cotton Julius D. ix, ed. C. D'Evelyn and A. J.
Mill. Vol. I, Text, 1959 (*for* 1957), *reprinted* 1967.

236 **The South English Legendary,** Vol. II, Text, ed. C. D'Evelyn £3·15
and A. J. Mill. 1956 (*for* 1952), *reprinted* 1967.

237 **Kyng Alisaunder,** Vol. II, Introduction, commentary and £2·50
glossary, ed. G. V. Smithers. 1957 (*for* 1953), *reprinted with*
corrections 1969.

238 **The Phonetic Writings of Robert Robinson,** ed. E. J. Dobson. £1·50
1957 (*for* 1953), *reprinted* 1968.

239 **The Bibliotheca Historica of Diodorus Siculus translated by** £1·50
John Skelton, Vol. II, Introduction, notes and glossary, ed.
F. M. Salter and H. L. R. Edwards. 1957 (*for* 1954), *re-*
printed 1971.

240 **The French Text of the Ancrene Riwle,** Trinity College Cam- £2·75
bridge MS. R. 14. 7, with variants from Paris Bibliothèque
Nationale MS. fonds fr. 6276 and Bodley MS. 90, ed. W. H.
Trethewey. 1958 (*for* 1954), *reprinted* 1971.

241 **Þe Wohunge of Ure Lauerd** and other pieces, ed. W. Meredith £2·25
Thompson. 1958 (*for* 1955), *reprinted with corrections* 1970.

242 **The Salisbury Psalter,** ed. Celia Sisam and Kenneth Sisam. £4·50
1959 (*for* 1955–6), *reprinted* 1969.

243 **The Life and Death of Cardinal Wolsey by George Cavendish,** £2·25
ed. R. S. Sylvester. 1959 (*for* 1957), *reprinted* 1961.

244 **The South English Legendary,** Vol. III, Introduction and £1·50
glossary, ed. C. D'Evelyn. 1959 (*for* 1957), *reprinted* 1969.

O.S. 245 **Beowulf:** facsimile of British Museum MS. Cotton Vitellius £5·00
A. xv, with a transliteration and notes by J. Zupitza, a new
reproduction of the manuscript with an introductory note by
Norman Davis. 1959 (*for* 1958), *reprinted* 1967.

246 **The Parlement of the Thre Ages,** ed. M. Y. Offord. 1959, £2·00
reprinted 1967.

247 **Facsimile of MS. Bodley 34:** St. Katherine, St. Margaret, £3·15
St. Juliana, Hali Meiðhad, Sawles Warde, with an introduc-
tion by N. R. Ker. 1960 (*for* 1959).

248 **Þe Liflade ant te Passiun of Seinte Iuliene,** ed. S. R. T. O. £2·00
d'Ardenne. 1961 (*for* 1960).

249 **The English Text of the Ancrene Riwle: Ancrene Wisse,** £2·50
Corpus Christi College Cambridge MS. 402, ed. J. R. R.
Tolkien, with introduction by N. R. Ker. 1962 (*for* 1960).

250 **Laȝamon's Brut,** Vol. I, Text (lines 1–8020), ed. G. L. £5·00
Brook and R. F. Leslie. 1963 (*for* 1961).

251 **The Owl and the Nightingale:** facsimile of Jesus College £2·50
Oxford MS. 29 and British Museum MS. Cotton Caligula
A. ix, with an introduction by N. R. Ker. 1963 (*for* 1962).

252 **The English Text of the Ancrene Riwle,** British Museum MS. £2·50
Cotton Titus D. xviii, ed. F. M. Mack, and the Lanhydrock
Fragment, Bodleian MS. Eng. th. c. 70, ed. A. Zettersten. 1963
(*for* 1962).

253 **The Bodley Version of Mandeville's Travels,** ed. M. C. £2·50
Seymour. 1963.

254 **Ywain and Gawain,** ed. Albert B. Friedman and Norman £2·50
T. Harrington. 1964 (*for* 1963).

255 **Facsimile of British Museum MS. Harley 2253,** with an £5·00
introduction by N. R. Ker. 1965 (*for* 1964).

256 **Sir Eglamour of Artois,** ed. Frances E. Richardson. 1965. £2·50

257 **The Praise of Folie by Sir Thomas Chaloner,** ed. Clarence H. £2·50
Miller. 1965.

258 **The Orcherd of Syon,** Vol. I, Text, ed. Phyllis Hodgson and £5·00
Gabriel M. Liegey. 1966.

259 **Homilies of Ælfric, A Supplementary Collection,** Vol. I, £5·00
ed. J. C. Pope. 1967.

260 **Homilies of Ælfric, A Supplementary Collection,** Vol. II, £5·00
ed. J. C. Pope. 1968.

261 **Lybeaus Desconus,** ed. M. Mills. 1969. £2·50

262 **The Macro Plays:** The Castle of Perseverance, Wisdom, £2·50
Mankind, ed. Mark Eccles. 1969.

263 **The History of Reynard the Fox translated from the Dutch** £2·50
Original by William Caxton, ed. N. F. Blake. 1970.

264 **The Epistle of Othea translated from the French text of** £2·50
Christine de Pisan by Stephen Scrope, ed. C. F. Bühler. 1970.

265 **The Cyrurgie of Guy de Chauliac,** Vol. I, Text, ed. Margaret S. £5·00
Ogden. 1971.

266 **Wulfstan's Canons of Edgar,** ed. R. G. Fowler. 1972. £1·50

267 **The English Text of the Ancrene Riwle,** British Museum MS. £3·50
Cotton Cleopatra C. vi, ed. E. J. Dobson. 1972.

SUPPLEMENTARY SERIES

FORTHCOMING VOLUMES

ORIGINAL SERIES 1864–1938
EXTRA SERIES 1867–1920

In the following list books marked K are reprinted by the Kraus Reprint Co.

O.S. 1. Early English Alliterative Poems, ed. R. Morris. (*Reprinted* 1965.) £2·70   1864
     2. Arthur, ed. F. J. Furnivall. (*Reprinted* 1965.) 50p   ,,
     3. Lauder on the Dewtie of Kyngis, &c., 1556, ed. F. Hall. (*Reprinted* 1965.) 90p   ,,
     4. Sir Gawayne and the Green Knight, ed. R. Morris. (*Out of print, see* O.S. 210.)   ,,
     5. Hume's Orthographie and Congruitie of the Britan Tongue, ed. H. B. Wheatley. (*Reprinted* 1965.)
        90p   1865
     6. Lancelot of the Laik, ed. W. W. Skeat. (*Reprinted* 1965.) £2·10   ,,
     7. Genesis & Exodus, ed. R. Morris. (*Out of print*.)   ,,
     8. Morte Arthure, ed. E. Brock. (*Reprinted* 1967.)   1·25   ,,
     9. Thynne on Speght's ed. of Chaucer, A.D. 1599 ed. G. Kingsley and F. J. Furnivall. (*Reprinted* 1965.) £2·75   ,,
   10. Merlin, Part I, ed. H. B. Wheatley. (*Out of print*.)   ,,
   11. Lyndesay's Monarche, &c., ed. J. Small. Part I. (*Out of print*.)   ,,
   12. The Wright's Chaste Wife, ed. F. J. Furnivall. (*Reprinted* 1965.) 50p   ,,
   13. Seinte Marherete, ed. O. Cockayne. (*Out of print, see* O.S. 193.)   1866
   14. King Horn, Floriz and Blauncheflur, &c., ed. J. R. Lumby, re-ed. G. H. McKnight. (*Reprinted* 1962.) £2·50   ,,
   15. Political, Religious, and Love Poems, ed. F. J. Furnivall. (*Reprinted* 1965.) £3·15   ,,
   16. The Book of Quinte Essence, ed. F. J. Furnivall. (*Reprinted* 1965.) 50p   ,,
   17. Parallel Extracts from 45 MSS. of Piers the Plowman, ed. W. W. Skeat. (*Out of print*.)   ,,
   18. Hali Meidenhad, ed. O. Cockayne, re-ed. F. J. Furnivall. (*Out of print*.)   ,,
   19. Lyndesay's Monarche, &c., ed. J. Small. Part II. (*Out of print*.)   ,,
   20. Richard Rolle de Hampole, English Prose Treatises of, ed. G. G. Perry. (*Out of print*.)   ,,
   21. Merlin, ed. H. B. Wheatley. Part II. (*Out of print*.)   ,,
   22. Partenay or Lusignen, ed. W. W. Skeat. (*Out of print*.)   ,,
   23. Dan Michel's Ayenbite of Inwyt, ed. R. Morris and P. Gradon. Vol. I, Text. (*Reissued* 1965.) £2·70   ,,
   24. Hymns to the Virgin and Christ; The Parliament of Devils, &c., ed. F. J. Furnivall. (*Out of print*.)   1867
   25. The Stacions of Rome, the Pilgrims' Sea-voyage, with Clene Maydenhod, ed. F. J. Furnivall. (*Out of print*.)   ,,
   26. Religious Pieces in Prose and Verse, from R. Thornton's MS., ed. G. G. Perry· (*Out of print*.)   ,,
   27. Levins' Manipulus Vocabulorum, a rhyming Dictionary, ed. H. B. Wheatley. (*Out of print*.)   ,,
   28. William's Vision of Piers the Plowman, ed. W. W. Skeat. A–Text. (*Reprinted* 1968.) £1·75   ,,
   29. Old English Homilies (1220–30), ed. R. Morris. Series I, Part I. (*Out of print*.)   ,,
   30. Pierce the Ploughmans Crede, ed. W. W. Skeat. (*Out of print*.)   ,,
E.S. 1. William of Palerne or William and the Werwolf, re-ed. W. W. Skeat. (*Out of print*.)   ,,
     2. Early English Pronunciation, by A. J. Ellis. Part I. (*Out of print*.)   ,,
O.S. 31. Myrc's Duties of a Parish Priest, in Verse, ed. E. Peacock. (*Out of print*.)   1868
   32. Early English Meals and Manners: the Boke of Norture of John Russell, the Bokes of Keruynge, Curtasye, and Demeanor, the Babees Book, Urbanitatis, &c., ed. F. J. Furnivall. (*Out of print*.)   ,,
   33. The Book of the Knight of La Tour-Landry, ed. T. Wright. (*Out of print*.)   ,,
   34. Old English Homilies (before 1300), ed. R. Morris. Series I, Part II. (*Out of print*.)   ,,
   35. Lyndesay's Works, Part III: The Historie and Testament of Squyer Meldrum, ed. F. Hall. (*Reprinted* 1965.) 90p   ,,
E.S. 3. Caxton's Book of Curtesye, in Three Versions, ed. F. J. Furnivall. (*Out of print*.)   ,,
     4. Havelok the Dane, re-ed. W. W. Skeat. (*Out of print*.)   ,,
     5. Chaucer's Boethius, ed. R. Morris. (*Reprinted* 1969.) £2·00   ,,
     6. Chevelere Assigne, re-ed. Lord Aldenham. (*Out of print*.)   ,,
O.S. 36. Merlin, ed. H. B. Wheatley. Part III. On Arthurian Localities, by J. S. Stuart Glennie. (*Out of print*.)   1869
   37. Sir David Lyndesay's Works, Part IV, Ane Satyre of the thrie Estaits, ed. F. Hall. (*Out of print*.)   ,,
   38. William's Vision of Piers the Plowman, ed. W. W. Skeat. Part II. Text B. (*Reprinted* 1964.) £2·10   ,,
   39, 56. The Gest Hystoriale of the Destruction of Troy, ed. D. Donaldson and G. A. Panton. Parts I and II. (*Reprinted as one volume* 1968.) £5·50   ,,

E.S. 85. Alexander Scott's Poems, 1568, ed. A. K. Donald. (*Out of print.*) 1902
   86. William of Shoreham's Poems, re-ed. M. Konrath. Part I. (*Out of print.*) „
   87. Two Coventry Corpus Christi Plays, re-ed. H. Craig. Second Edition. (*Reprinted* 1967.) £1·50 „
O.S. 122. The Laud MS. Troy-Book, ed. J. E. Wülfing. Part II. (*Out of print.*) 1903
   123. Robert of Brunne's Handlyng Synne, and its French original, re-ed. F. J. Furnivall. Part II. (*Out of print.*) „
E.S. 88. Le Morte Arthur, re-ed. J. D. Bruce. (*Out of print.*) „
   89. Lydgate's Reson and Sensuallyte, ed. E. Sieper. Vol. II. (*Reprinted* 1965.) £1·75 „
   90. English Fragments from Latin Medieval Service-Books, ed. H. Littlehales. (*Out of print.*) „
O.S. 124. Twenty-six Political and other Poems from Digby MS. 102, &c., ed. J. Kail. Part I. (*Out of print.*) 1904
   125. Medieval Records of a London City Church, ed. H. Littlehales. Part I. (*Out of print.*) „
   126. An Alphabet of Tales, in Northern English, from the Latin, ed. M. M. Banks. Part I. (*Out of print.*) „
E.S. 91. The Macro Plays, ed. F. J. Furnivall and A. W. Pollard. (*Out of print; see* 262.) „
   92. Lydgate's DeGuilleville's Pilgrimage of the Life of Man, ed. Katherine B. Locock. Part III. (*Out of print.*) „
   93. Lovelich's Romance of Merlin, from the unique MS., ed. E. A. Kock. Part I. (*Out of print.*) „
O.S. 127. An Alphabet of Tales, in Northern English, from the Latin, ed. M. M. Banks. Part II. (*Out of print.*) 1905
   128. Medieval Records of a London City Church, ed. H. Littlehales. Part II. (*Out of print.*) „
   129. The English Register of Godstow Nunnery, ed. A. Clark. Part I. *K* £6·25 „
E.S. 94. Respublica, a Play on a Social England, ed. L. A. Magnus. (*Out of print. See under* 1946.) „
   95. Lovelich's History of the Holy Grail. Part V. The Legend of the Holy Grail, ed. Dorothy Kempe. (*Out of print.*) „
   96. Mirk's Festial, ed. T. Erbe. Part I. (*Out of print.*) „
O.S. 130, 142. The English Register of Godstow Nunnery, ed. A. Clark. Parts II and III. *K* £8·00 1906
   131. The Brut, or The Chronicle of England, ed. F. Brie. Part I. (*Reprinted* 1960.) £2·75 „
   132. John Metham's Works, ed. H. Craig. (*Out of print.*) „
E.S. 97. Lydgate's Troy Book, ed. H. Bergen. Part I, Books I and II. (*Out of print.*) „
   98. Skelton's Magnyfycence, ed. R. L. Ramsay. (*Reprinted* 1958.) £2·75 „
   99. The Romance of Emaré, re-ed. Edith Rickert. (*Reprinted* 1958.) £1·50 „
O.S. 133, 144. The English Register of Oseney Abbey, by Oxford, ed. A. Clark. Parts I and II. *K* £4·80 1907
   134, 135. The Coventry Leet Book, ed. M. Dormer Harris. Parts I and II. *K* £9·50 „
E.S. 100. The Harrowing of Hell, and The Gospel of Nicodemus, re-ed. W. H. Hulme. (*Reprinted* 1961.) £2·50 „
   101. Songs, Carols, &c., from Richard Hill's Balliol MS., ed. R. Dyboski. (*Out of print.*) „
O.S. 135. The Coventry Leet Book, ed. M. Dormer Harris. Part II. (*See* O.S. 134) 1908
   136. The Brut, or The Chronicle of England, ed. F. Brie, Part II. *K* £5·25 „
E.S. 102. Promptorium Parvulorum, the 1st English-Latin Dictionary, ed. A. L. Mayhew. (*Out of print.*) „
   103. Lydgate's Troy Book, ed. H. Bergen. Part II, Book III. (*Out of print.*) „
O.S. 137. Twelfth-Century Homilies in MS. Bodley 343, ed. A. O. Belfour. Part I, the Text. (*Reprinted* 1962.) £1·40 1909
   138, 146. The Coventry Leet Book, ed. M. Dormer Harris. Parts III and IV. *K* £6·60 „
E.S. 104. The Non-Cycle Mystery Plays, re-ed. O. Waterhouse. (*See Supplementary Series* I. 1970.) „
   105. The Tale of Beryn, with the Pardoner and Tapster, ed. F. J. Furnivall and W. G. Stone. (*Out of print.*) „
O.S. 139. John Arderne's Treatises of Fistula in Ano, &c., ed. D'Arcy Power. (*Reprinted* 1969.) £2·25 1910
   140. Capgrave's Lives of St. Augustine and St. Gilbert of Sempringham, ed. J. Munro. *K* £3·25 „
E.S. 106. Lydgate's Troy Book, ed. H. Bergen. Part III. (*Out of print.*) „
   107. Lydgate's Minor Poems, ed. H. N. MacCracken. Part I. Religious Poems. (*Reprinted* 1961.) £3·50 „
O.S. 141. Erthe upon Erthe, all the known texts, ed. Hilda Murray. (*Reprinted* 1964.) £1·50 1911
   142. The English Register of Godstow Nunnery, ed. A. Clark. Part III. (*See* O.S. 130.) „
   143. The Prose Life of Alexander, Thornton MS., ed. J. S. Westlake. *K* £1·85 „
E.S. 108. Lydgate's Siege of Thebes, re-ed. A. Erdmann. Part I, the Text. (*Reprinted* 1960.) £2·50 „
   109. Partonope, re-ed. A. T. Bödtker. The Texts. (*Out of print.*) „
O.S. 144. The English Register of Oseney Abbey, by Oxford, ed. A. Clark. Part II. (*See* O.S. 133.) 1912
   145. The Northern Passion, ed. F. A. Foster. Part I, the four parallel texts. *K* £4·00 „
E.S. 110. Caxton's Mirrour of the World, with all the woodcuts, ed. O. H. Prior. (*Reprinted* 1966.) £2·50 „
   111. Caxton's History of Jason, the Text, Part I, ed. J. Munro. (*Out of print.*) „
O.S. 146. The Coventry Leet Book, ed. M. Dormer Harris. Introduction, Indexes, &c. Part IV. (*See* O.S. 138.) 1913
   147. The Northern Passion, ed. F. A. Foster, Introduction, French Text, Variants and Fragments, Glossary. Part II. *K* £3·60 „
E.S. 112. Lovelich's Romance of Merlin, ed. E. A. Kock. Part II. (*Reprinted* 1961.) £2·25 „
   113. Poems by Sir John Salusbury, Robert Chester, and others, from Christ Church MS. 184, &c., ed. Carleton Brown. (*Out of print.*) „
O.S. 148. A Fifteenth-Century Courtesy Book and Two Franciscan Rules, ed. R. W. Chambers and W. W. Seton. (*Reprinted* 1963.) £1·50 1914
   149. Lincoln Diocese Documents, 1450–1544, ed. Andrew Clark. *K* £6·00 „
   150. The Old-English Rule of Bp. Chrodegang, and the Capitula of Bp. Theodulf, ed. A. S. Napier. *K* £2·25 „
E.S. 114. The Gild of St. Mary, Lichfield, ed. F. J. Furnivall. £1·35 „
   115. The Chester Plays, re-ed. J. Matthews. Part II. (*Reprinted* 1967.) £1·90 „

Orders from non-members of the Society should be placed with a bookseller. Orders from booksellers for volumes in part 1 of this list should be sent to Oxford University Press, Ely House, 37 Dover Street, London W. 1. Orders from booksellers for volumes in part 2 of this list should be sent to the following addresses: orders from the United States and Canada to Kraus Reprint Co., 16 East 46th Street, New York, N.Y. 10017, U.S.A.; orders from Germany and Japan to Kraus Reprint Co., FL 9491 Nendeln, Liechtenstein, or Oxford University Press; orders from Great Britain and all other countries to Oxford University Press, Ely House, 37 Dover Street, London W. 1.

University Press, Oxford
England